ANTONÍN DVOŘÁK

OTAKAR ŠOUREK

THE ORCHESTRAL WORKS

OF

ANTONÍN DVOŘÁK

OTAKAR ŠOUREK

ENGLISH VERSION

BY

ROBERTA FINLAYSON SAMSOUR

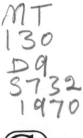

GREENWOOD PRESS, PUBLISHERS
WESTPORT, CONNECTICUT

Originally published in 195_ ?
by Artia, Prague

Reprinted from an original copy in the collections
of the Brooklyn Public Library

First Greenwood Reprinting 1970

Library of Congress Catalogue Card Number 77-109851

SBN 8371-4342-X

Printed in the United States of America

CONTENTS

2-7-77 16.00

B+T

LIST OF ILLUSTRATIONS:

INTRODUCTION

It is no exaggeration to say that the medium of expression most suited to Antonín Dvořák's creative imagination was the orchestra. For while it is true that this artist also created a large body of chamber music, enriching thereby both Czech and world music with works of rare beauty and originality, he returned to this form only at intervals, some longer, some shorter, and, as a rule, only for a relatively short time. And even his compositions for the human voice, which provided him with equally congenial material, were produced only in the pauses demanded by intensive work in symphonic and chamber music forms. With the orchestra, however, he was in almost permanent contact, for he was engaged in problems of orchestration not only in writing his symphonies, but also in the composition of operas, oratorios, and cantatas; from the time of his first youthful essays in original work up to the last pages of the opera "Armida" which brings his life's work to a close—that is, for a period of no less than four full decades.

For Dvořák this creative contact with the orchestra was an emotional necessity, which had its roots deep in the musical environment of his boyhood, when he played in the well-trained village band of his teacher, Antonín *Liehmann*, in Zlonice. This was then nourished, fertilized and strengthened by the practical experience gained in his student years as a member of the Saint Cecilia Society, and still further during his ten years' membership of the Czech Interim Theatre orchestra.

Even at that time there was no important stylistic link in the evolution of orchestral music with whose characteristic features Dvořák was not acquainted—from the foremost masters of pre-classical and classical music to Berlioz and on to the mighty growth of orchestral technique in the music of Wagner and Liszt. Dvořák had, too, a rare opportunity of penetrating to the inner structural and functional core of the orchestral organism, and so to realize its immense possibilities and the wide and finely-graded range of its tone-colour values. And if a highly developed feeling for the aesthetic qualities and natural beauty of sound was one of the most outstanding constituents of his creative genius, he acquired very soon, and much sooner than in other departments of musical composition, the ability to express his musical thought through the medium of the orchestra, with a unique economy of means, while yet making the fullest use of its expressive resources.

The strong creative ferment which is discernible in Dvořák's work in the period around 1870, and which, having its origin in the composer's enthusiastic admiration for the music of Wagner and Liszt, manifested itself in a liking for a certain complexity and ruggedness of expression, was not without influence on his orchestral works. In his first orchestral compositions, whether for orchestra alone, as for example his first three symphonies, or combined with vocal music, as in his first opera, there is observable, at times, an overloading of the score in respect of the number and massiveness of the instrumental means which, in Dvořák's later work, is altogether unknown. There is also a predilection for certain instruments less common at that time, such as the cor anglais or the bass clarinet, which arose more out of the keen desire to follow the example of his admired models than from his own extraordinarily sensitive feeling for the functional effectiveness of every nuance in the scale of instrumental tone colour out of which is born the rare beauty of all Dvořák's later orchestral scores. And yet this ferment was also richly productive, contributing in no small measure to the rapid maturing of Dvořák's orchestral technique and towards raising that technique to the level which made Dvořák one of the greatest masters of instrumentation since Berlioz, and undoubtedly the greatest up till then in Czech music.

Let it be said at once that he achieved that eminence with an art from which nothing was so far removed as the desire for superficial brilliance or novelty. His scores are, above all, interesting and instructive for the impression they give of being, despite all their extraordinary beauty of ultimate sound effect, perfectly simple and transparent. It is, indeed, difficult on hearing them performed to realize with what a small combination of instruments Dvořák was able to create an effect of expressive colourfulness, profusion and harmony.

As a rule, the core of his instrumentation is the string orchestra, his early experience as viola player having taught him from the first to rate highly the flexibility, adaptability and importance of string tone. He frequently entrusted it with the chief role, exploiting its entire range of colouring with a wizardry which is specifically Dvořák, whether it be the fascinating brilliance of the sustained or running passages in the high violin registers, or the full-bodied expressiveness of pizzicato in the medium and low pitched instruments as, for instance, in his use of the 'cellos. Both groups of wind instruments are employed with obvious economy, and yet with a rich use of all their instrinsic sound qualities and technical resources. At the same time there is a fine appreciation of their effectiveness in different combinations within the group, as also with the strings. And though, considering his historic context, we cannot be surprised at his extensive use of the wood-wind, certainly far from common was the attention he paid to the brass, which he employed with admirable effect, especially in their melodic function. As to his skill in handling the great variety of percussion instruments, a more than sufficient guaranty was his characteristically acute and elemental sense of rhythm, which was, however, sufficiently disciplined to avoid any danger of misuse.

The key to the secret of Dvořák's orchestral art is to be found in his scores Theoretically he gave a clue to it when he explained to his pupils at the Conservatoire that a beautiful, or as he himself modestly put it, a good effect, is one of the essential conditions a composition must fulfil if it is to come to life as a work of art. His view was that everything must sound well as written for each individual instrument, and in his own work he applied this rule with unrelaxing stringency. The fact that his every musical thought sounded well, because it was born and imagined in a given musical context, and was thus inseparably bound up with that instrument's tone-colouring, was precisely the secret of his creative genius. From this it follows that the tone-colouring was never an end in itself, but was the most apt and natural expression of the qualities demanded by the musical content. Thus scoring was never for Dvořák a question of superficial colourist virtuosity, or a seeking after subtle refinements of tone-painting for its own sake, but first and foremost a question of adequate, natural and true musical expression. Thus, unperturbed, he could allow every new trend in symphonic music, including the impressionist, to impinge upon his consciousness, and, while keeping in step with all new developments, cull from them what he found of value for his art, without in any way transgressing his own principles of absolute creative honesty and without suppressing in the smallest degree his own highly individual musical personality.

If we realize this, and also how his creative consciousness was constantly agitated by an abundance of subjects and designs which sought the most various forms of musical realization, we shall find it quite natural that Dvořák's elemental interest in the orchestra manifested itself ever and again in purely instrumental compositions. These works showed great diversity of character, both as regards content and form, and even led to the instrumentation of compositions not originally written for orchestra.* We shall find it all the more comprehensible, too, if we recall with what delight Dvořák entered every department of musical composition, finding in each a suitable field for the exercise of his creative imagination.

* It may be noted in this connection that between October 29th and November 6th, 1880, Dvořák scored the third volume of Brahms "Hungarian Dances" (Nos. 17—21) to the complete satisfaction of the composer.

In the period between 1865 and 1898 we can number up to over half a hundred orchestral compositions (including opera overtures), even when couting whole cycles such as the "Slavonic Dances" and the "Legends" as single compositions.

The largest in extent and the artistically most significant sector of Dvořák's orchestral compositions is, however, the series of nine symphonies which gives Dvořák his place among the greatest and most original symphonists in musical history. Among his other orchestral works there are also compositions of outstanding musical value, power and vitality. Some of these form part of the most successful concert repertoire, as the expression of a genius bearing the indelible hallmark of personal and national individuality, both in the character of the musical invention and in the truly masterly command of the art of musical composition.

In addition, his orchestral works include "cycles"—compositions of several movements which, in structure, closely approach the symphonic form (concertos for solo instruments and orchestra, serenades, suites); then compositions which, while individually independent, form groups having a common basic character, (rhapsodies, the "Slavonic Dances", the "Legends") and, finally, compositions in one part. The latter include a special group of works belonging to the genre of "programme" music, that is, works that owe their inspiration to some personal experience or poetic theme which they describe in tone.

The haphazard way in which Dvořák realized the creative ideas which kept seeking outlet in these orchestral compositions does not very well allow us to follow them simply in the order in which they arose. Nor is it necessary, for the chronological grouping does not show any particularly marked inner relationship. Such a relationship is, however, observable within the different form groups, and this is even more clear if we preserve the chronological order within the group.

The analytical survey of all these works provides convincing proof that Dvořák, with the inexhaustible resources and freshness of his creative inspiration, was able to make abundant use of gifts of an unusually high order in expressing his musical thought, and of a unique mastery of the orchestra as its medium. Placing this art in the service of his spontaneous yet deeply experienced musicality, he created a body of orchestral works which has enriched the treasure-house of musical literature with a legacy of rare artistic value, richly varied musical content and unusual originality of expression.

I

SYMPHONIES

In the impressive complex of Dvořák's orchestral music, the series of nine symphonies holds a position all the more important and remarkable because, as in the imposing group of chamber music compositions, it testifies particularly eloquently and convincingly to the composer's creative powers in absolute music, that is, instrumental music independent of the poetic word or idea. This phenomenon was by no means so common in the second half of the 19th century when, under the influence of Richard *Wagner* and Franz *Liszt*, the view gained considerable ground that such music represented a phase that had been surpassed and had no place in the future of music. Still more was this true of Czech music, which so far had been an almost untilled field in this branch of musical composition. Dvořák's series of symphonies, growing with each new work in beauty of musical content, in strength of symphonic presentation and, not least, in the stamp they bore of national and personal individuality, not only raised him to the front ranks of the greatest symphonic writers in world music, but also become one of the foundation stones on which his special importance for Czech musical art is based. For there can be no doubt that Antonín Dvořák was *the founder of the Czech symphony* and, in the first period, its greatest master.

The symphony is among the musical forms in which Dvořák made his first essays in musical composition not very long after completing his studies at the Prague Organ School. In 1865, at the age of barely twenty-four, he wrote two symphonies in close succession, the *first* in C minor the *second* in B flat major. Undeterred by the fact that he was unable to get them performed, he returned to this branch of musical creation after a number of years, and kept returning at varying intervals over a period spanning three decades, when he was already a well-known composer, whose works were frequently performed both at home and abroad. Almost all the many different phases in this period of Dvořák's development as an artist and as a man find expression in one or other of his symphonies. From this, too, it follows that each of Dvořák's nine symphonies is different, each embodying in its spiritual atmosphere the phase it reflects as well as the corresponding level of achievement in compositional technique.

Dvořák's first two symphonies belong to the period of his artistic initiation, when the influences of Classical and Romantic music waged a battle for his allegiance, and when, in his personal life, he was experiencing the pangs and passion of a naively sincere young love, and the encouragements and rebuffs in his art which are the fate of young artists. They are still very clearly the works of a beginner, showing, especially in the opening and closing sonata movements, a still clumsy and inadequate command of form, a lack of individualization in the thought content and, as yet, only giving promise of his future mastery of orchestral technique. Nevertheless the immaturities are such as needs must mark the first works of an unusually gifted artist destined one day to achieve greatness, with their flashes of genius in the quality of the melodic, rhythmic and harmonic inventiveness, in the treatment of the themes and in the imaginative power animating the design and tone-conception. Thus, through the shell of the first creative immaturities there breaks the promise of uncommon gifts for the high demands of symphonic expression, a promise also apparent in the inner content of both symphonies. Of these the first, entitled in the author's reminiscences, "*Zlonice Bells*", is dedicated to his boyhood, in which an inborn love for music had to fight a hard struggle to establish its claims, while the second mirrors the contemporary phase of young manhood, full of courage and faith in his personal future.

In the eight years which separate these two symphonies from the birth of a *third*, in E flat major (1873), Dvořák went through a process of strong creative ferment under the confusing influence of

the German neo-Romanticists which reached its crisis at the turn
of the 'sixties and 'seventies. The E flat major symphony is a typical
example of this period from the clear traces it still bears of the influence of Wagner and Liszt in the expressive means, in the monothematism and in other typical features of their compositional
technique (diffuseness of themes, peculiarities of scoring, etc.).
On the other hand, it shows equally clearly that it arose at a
time when that influence was already in the descendant, and when
Dvořák was working his way forward on to the firm ground of his
own creative mission. For this reason, the second symphony stands
incomparably higher than the first, for, in spite of being marred by
certain structural defects, it fully reveals all those typically Dvořák
qualities in which lies the strength of his symphonic expression and
whereby he ensured himself a distinguished place in contemporary Czech and world music. This is evident in many characteristic ways, from the choice of themes, expressive and richly plastic
in form, their structural integration and treatment, which develops
clearly, spontaneously and effectively, the many masterly and daringly original strokes with which he surprises us, to the general
design of the movements, sometimes still excessively broad, but at
the same time plastic, firmly constructed and with climaxes of strong
dramatic power.

The next two symphonies which arose within the two following
years, the *fourth* in D minor (1874) and the *fifth* in F major
(1875), reveal an artist who, having won through to calm self-
reliance, is now striving to achieve his own personal and nationally
characteristic expression along the lines which a study of the works
of Smetana had suggested him. There are clear indications of this in
the D minor symphony, in which, the crisis past, he still, in occasional echoes of musical invention, looks over his shoulder at tempta-
tions overcome, but otherwise advances firmly towards greater purity of style, economy of means and more harmonious proportions
in the build-up of the movements as well as an improved technique.

Still more striking, however, is the advance in the individuality of
expression in the F Major symphony, in the last movement of which
its creator achieved the level of true symphonic mastery. If in the
content of these two works he still appears as a Romanticist, now
with a soul restless and agitated by passion (D minor), now idyllically peaceful and smiling (F major), but always with the fresh
and courageous confidence of youth, and always rising in the end
to heights of joyful triumph, in his compositional art he now takes
as his sole model Beethoven with whom he feels a spiritual kinship
and to whom, as an artist, he owes much. This is especially noticeable in his thematic treatment, which is abundantly free, inventive
and bold, delighting in the lively play of characteristic imitation,
figural embroidery and countermelody (especially in the bass) which,
at the same time, always develops naturally and logically, entitling
him to take his place beside the great German master in the command he possesses of this aspect of composition, of which few since
Beethoven had shown themselves capable. The fact that here and
there reminiscences of the Master creep into the expression is not
only understandable but forgivable.

After these three symphonies, following each other at intervals
of about a year, there is a lull of five years in Dvořák's symphonic
composition. In this period Dvořák was maturing in inventive individuality, and harvesting one success after another at home and
abroad where, with the help of Johannes Brahms, he was beginning
to win triumphant recognition. There followed then the celebrated
"Slavonic", or rather, the completely Czech period of his creative
production—a period abundantly fruitful, musically sharply erup-
tive and nationally characteristic, fertilized by the spirit of the
folksong and folk-dance whose typical forms he took delight in
idealising; it is a period of passionate joy in living, in creating and
in his artistic successes, bright with inward happiness and effer-
vescing with unaffected gaiety; it is the period of the "Slavonic
Dances", the "Rhapsodies", the String Sextet, the "Czech Suite",

the E flat major Quartet and the Violin Concerto. To this period, too, belongs the *sixth* D major symphony (1880), as one of its last but most typical and outstanding manifestations. Gay in content, undeniably Czech in expression, with a "Furiant" in place of a Scherzo, and in conception and design a work of classical purity, beauty and clarity. The perfection of craftsmanship and the powerful symphonic utterance which Dvořák had achieved in the last movement of the preceding symphony becomes the rule from now on. Artistic contact with Brahms contributes substantially to this result in some important aspects of composition and is not without considerable influence on both this and the following symphony. This time, however, the influence is altogether beneficial, for, combined with the spirit of the Beethoven symphony, instead of strangling the personal utterance of an original artist, it raised his creative powers to greater heights.

A gap of almost five years again separates this symphony from the next, the *seventh*, and the second in D minor (1884-5). Dvořák was then reaping brilliant successes in England, besides being engaged upon several large-scale works; the opera "Dimitri" and his cantatas "The Spectre's Bride" and "Saint Ludmilla", but at the same time he was inwardly devoured by hesitations and doubts as to whether it was possible — for the prize of success offered him in the field of opera abroad — to suppress in himself what made him a true son of the Czech soil and a typically Czech artist. This spiritual struggle is mirrored most clearly in the chamber and orchestral music of this period and culminates in the above-mentioned D minor symphony. From this derives the immense inner tension of the work, from this its passionate and agitated thought-content, but also the Brahms-like terseness and severity of its general character, in which the translucent, humanly simple and open core of Dvořák's personality is clouded over. From this, too, derives a certain bareness and austerity in the orchestral tone-colouring—a feature otherwise foreign to Dvořák's works. The symphony is thoroughly

South Bohemian in character—hard, unyielding and strong, with a finale which tells us quite unmistakably how this short inner crisis ended.

In the succeeding period of relaxed tension, of spiritual clarification and idyllic calm, and also of full artistic maturity, Dvořák creates, after another pause of four years, his *eighth* symphony in G major (1889). In it there speaks once more the simple, genuine, moodily excitable Dvořák, with the soul of a child and the contemplativeness of a poet, and withal an artist of high individuality in the full strength of his creative powers. Living in calm and happy contentment in the Czech countryside, among simple people, he created this symphony which, uncomplicated by intellectual or compositional problems, gave the composer a unique opportunity to avoid all that is trite or schematic as regards form, and to develop his creative freshness, flexibility and originality in all directions.

Then comes the time of Dvořák's three years' residence in America (1892—95), and here, too, the Master renders the symphony its due. Shortly after his arrival in New York, he writes there his *ninth* symphony in E minor (1893), named after the place of its birth, "From the New World", and in the order of his published works designated the "fifth". This becomes the most loved of all his symphonies and makes its way with unbroken success on to the concert platforms of every city in the world. As the first composition to take shape in America, it is also the expression of the first vivid impressions with which the world across the ocean flooded Dvořák's mind and senses, and one of the few works in which the atmosphere of the New World, the spirit and mood of its music, are strongly reflected. But it is at the same time the first expression of his longing for home, which never left him during his sojourn in America, and which find an echo in almost every work that arose there. In form and thematic structure, this symphony is actually not the most original, for the return to classicism is, after the preceding D major symphony, rather surprising; but it is certainly the most mature, especially if we think of the complete command of form and of the structural unity of individual movements. In the advance made in this respect between Dvořák's first and last symphonies, there is revealed the imposing growth of the artist's compositional mastery in its full extent.

The New World Symphony closes the series of Antonín Dvořák's nine symphonies. The last, post-American period of his life's work, a period characterized almost exclusively by a predilection for the world of fairy-tale, sought an outlet only in symphonic poems and operas. To the symphony, although encouraged and even urged by his publisher to continue the series, Dvořák did not return.

*

It was formerly the custom to speak about Dvořák as about a formalistic conservative. His symphonies taken all together might serve as an instructive example of how such a judgment may easily be superficial. It is true that he kept to the old forms, especially if we have in mind the cyclic sonata form. Dvořák was certainly no iconoclast. Tradition was for him as sacred as were the works upon which famous generations had built and which, in the course of development, had been constantly perfected and enriched. In the symphony, too, he links up with the old forms and takes them for his foundation. But what endless modifications he finds for them, how varied their nuances and deviations, and with what art does he change their sense and shift the centre of gravity of their sections! From this point of view, too, each of Dvořák's symphonies is different and expressed in a different way. If we compare only their respective first and last movements, the first movement of the "New World" symphony alone keeps strictly to the regular features of the classic sonata form. All the others are more or less divergent variants, some of them, such as the opening movement and finale of the G major symphony, or the finale of the E minor symphony, are very bold and original variants, always interesting as testifying to a master hand in the treatment of form. The same is true of his scherzo movement, which varies in type from one symphony to another, going through a clear course of development from the simple classical Minuet, by way of the idealized Czech folk-dance, to a definite, individual form which, however, has its roots in the Beethoven scherzo. Everything is determined by the general character and style of the individual symphony for, with Dvořák, too, form grows out of *content*, and the inner relation between content and form is governed by strict *stylistic* laws for which Dvořák had a very sensitive feeling, though it may have been more instinctive than conscious. In keeping with the general character of the work is also the form of the slow movement, even though it is of all the movements the one that undergoes relatively least outward change. It is particularly characteristic, and a repeatedly observed fact that the emotionally deep, sincere, ardently contemplative and truly religious soul of the artist was able to create in these movements, both in symphonies and, in an equally significant measure, also in chamber compositions, music of rare beauty and great power.

If it has already been said that Dvořák is the creator of the Czech symphony, it is not so much in respect of its form as of its *content*. Nor is it merely in the narrow sense of its purely musical content, to which reference has already been made a number of times, and whose aesthetic values and rich variety were the expression of Dvořák's powerful creative genius, his gift of free-blossoming and cultivated melody and his elemental, supple and distinctive rhythms, his art of formulating, developing and working up his musical materials, and, not least, his remarkable feeling for the colour, texture and glowing ecstatic intoxication of orchestral tone. Here a decisive element is also the specifically Czech colouring of the emotional content of his symphonies, so inseparably bound up with the spiritual climate of Czech life, its sentiments, joys and griefs. This element was not present in any noticeable degree at the beginning of Dvořák's symphonic production, but, from the time his own personality began to awaken, the Czech soul in him demanded to be heard. And in Dvořák's symphonies it speaks a clear and unmistakable language. In them he tells of his love of country and of his purely human emotions, of all for which he lived, dreamed, fought and conquered. In this personally experienced content, in its correspondence with the artist's life, his spiritual and emotional states and moods, projected against the background of his artistic and human destiny, resides what might be called the "programme" of these symphonies, and herein lies the proof that they are the true manifestations of his personal experience. Dvořák passes the tradition of the classic symphony through the fire of his own living experience and gives to it the form of an original, individually and nationally coloured work of art. Thus he was one of the first to demonstrate the right to the continued existence and artistic recognition of a purely musical form of expression, and in doing so he proved once more the irrelevance of dividing music into "absolute" and "programme" music, or the still greater absurdity of preferring the latter to the former. He created works which, having their roots deep in Czech soil, sing its praises, its beauty and its joys. Above all, its joys! For the happily optimistic view of life of which Dvořák was always so ardent an upholder, that passionately devout affirmation of life and Nature, and that belief in the benignly purifying influence of their beauty, which filled his heart and shaped and gave direction to his individual personality, break through in his symphonies, too, with victorious conviction.

SYMPHONY IN C MINOR

"ZLONICE BELLS"

Instrumentation: piccolo, 2 flutes, 2 oboes, cor anglais, 2 clarinets, 2 bassoons, 4 horns, 2 trumpets, 3 trombones, tympani, strings.

Written in score between February 14th and March 24th 1865, in Prague.—First performed at a concert of the Provincial Theatre in Brno on October 4th, 1936, conducted by Milan *Sachs.*—Unpublished.—Duration: 44 minutes.

It was for long supposed that the first of Dvořák's nine symphonies, which was possibly the artist's first orchestral work, had been destroyed by its author. He himself gave substance to this supposition by listing it among *"the compositions I have torn up and burned"*. It was, however, a mistake on his part, but whether unintentional or deliberate it is impossible to say. This much is known, that the symphony was entered for some competition in Germany, and when it was not returned the composer did not trouble himself any further about it.* The score of the work then found its way into a German second-hand music shop, where it was bought by a student from Bohemia who, however, refrained from making the fact of its acquisition public. The score of the symphony was not discovered till almost twenty years after the composer's death, while a number of years passed again before its first public performance.

Possessing now the necessary perspective which allows us to rank Dvořák among the most outstanding symphonists in musical history, it is not difficult to see that this first symphony was full of promise of what was to come. It is not, however, without the marks of a beginner's uncertainties and perplexities, nor are these altogether overcome in the second symphony which follows closely after. They stem, above all, from the features which are, in general, character-

---

* Many years later when he told his pupils at the Prague Conservatoire about it and was asked what he did to get the work back, he is said to have replied: "Nothing. I sat down and wrote a new symphony."

istic of the first period of Dvořák's creative work, namely an abundance of musical thoughts he is not yet certain how to incorporate, especially in the difficult sonata form, functionally and most effectively into the musical structure, so as to achieve the necessary balance of parts and the logical unity of the whole. In the first symphony the themes are predominantly periodic units and do not, except occasionally, show a tendency to melodic irregularity and harmonic instability. This tendency is much more marked in the second symphony and was undoubtedly due to Dvořák's growing enthusiasm for the German neo-Romanticists, which reached its height at the beginning of the 'seventies. And yet the structure of the movements gives the impression of lack of cohesion, both in the thought-content and in the design, an impression strengthened in no small degree by the circumstance that the composer, in addition to the usual basic themes, crowds into the movements numerous motifs, unrelated or only remotely related to the main thematic material and, for that reason, insufficiently assimilated into the flow of the movement.

While fully admitting these reservations, we cannot be deaf to the fact that this work proclaims the advent of a creative spirit of exceptional inventive power and spontaneity and, what is especially important, one possessing that rare sense of the true nobility and spaciousness of symphonic style. This reveals itself, first of all, in the expressiveness of the thoughts and the lively development of the movements; then in the way the composer is able to illuminate the different facets of his themes, in the ingenuity of the imitational and figural embroidery and in his endeavour to delight the ear with richly varied polyphonic passages; finally, and not least, in the extremely imaginative use of tone-colour, even though at times an exaggerated density of application shows that he has not yet reached full mastery of orchestral technique. The music of this symphony already possesses remarkable inner vitality, its sharp rhythms attract, startle and excite the listener and impress upon the mind an essential unity of mood. And this because it is music springing from a healthy, spontaneous and pure emotional base, the expression of a serious creative urge combined with the gift of inborn musicality, even though it is, for the most part, far from what we have come to regard as typically Dvořák expression. As in the two chamber music works preceding it, the String Quintet in A minor, op. 1, and the String Quartet in A major, op. 2, in this first symphony Dvořák has taken Beethoven and Schubert as his chief models, occasionally allowing them to colour his own musical utterance. From that, too, we see on what a sound basis he placed his symphonic composition and how high the aim he set himself.

An important quality in the C minor symphony is its genesis in the author's emotional experience and the unity of content. The individual movements do not merely string a number of moods together in some chance sequence, but have an inner conscious tendency giving its impress to the whole work, which shows a clear logical and emotional development and reflects a fiercely passionate spiritual struggle.* The first movement, written in sonata form, is, in mood, one of the darkest and most agitated in Dvořák's whole creative production. It is full of passionate unrest in which, as it were, the stealthy movement of fear-stricken lines of melody alternate with sudden outbursts of hammer-blows and the stormy swell of angry waves, and in which fighting courage and unyielding determination wage a stubborn struggle with the consciousness of almost hopeless uncertainty and wounded sensibilities. The second movement, perhaps the best part of the work, is borne on the stream of specifically Dvořák melody, providing a contrast to the first in its sudden tranquilisation which, at times, is not without signs of exhaustion. The melody rises and falls, now on waves of yearning and desire, now upheld by the spirit of fervent prayer, but able ever

* And this despite the fact that the first, second and fourth movements are numbered consecutively 1—239 and that the third movement (Scherzo) is independently numbered 1—44, having evidently been inserted later.

and anon to gather itself for a gesture of firm and assured faith in
the outcome, and concluding in a mood of quiet, deep confidence.
The third movement, a thematically condensed and rhythmically
vivacious scherzo, is brightened by flashes of humour more grotesque than sportive in character, in keeping with the dark key in
which it is set, and then warms up in the trio to a charming cheerfulness. It steps out proudly at last in the coda, but in the last few
bars there is a sudden strange breakdown, as if the author had
decided to dismiss the whole thing as a joke. The note of proud,
fighting determination returns to stay, however, in the last movement, which is again in sonata form. It swings along with a firm,
elastic step, and, in spite of the darker character of the subsidiary
theme, confidently works up to an imposing and ecstatically hymn-
like climax.

For the character of the content of the first symphony one other
significant circumstance must be taken into account. Dvořák is said
to have mentioned once that the symphony originally bore the
title "*Zlonice Bells*" (the score had no such inscription), and this title
has long been associated with the work. And not without reason.
From the musical substance of the symphony, however, it is at
once clear that, if such a connection did exist, it was not expressed
in any superficial tone-painting, either in the themes or instrumentation, but alone in the inner character of the symphony, in its
content. The most natural and probable explanation is that Dvořák
connected the content of his first symphony with recollections of the
years of his boyhood spent in Zlonice near Slaný in Bohemia
(1854—1857), where he found an excellent teacher and advocate
for the claims of his musical talent in Antonín *Liehmann*, one of the
most competent of the splendid band of teacher-musicians who kept
the Czech musical tradition alive in the countryside. It was for him
the period of his first joyful, unrestricted and enthusiastic initiation
into his art, but at the same time one of torturing uncertainty. In
Zlonice his fate hung in the balance, for while family reasons spoke

for his keeping to the trade of butcher, in which he had served his apprenticeship, his soul burned with the desire to dedicate himself wholly to music. It was a time when moments of bitter hopelessness alternated with gleams of firm confidence, storms of despair with ardent prayers, and in which at last the decision was taken which filled him with a feeling of blissful happiness and a steadfast faith in a happy and fruitful future.

The above-indicated emotional content of the symphony would, as is evident, be in striking agreement with such an explanation. Nor would then the key of C minor, in which this work is written and which is not to be found in any other of Dvořák's cyclic work, either of symphonic or chamber music character, be without a certain significance. Not only because it is exceedingly characteristic for the emotional origins of the symphony, but also because the movements show a sequence of keys: C minor, A flat major, C minor, C major, which is strongly reminiscent of Beethoven's C minor "Fate" symphony. And then two remarkable and closely interrelated ideas in the thematic structure of the individual movements convincingly support such an interpretation. The first of these is to be found in a small but significantly rhythmic motif in the opening movement (see Ex. 2), which reappears at important junctures in the other movements like a constant reminder of the inevitability of fate, and thunders forth at the height of the monumental peroration of the finale. Is it not possible that here Dvořák connected the memory of the bells of the Zlonice church, where he so often played the organ, with the spiritual states of that period, now darkly overcast, now encouragingly clear and sunny, in whose sharp contrasts he had a foreshadowing of his future fate? And the second idea is contained in the principal theme, which steps out briskly in the finale (Ex. 15) and is heard on two occasions in the first movement—at its beginning and then again at the end, as if, on the very threshold of the work, still agitated and full of unrest, there should be presaged the glorious climax in which it would culminate. Both these examples of thematic reminiscence linking one movement with another are of interest, too, as showing that Dvořák, at the very beginning of his symphonic composition, introduces a characteristic structural principle of the Romanticists (especially Schumann) to which he returns in several of his later symphonic works, but which is employed most systematically in his last symphony.

Nevertheless, the foregoing interpretation of Dvořák's first symphony, though exceedingly probable and generally acceptable, cannot be conclusively vouched for. It is, therefore, only put forward as a hypothesis and does not exclude the possibility that this work, whose content so aptly illustrates the emotional states of turbulent youth struggling hard to secure a foothold and suffering in the way that only youth can suffer, yet not losing courage or faith in the future was, for its creator, also the expression of emotional experiences, longings and hopes much nearer in time. Certainly the fact

* The intimate relation in which Dvořák stood to these three early works is best seen from the fact that he made use of their musical thoughts later in other compositions. As regards the two symphonies, the thematic material was then worked up, especially in the cycle of piano compositions, "Silhouettes", which he wrote towards the end of 1879 and published soon afterwards as op. 8. From the first symphony he took over mainly the principal theme of the opening movement (Ex. 3), which provides the leading motif of the first and last "Silhouettes", transposed, however, into the tonic key of C sharp major and for the most part in its diminished second four-bar strain; in the last "Silhouette", however, alongside the delightful variation in A flat major, in its full original form. In addition this theme is also employed in the fifth "Silhouette". (In the original manuscript of the cycle, the theme in question is also appended to the close of the second movement of the third unpublished "Silhouette", and it is possible to suppose that it was meant to be a kind of unifying element throughout the whole cycle.) In addition, Dvořák used the theme of the Scherzo (ex. 11) for the second part of the eighth "Silhouette" and the principal pastoral theme of the finale (15) transposed into B major for the ninth "Silhouette". Dvořák also returned to one of the themes from the middle part of the Scherzo (12) in his Rhapsody, op. 15 (1874). (Reference will be made to the themes from the second Symphony, also used for the "Silhouettes", in the analysis of the work in question).

cannot be overlooked that Dvořák wrote the C minor symphony at a time when his heart was torn with the unhappiness and pain of his unrequited love for Josefina *Čermák*, a member of the Czech Theatre and the elder sister of his future wife, who was later to marry the Count Václav *Kaunic*. This emotional state found expression soon after the symphony in a cycle of love songs, "The Cypresses", based on poems by Gustav *Pflegr-Moravský* and possibly, in part at least, in the following second symphony in B flat major.

FIRST MOVEMENT

(*Tempo not indicated*, C minor, $^3/_4$)

The first movement of the C minor symphony is written in sonata form. The tempo indications are not given in the manuscript of the score, but it is evidently intended to be fairly brisk. The actual exposition, which is repeated, is preceded by an eight-bar introductory theme in duple time alle breve, which appears again at several culminating points in the development, but otherwise makes itself felt only through its characteristic rhythm. The introductory unison of bassoons and horns accompanied by the accented chords of the orchestra has a chorale-like character:

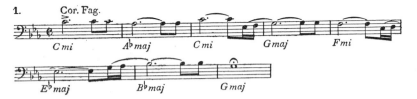

1. Cor. Fag.

C mi   A♭ maj   C mi   G maj   F mi

E♭ maj   B♭ maj   G maj

The exposition is built up from three main themes and then from the rhythmic figure mentioned above, which is heard at intervals

throughout the movement, now in the faint, shy tones of the basses
or violins, again in the wild exclamations of the wood-wind and
horns or in the hammered rhythms of the tympani:

Three times this motif introduces the first principal theme—an
eight-bar period with a smoothly flowing first section and a sharply
rhythmical second section, from which the movement derives its basically agitated character:

Calmer and warmer in character is the expression of the melodic
subordinate theme:

but into its continuation new thoughts are woven introducing, at
places, a new element of unrest and even of inner convulsion.

The final theme is again in two sections, alternating grave major
chords with an impassioned thought in the minor mode related to
the principal theme:

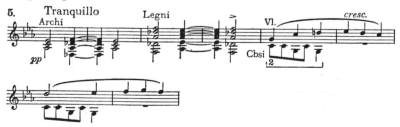

The development opens with a mighty entry in C minor, works mainly with the material of themes 2 and 3, at important junctures restates the serious introductory theme (1) and shortly before the recapitulation allows the augmented subordinate theme (4) to be heard in a $^2/_4$ passage intoned over sustained chords in the woodwind, the delicate rustling of the violins and the mysterious pizzicato of the violoncellos and basses, and by the cor anglais on the only occasion of its use in this symphony.

The recapitulation, which runs true to type in introducing the subordinate theme, concludes with a dynamically powerful coda embroidered with lively and extremely varied polyphonic and figural work. At the end of this coda the principal theme (3) appears in a unison of horns and bassoons above the wild whirlings of motif 1 in the tympani, and then, against the rhythmic dancing of the horns, there is an anticipatory statement of the main theme from the finale (15), whereupon the movement comes to an agitated close.

SECOND MOVEMENT

(*Adagio di molto*, A flat major, $^2/_4$)

The second movement, inscribed in the manuscript "*Second Part*", opens with a grave four-bar motif lengthened by pause-signs, given out first in A flat major and then repeated in C minor:

Close upon it there rises in the oboes a broad principal theme full of longing, with a calm wavy accompaniment in the strings and supported by a typically Dvořák flexible bass (indicated in the example in small notes two octaves higher:

After a short interruption, the theme develops another thought, whose rising sequences are tinged with longing (Ex. 8). The principal theme (7) returns above a more agitated clarinet accompaniment, and yields to the grave introductory motif (6), whereupon it is delivered once more by the oboes, this time with a contrapuntal counter-melody in the violas which, in a dramatic change to G flat major, weave an inner melodic line of lovely and warmly emotional expression (Ex. 8a):

A sudden modulation to E flat major prepares the way for a new theme, like the sound of solemn fanfares (Ex. 9a), to which, in the course of further development, another festive little motif is added, (Ex. 9b), interesting for the reminiscence it evokes of Smetana:

In strong contrast to the temporal splendour of these motifs is the calm atmosphere of religious fervour radiated by the next theme (Ex. 10), which alternates twice with the preceding motifs (9a and 9b):

This theme is then followed by a kind of development section, the second part of which is treated in the form of a double fugato in the introductory theme (6). With the return of the principal theme (7), the movement enters C major, in which key theme 9 is taken up by the full orchestra, whereupon theme 7 is heard for the last time. After a delicate diminuendo (with motif 2 on the sixth = *e flat—g* in the tympani!) this theme yields to theme 8, which closes the movement with a prayer of touching sincerity.

THIRD MOVEMENT

(Allegretto, C minor, $^2/_4$)

The scherzo movement is written in the usual three-part or 'ternary' form. The first part is built up from a single small, lively motif with typical canon imitation worked out with plenty of variety:

11. Allegretto

In the middle section, which is in the key of E flat major, three themes appear. The first, not without a sense of humour, is the most important and is in march rhythm:

12. Ob.

The second, punctuated by leaps of a seventh, is really a continuation of the first:

13.

The third, which makes its entry in the middle of the trio, is melodically more leisurely, calmer and, in feeling, somewhat graver: Ex. 14

14.

After a literal repetition of the first section there follows a coda which deals with themes 11 and 12 and various derivatives from them, and then proceeds to build up the tension in energetic rhythmic gradations which, however, at their very culmination (beneath the principal theme, motif 2 is heard in the tympani) collapse, and the movement—quite unexpectedly and almost involuntarily—comes to an end.

FOURTH MOVEMENT

(*Allegro animato*, C major, $^2/_4$)

From the last movement we quote the three most important themes. The first and principal theme is delivered in the characteristic timbre of the oboes above a dominant pedal, with pizzicato chords, and is gaily pastoral in mood:

15. Allegro animato

In the course of the movement, however, this theme becomes more and more energetic and self-assertive till, at the close, it sounds forth in an augmentation of triumphant rejoicing.

A proud, confident tone characterizes the second theme and its derivatives:

16.

The third theme, on the other hand, from which the subordinate theme is developed, contrasts strongly in its minor mode with the two preceding themes as well as in its melancholy colouring, which seems indeed to belong to a different world. It consists of two strains of which especially the first (17a) shows a rich variety of musical and rhythmic development.

These three main themes, along with several derivatives, form the musical material of a movement whose form lies somewhere between a rondo and a sonata movement, while showing important deviations from both, especially in the process of the thematic exposition (which is broadly discursive) and in a tendency to disregard the demands of strict functional economy in the proportions and the structure of the movement.

A dynamic crescendo leads into the coda, which assumes the character of an impressive, grave and solemn hymn in $^3/_2$ time, built up of fragments of the main theme. At its climax, motif 2 is heard, for the last time, in augmentation in the tympani. The final paragraph of the work returns to the original tempo and closes with an energetic recapitulation of the main theme 15 in the horns and in a mood of happy excitement.

SYMPHONY IN B FLAT MAJOR, OP. 4

Instrumentation: piccolo, 2 flutes, 2 oboes, 2 clarinets, 2 bassoons, 4 horns, 2 trumpets, 3 trombones, tympani, strings.

Sketch completed between August 1st and September 9th, 1865, scored by October 9th, 1865 in Prague. Revised at the beginning of 1888. First performed on March 11th, 1888 in Prague, by the orchestra of the National Theatre with Adolf Čech conducting. —Unpublished.—Duration: about 45 minutes.

The short interval of time separating these two symphonies is sufficient explanation for the close kinship between them and the large number of shortcomings as well as attractive features which they have in common. The former come out most clearly in the opening and closing movements where the sonata form suffers from a too great profusion of thematic material, which crowds in upon the composer more thickly than can be organically assimilated into the structure of the movement. This weakness, which is underlined by the excessive breadth of the two movements, was obviously in part attributable to the circumstance that Dvořák had already come under the influence of the neo-Romanticists, Wagner and Liszt, in choosing themes of very loose construction, unperiodic and harmonically shifting. And then, also, to the fact that the contrapuntal texture of his musical sentences is, in places, too dense, a fault he corrected to a large extent in the process of a later clarifying revision. From the point of view of form, the inner movements, the adagio and scherzo, are immeasurably more mature. In them too, there is at times a tendency to diffuseness, although the three-part rondo form imposes greater concentration on the design and better proportions in the individual sections. A characteristic, formal feature of the symphony is that each movement is preceded by a longer or shorter introduction which always, however, keeps to the basic tempo of the movement.

On the other hand, if we except the occasional overloading of the score (partially rectified in a later revision of the instrumentation), this symphony again gives clear proof of the uncommon musicality of its creator. For though some of the themes may be somewhat lacking in expressiveness or plasticity (especially in the last movement), the majority are of truly symphonic stamp, delighting the ear with the noble variety of their melodic, harmonic and rhythmic invention. As regards expression, Dvořák is still clearly influenced by his great models, more especially Beethoven and Schubert, in spite of which there are not wanting in the composition the signs of a strongly inventive individuality. This is reflected, on the one hand, in the character of certain themes, and, on the other, in the vigorous treatment of the bass and inner melodic line, as well as in the way the composer alternates and combines elements of the different themes and is able with these materials to work up the movement to highly effective climaxes.*

A much more substantial difference between the two symphonies is observable in the whole character of the content and of the mood. This work is, like the first, a completely convincing expression of youth. But of youth no longer haunted by the memories of past griefs and joys. It would seem that even the wound of his still recent disappointment in love has healed, his pent-up emotion having found outlet in the passionate confession of the cycle of songs entitled "*The Cypresses*". Evidently the delight in Nature aroused by a summer holiday in the country, during which the second symphony was born, had exercised a benignly soothing and healing influence on the author's soul. In this symphony youth finds expression, but youth which is already conscious of its power and is looking forward with clear and confident eyes to its own future. Thus

---

* For his cycle of piano compositions, "Silhouettes", op. 8, Dvořák used the principal theme of the last movement from the second symphony (Ex. 23) which, with its rocking movement and wistfulness of mood, forms the thematic core of the sixth "Silhouette". The theme of the Scherzo (Ex. 17), which was used first in the unpublished third "Silhouette", employed later in a more decorative and attractive variation in the eleventh of the series.

the musical content of the symphony is, for the most part, of a happy spring-like freshness, full of movement and youthful, buoyant élan, which find most convincing utterance in the first and last movements, and also, to a certain extent, in the Scherzo. If the yearnings of a lover's heart still find expression in the broad melodic phrasing of the deeply emotional and specifically Dvořák Adagio, it is a heart that passion has purified and tempered. Should we take as the gauge of the inner contrast between these two symphonies the works which had the strongest influence on their creation, then we might think of Beethoven's Fifth Symphony, in connection with Dvořák's first symphony, while the second reminds us in parts especially of his Pastoral Symphony.

FIRST MOVEMENT

(*Allegro con moto*, B flat major, $^2/_4$)

In the opening movement of the symphony two themes are stated straight away, one of which proves to be the principal theme, while the other plays a transitional role. Both are designed to portray the soul of a young man, vigorous, unrepining and looking ahead with youthful confidence. The first bears the imprint of a good-natured countenance, with expressive eye and a sincere, open, if at times dreamily overcast expression:

while the second, which develops out of basic elements of the first, is the reflection of a youthfully joyous and overflowing vitality:

These two themes appear in the opening section of 62 bars which precedes the actual exposition and is immediately followed by another theme, very broad and straightforward, which is not, however, made any further use of constructionally. It grows out of two figures:

Only now, with the principal theme in the form quoted above (1), does the exposition proper begin, the section being marked off with repeat signs. The theme, at first mild and soft, soon grows more tense (a clear indication of which is the rhythmically firmly accented motif (Ex. 4) and leads then to the transitional theme (2)

culminating in the diminished chord *(f-aflat-b-d)* into which the trombones and basses storm with a new energetic thematic figure otherwise of only subsidiary importance:

5.

With the establishment of the bright key of C major a dramatic tranquilisation follows, both in the dynamics and tone-colouring, which sets the scene for the long-awaited entry of the second subject. It is a theme melodically fully articulated and expressively well sustained. Presented according to rule in the key of the dominant (F major), it begins with a tenderly yearning duet between clarinet and violin, to which a pedal-point on a bare fifth and a two-bar diminution of the main theme (16), in decorative imitation, gives a pastoral, idyllic colouring:

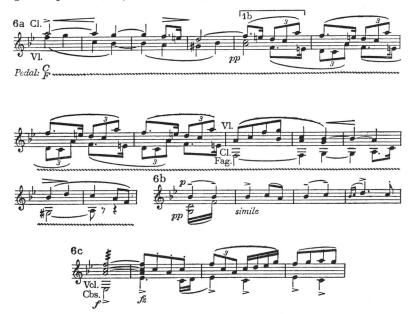

The closing theme, sung by the flute and oboe over the counter-melody of the second violins and 'cellos, returns to the mood of the subordinate theme (Ex. 6a) with which it is, in any case, melodically related (see the even pairs of bracketed bars); indeed, the expression of yearning is further enhanced by the passionate sighs with which it is punctuated:

7.

The sudden change from B flat major to A major strengthens the impression of rising jubilation in which the strings and wood-wind introduce new motifs derived from the regrouping of elements of previous themes and also accompanying them.

8.

The development, modulating freely, first of all works up the main elements of the principal theme (1a, b), until interrupted by a change to the warm key of A flat major in which the subordinate theme (6a), presented by the clarinet, makes its way through the flowing melody of the flutes in new guise:

9.

In the further course of the development, in which the changing moods are well contrasted, two new thoughts not otherwise employed in the movement surprise us by their appearance towards the end of the section:

The movement then ends with a fairly broad recapitulation diverging somewhat from the exposition and culminating in the presentation of theme 7, sung in jubilant cantabile by the full orchestra.

SECOND MOVEMENT

(*Poco adagio*, G minor, $^{12}/_{8}$)

The slow movement of the second symphony has the character of a nocturne in which a heart moved by longing and desire listens to the mysterious voices of Nature as she sinks to sleep and at the same time holds converse with itself. Borne on a calm, broad and uninterrupted stream of melody, this movement is reminiscent of the corresponding mood of the movement in Beethoven's Pastoral Symphony, and, though of considerable length, is a worthy precursor of the masterly adagios of the composer's maturity. The form is that of a three-part rondo.

The first section opens with an eight-bar introduction in which, above the stealthily gliding steps of the basses and the long-drawn-out and muffled tones of the horns and bassoons, there weaves in and out a delicate wavy figure of semiquavers in the violins and violas, supported by soft chords in the woodwind alternating with the sharp accents of the 'cellos. This introduction, like the evening wind gently rocking the forest, creates the atmosphere for the entry of the principal theme which is given ample room to display itself in 16 bars of slow-moving $^{12}/_8$ time. It is delivered by the violins which, accompanied by an independent counterpoint in the solo horn, draw their line of melody over the chords of the clarinets and the undulating semiquaver movement of the second violins and violas and the sinuous, typically Dvořák line of the 'cellos and basses, punctuated by yearning bird-like sighs in the oboe and flute:

The exposition is followed by an intermezzo of several bars passing through the keys of G and F minor, in which the running passages of the clarinet mingle with the melodic curves of the 'cellos, both alternating with the calm, smoothly-phrased line of the violins, to the accompaniment of short semiquaver figures in the flutes and oboes:

It seems as if the countryside were all at once flooded with silvery moonlight, in whose brightness the sweet song of the nightingale falls upon the ear.

The middle section at first develops in the form of a double fugato on two themes, the quicker and more lively of which is assigned to the strings, while the other, calmer and more sustained, is delivered by the wind instruments:

The fugato suddenly ascends dynamically until stopped short by the dramatic entry of the diminished chord *g sharp-b-d-f*, when calm is again restored with a soft dreamy theme given out by the clarinets and bassoons, enlivened by the delicate rustle of the strings and again punctuated by the yearning sighs of the violoncello, in a contrapuntal design derived from elements of theme 13 (in the violins) and of 14 (in the oboes):

But again the expression becomes agitated and mounts to a crest of chords in the full orchestra (in the harmonic series: A major,

E major, A flat major, E flat major, G minor, D major), the last of
which concludes the movement and at the same time leads up to
the third section which, after a general pause, embarks straight
away on the main theme (12), the scoring being similar to that of
the exposition. This is followed by the second part of the middle
sector theme (15), whereupon a miniature mosaic is built up of
fragments from the main themes, till calm returns with the soft
sighs of the main theme, the movement closing dreamily in the clear,
delicate key of G major.

THIRD MOVEMENT

(Scherzo, *Allegro trio*, B flat major, $^3/_4$)

In the scherzo the dominant mood is again one of vigorous, care-
free and happy youth. The form is ternary, the first and last section
being separated by a trio and the whole ending in a broad coda. By
way of introduction, there is a series of sustained chords struck alternately by the strings and the brass:

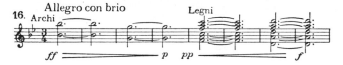

This is repeated three times, transposed successively a fifth
lower, whereupon a slowly swelling and diminishing pedal point develops on the dominant chord of F major, over which the strings
weave a gay variation of the middle theme from the scherzo (quoted

below under 18*b*), which finishes with a lively passage. Now the principal theme of the scherzo dances in with an expressively graceful and flexible menuet motion, of which the bass and inner complementary parts move independently in the chamber music style of a quartet:

Close on its heels there rises in the clarinets and oboes, and then in the strings, a subordinate theme, a variant of which appeared in the introductory bars and which offers a gay, frolicking contrast to the cantabile of the principal theme:

The movement grows in expressiveness and power up to a general pause, after which the full orchestra plunges into the proud, energetic third theme (Ex. 19). This, after mounting to a jubilant fanfare of trumpets and horns and then alternating with its sequel, brings the first part of the scherzo to a close.

A short transition following the chords of the introductory bars (16) leads into the trio in A major in which the solo 'cello sings an expressively phrased melody of eight bars (Ex. 20):

As a sequel to this theme, which again for a while assumes a strongly passionate quality, the wood-winds introduce a sportive thought which, in melody, rhythm and modulation, is already very recognizably Dvořák:

The coda, following a regular repetition of the first part, works only with theme 21*b*, finally going over to a boisterous *presto assai* whose strength, however, falls away again, allowing the movement to close with serenely quiet chords, which accompany a calm, final statement of the augmented theme 21*b*, played by a solo horn.

FOURTH MOVEMENT

(Finale, *Allegro con fuoco*, B flat major, $^2/_2$)

The last movement of the symphony rounds off the whole work very conclusively as regards content, its buoyancy and verve swinging the happy mood of high-spirited youth to a climax. In form and design it has not the clarity and concentration of the two preceding movements, but in its return to the sonata form reveals features similar to those described in the first movement. Here again there is a superfluity of themes, for which there is not always sufficient functional justification, and a considerable amount of digression, along with an insufficiency of structural logic and of thematic organisation. On the other hand it is only fair to point to a number of original ideas and strokes of construction which raise this movement, too, above the common run, as being the work of an author with gifts of no mean creative order.

Such is, for instance, the choice of the key of A major for the several bars of introduction preceding the entry of the principal theme, which reaches the tonic by a simple rise of a semitone. The A major key is first announced by the violas with a vigorously accented C sharp, to which the tympani provide the tonic A and the clarinet and horn the E of the dominant. The 'cello alternates with the violins and some of the wood-wind in introducing a short figure within the compass of this chord, which plays a considerable part throughout the movement:

A short dynamic build-up of this figure (10 bars) leads to the principal theme, delivered by the violins above the sharply rhythmical accompaniment of the clarinets, bassoons and horns:

The development of this theme is again very broad and vague in melodic line and harmonisation, and only takes on firmer contours when, after a rise to a powerful climax, it opens out into D major, with the full orchestra passing to a solemnly expressive and rhythmically plastic continuation of the principal theme:

A dynamic falling-off leads to the subordinate theme, which remains at first in the key of D major and then modulates towards its close to B flat major, in which it is restated with a similar swing round to G flat major:

This theme, decidedly calmer as compared with the first, and not without an echo of passionate desire at its close, is given out first by the horn, together with the viola and 'cello, while clarinet and bassoons join in on its repetition. There follow several bars based on the first figure of the principal theme (23), whereupon the full orchestra vigorously and resolutely proceeds to a transitional theme rhythmically derived from the second subject:

26.

This carries the movement forward with almost festive stateliness, till there is a sudden falling away of tone and the clarinet comes in with the passionately and richly melodious closing theme in the key of D flat major:

27.

The relatively short development, without any well-defined transition, works up—kaleidoscopic fashion—the materials of almost all the themes quoted, in addition to some others introduced for the first time.

The recapitulation begins with the same figure 22 that introduced the movement, but then wanders restlessly through a wide range of keys, taking as its chief thematic material the first bar of figure *a* of the principal theme (23) and, towards the end, a part of theme 24. The subordinate theme (25) and the transitional theme (26) are omitted in the recapitulation and this section proceeds immediately to the closing theme (27), this time in G flat major.

A very broadly designed coda, jubilant and massively scored, brings the work with a short, vigorous Vivace to a punctual conclusion.

SYMPHONY IN E FLAT MAJOR, OP. 10

Instrumentation: piccolo, 2 flutes, 2 oboes, cor anglais, 2 clarinets, 2 bassoons, 4 horns, 2 trumpets, 3 trombones, tuba, tympani, harp, triangle, strings.

Manuscript completed on July 4th 1873. First performance in Prague at a Philharmonic concert (with the combined orchestras of the Czech and German theatres), conducted by Bedřich *Smetana.*—Published in score, parts and piano arrangement for four hands (Vilém *Zemánek*), by Simrock, Berlin, 1912. Duration: 37 minutes.

The second and third symphonies are separated by a long interval of eight years in which Dvořák was creatively very active, having written, in addition to several chamber and vocal works, two operas ("Alfred" and the first version of "King and Charcoal-Burner") and the "Hymnus" ("The Heirs of the White Mountain"), which earned him his first clear successes in Prague. It was a period of important growth in which he achieved a high degree of technical mastery in artistic expression but, at the same time, a period of creative crisis precipitated by the very considerable extent to which he had fallen under the influence of the neo-Romanticists, especially Wagner and Liszt. The E flat major symphony shows very characteristic signs of both processes. The advance made by Dvořák in the art of composition since the preceding symphony can be most clearly seen in the structure of the three movements, whether it be in the incomparably greater sureness in the handling of the sonata form, or in the daring with which he combines this form with that of the rondo, or finally, in the more harmonious proportions of the song-form of the slow movement. Further, a great step forward is apparent in the much greater degree of *coherence* in the subject matter of the different movements, and, consequently, in the neatness of design and the organisation of the thematic material. If some extra-organic thematic elements still appear, they do so only as countermelodies to some main themes or to strengthen the dynamic build-up, while the impression of apparently super-

fluous thematic ideas, in the Adagio and the last movement, is considerably weakened by their recognizable inter-relationship. The
themes in each of the movements are, for the most part, derived from
a single basic theme, elements of which occur also in the other
movements, so that it is here really a *question of monothematism*,
a feature which gives the E flat major symphony a unique position
in the series of Dvořák's nine symphonies, as it is also the only symphony consisting of *three movements*.

The two last characteristics confirm, at the same time, the close
relation in which this symphony stands to the music of the neo-
Romanticists. This connection is revealed, first of all, in the form:
both in the reduced number of movements and in the monothematism, innovations in which Dvořák was following the path opened up by Berlioz and Liszt; and again in the expression which shows
traces of the author's predilection for the individualistic features
of Wagner's music from which, however, the composer had, by that
time, to a great extent emancipated himself. Reminders of this influence are to be found in a number of direct reminiscences, melodic
and harmonic, in the broad, irregular and harmonically unsettled
slackness of the melodic line, and, again, in several typical features
of Wagnerian instrumentation, such as a fondness for the cor anglais and the harp, or the device of dividing the strings for flexibly
undulating passages, frequently used in places which, also in their
musical invention, recall Wagner. All this, however, in no way
affects our recognition of the fact that it is just in these aspects of the
work that Dvořák shows himself a master of the orchestral palette
and one of the greatest of his time.

Thus, while in these purely musical features of the third symphony
we have the proof that this is a work which, in its conception and
form, has already reached a considerable degree of maturity and
artistic vitality, we are confirmed in our judgment by the strength
and purity of the emotional quality of its content. The third symphony clearly has its source in the same fervent, patriotic feeling

as inspired the preceding "Hymnus"—The Heirs of the White Mountain. The grave, heroic and elevated mood of the first movement may at least find a partial explanation as being the musical expression of the conflicting emotions of pride in past glory and grief at past humiliations, awakened in the composer's mind by the contemplation of the history of his country: the gloomy, but softly melting Slav melancholy of the opening and closing sections of the Adagio, regret at the joylessness of the present, along with the grave optimism of the marching rhythm of the middle section; the bright gleam of faith in a better future and, finally, the cheerful good spirits of the finale seem to express the author's determination to go forward to meet that future with all his forces gathered. It is not surprising then that such a content should have stimulated Dvořák's creative imagination to a work artistically vital and convincing. The fact, too, that in this composition the composer omitted the scherzo, the character of which is then merged with that of the last movement, was without doubt a procedure dictated in part by the content of the symphony, but also undoubtedly connected with his search for a new solution to the scherzo movement in cyclic compositions—a striving which is apparent in several chamber music works belonging to this period.

FIRST MOVEMENT

(Allegro moderato. E flat major, $^6/_8$)

As has already been indicated above, the first movement might be regarded as inspired by a backward look into the history of the composer's native land: elevating in the contemplation of periods of glory and strength, but depressing in those periods in which it lay prostrate under the blows of powerful outward foes and weakened by inward strife and faction. The former finds expression in the expositional and concluding section determining its predominantly festive, earnest and ardent character; the latter is reflected in the middle part (the development), which contrasts strongly in mood with the other two sections. From this follows, too, the prominence given to the two principal themes: in the exposition and recapitulation the main theme predominates—the subordinate theme in the development. As was customary in Dvořák's work at the beginning of the 'seventies, there is no closing theme at the end of this movement, its place being taken by the principal theme.

The movement opens with a simple rhythmic motif of a fourth, which proves to be the bass support for the principal theme, but which possesses independent significance for the rest of the symphony:

The principal theme is introduced in the third bar, first by the oboe and violins, which are joined by the clarinet, bassoon and 'cello. The core of the theme, one of the broadest and most expressive musical ideas in Dvořák's symphonic music, consists of a 14-bar period, curving in a broad flexible arch and falling into two important thematic strains:

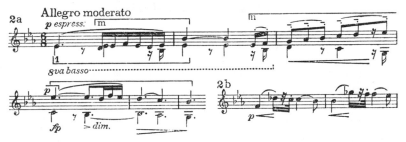

The diatonic descent in the bass in Ex. 2*a* should be noted as a feature of considerable significance, which moves up into the inner parts during the further development of the theme and is the material out of which is spun the melodic line of the subordinate theme (see Ex. 3*a*).

The above-cited period, though melodically complete in itself, does not yet, however, conclude the exposition of the main theme. There follows a further broad development typical of Dvořák's procedure at the time, melodically and harmonically meandering, in which there appear new variations of the theme (2*c*) and of both its principal strains (2*a*, *b*), as well as other motifs in various transmutations and combinations (2*d*, *e*). The character of the whole intro-

ductory passage is powerfully dramatic, with its changing and often sharply syncopated rhythms and its dynamic tension mounting to an imposing climax in which the full orchestra restates the main theme (2*a*, *b*) *grandioso*.

The subordinate theme in the key of G flat major is the very opposite in character to the main theme: a square section of eight bars, of great simplicity in melody, harmony and rhythm, and calm yet dignified in expression. Of its origin in the bass of the principal theme mention has been made above. Its connection with that theme is further underlined by figure—*m*—which forms a melodically characteristic constituent of the second and fourth bars of the subordinate theme. It should be noted that this theme, too, is supported by

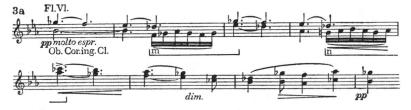

a thematically independent bass which, here scarcely perceptible, later, in the culminating entries of the theme, acquires exceptional significance:

The exposition of the subordinate theme is relatively short, limiting itself to two repetitions. Thereupon the elements of the principal theme provide the materials for the close of the expositional section, which is not repeated, and, with a direct modulation to E flat minor, enters directly on the development. After a passing allusion to the principal theme (2*a*), theme 3*a* assumes emotional colouring by its translation into a soft key or as a consequence of the specific *timbre* of the instruments to which it is assigned (cor anglais, 'cello, horn or violins). In the gradations of the theme an agitating role is filled by two short, one-bar motifs, one melodic (4*a*), the other purely rhythmic (4*b*), which rise in steeply mounting sequences in the full orchestra (the first in passionate lamentation by the violins) and then, gathering up another thematic figure not yet used (4*c*), whose incisive rhythms in the alternating voices of the trombones and horns add their weight to the growing momentum of the passage, culminates as it were in shrieks of terror. There follows sudden

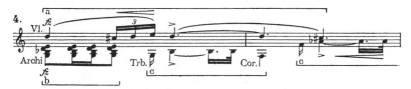

decline, and the next part of the development takes as its starting-
point the first two bars of the principal theme which are repeated
a semitone higher in the bassoon and 'cello, while into the wavy
movement of the strings new agitation is carried by the *ostinato* of
the rhythmic figure in the clarinet (5a), caricatured at intervals
by interpolations of the horn (5b):

Then comes a sudden short rise to the majestic entry of the subordinate theme (3a in G major) in the full orchestra. This constitutes the climax of the development and also its conclusion, for, eight
bars later, the episode opens out into the tremendous dominant seventh chord of E flat major, from the heights of which the violins
lead rapidly down into the calm stream of the recapitulation.

    The latter is leisurely, developing new aspects of the principal
theme (2), which fetches a wide compass through a great variety of
keys and in a wealth of orchestral colouring, whereupon a sharp
dynamic gradation leads to the short but impressive reappearance
of the subordinate theme (3) delivered with immense power of tone.
A brief interruption of this gives pause for a re-gathering of forces,
and, after another gradation, in which the motif 5a also plays an
important part, the stream of sound sweeps forward to a mighty conclusion, whose elevated and festive character is further heightened

by the trumpets and trombones reaffirming the monumental bass motif of the introduction (1), thus bringing the movement round full circle to its beginning.

SECOND MOVEMENT

(Adagio molto. Tempo di marcia, C sharp minor $^2/_4$*)*

The middle movement keeps, in its main features, to three-part rondo form. The first part is permeated by a pathos which, along with the measured movement of $^2/_4$ time, gives it something of the character of a funeral march. In its content it mirrors convincingly a state of spiritual gloom and dejection evoked by bitter and painful meditations. This finds utterance in several themes possessing sufficiently close inner relationship, being linked by certain common elements, while yet retaining a clear connection with the principal theme (2) of the first movement. The opening theme of the movement is delivered in the gloomily overcast tones of the strings and wood-wind. The sextolet in the fourth bar of this theme is a

significant reminder of a similar figure in the principal theme (2*a*) of the preceding movement and is a characteristic element in almost all the themes of this movement. Thus it appears at once in a short transitional thought,

and concludes the following auxiliary theme:

it also accompanies the plaintive motif, interpolated like sighs in the horn, being in reality nothing other than the detached second strain of the principal theme of the first movement (2*b*):

These are the main thematic ideas in the introductory part of the movement, which is repeated with a number of smaller deviations, but with clearer dynamic gradations, after which it dies away with delicate quotations of the sextolet figure leading into the middle section.

Piercing the grey oppressive clouds as with a shaft of sunlight, a sudden change to the bright key of D flat major disperses the gloom of C sharp minor. The middle part of the movement remains unaltered as regards pace and rhythm. In it the wood-wind and horns present a theme, serious and almost majestic, but full of prophetic confidence, in which the melodic and rhythmic conformity of the bass, with the introductory motif of the first movement (1), is, though perhaps unintentional, interesting as bringing out the connection between the subject-matter of the two movements:

There is something mythical in the nature of this theme and in the whole atmosphere of the middle section of the movement—an impression to which the frequent use of harp arpeggios and the rich rustling of the strings contribute very substantially. Some reminiscences of Wagner's Walhalla motif (from the "Ring of the Nibelungs") are a symptomatic feature of this symphony and of the time of its composition, which is as understandable as it is characteristic. The four-bar phrase, which joins on to the richly orchestrated repetition of the theme, has also a distinctly Wagnerian profile:

The next part of this section is again broadly worked out, but darkens the calm and clarity of its mood with new moments of emotional yearning and agitation indicated also by the chromatic chord of the motif which, in combination with the sextolet figure, reveals its connection with theme 6 and provides a nexus out of which endless new thematic ideas are developed without ever losing their kinship with the master-pattern. Here they are quoted in the order in which they appear:

* This motiv with the characteristic triplet accompaniment was used by Dvořák later (1880) without change in the middle of the sixth Legend op. 59.

After the exposition of the last of these themes, a short gradation is built up to prepare for the entry of the principal theme (10), which now sounds forth in all the glory of the combined brass, accompanied by the richly decorative and undulating motion of the strings.

The closing section of the movement, analogous to the first in key and thematic material, is reduced to about half the original volume. The analogy holds, too, for the content, the mood being wholly dominated by the original expression of gloom and suffering, but intensified to a degree not reached in the first section. This mood of dark despair is not able, however, to maintain itself to the very end of the movement. In the last few bars there rises once more in the horns the gravely confident, pathetic theme of the middle section (10), to the accompaniment of undulating arpeggiated chords in the strings and harp, mounting to ever higher registers of the wood-wind, (as if into rarefied, etherial spheres), till a calm D flat major chord brings the movement to a close.

THIRD MOVEMENT

(Finale. *Allegro vivace*, E flat major, $^2/_4$)

The brighter conclusion of the preceding movement foretold that the dominating expression of gloom is not one of permanent despair, but that belief in a better future has not yet evaporated from the soul. The last movement is then one great shout of exultation and joy at the anticipation of what is to come. Full of vital energy, the movement swings along, never faltering, never failing in its mood. The themes step out in youthfully vigorous and elastic rhythms, and the movement piles up with an irrepressible dynamism to a culminating orgy of rejoicing.

As regards the form of the movement, it is, in its main outlines, rondo, but not without certain features of sonata form. The themes, of which there are at first sight quite a number, prove to be, with one exception, all derivatives from a single basic theme, the *Urkeim* of the Lisztian doctrine, so that there we are entitled to speak of monothematism in a much more literal sense than in the preceding movements. In these themes there are no Wagnerian reminiscences —on the contary, there are distinct intimations of Dvořák's specifically individual traits. Structurally, too, this movement is the most original and the boldest in conception. Not based on any exact, accepted scheme, it develops freely within the framework of its individual paragraphs, and in its thematic construction is full of interesting and daring ideas and invention which, though not always completely clarified, are nevertheless convincing manifestations of real creative genius.

The key to the mood of this movement is immediately established in a basic eight-bar theme which is delightfully youthful, rhythmically crisp and gay:*

*Dvořák created this theme from the diminution of the melodic thought on which is based the big ensemble in D major, in the third act of the first version of the opera "King and Charcoal-Burner" (87), later rejected by the author, where the theme has this form:

13.   Allegro vivace

The theme is led up to by a fairly long introductory passage, which then makes way for the second theme in A flat major, whose kinship with the first is specially apparent in the rhythmic figures marked *a* and *b* in Ex. 14:

14.

The melody and the firm resilient rhythm of this theme seem to sum up the slogan: "Fearlessly forward to a better life!" and the spirit of this sentiment is given body by the use of the full volume of orchestral tone.

An energetic gradation leads to the third theme, which is related to the basic motif only in its general rhythmic outline. Its expression—manly, proud and unafraid—raises still further the mood of the preceding theme both in melody and scoring.

15.   *con 8* ....

A further theme, the first two bars of which are identical with the basic theme, then completely changes its melodic and rhythmic line, continuing, in sharply syncopated rising sequences, in the bold spirit of the preceding themes:

16.

With its rise into higher registers, the movement grows in tone-volume, from which there is a sudden decline when, after a short modulating process, it swerves into C major and, with a gradual augmentation in delicate octaves in the strings of figure *a* from theme 14, the way is paved for the fifth theme which rhythmically is the counterpart of the basic theme (13):

17. Picc.
    Ob.

This theme introduces a new element into the movement in as far as it is the first important deviation from the tonic key, but also in its teasing, playful mood and bizarre colouring which contrast strongly with the resolute character of the preceding themes. For this reason, too, if we bear in mind the sonata form of the movement, the first group of four themes (13—16) might be considered the principal theme and this new element the secondary theme.

This fact then plays an important role in the development and in the recapitulation, which omits themes 13, 14 and 16 and provides a surprising stroke in the modulation into the key of B major. In the culminating jubilation of the coda, the main theme (13) again comes into its own, punctuated by victorious fanfares in the trumpets and trombones based on a fragment from the first bar of theme 17. And with these exultant fanfares the work comes to a full and satisfying close.

SYMPHONY IN D MINOR, OP. 13

Instrumentation: 2 piccolos, 2 flutes, 2 oboes, 2 clarinets, 2 bassoons, 4 horns, 2 trumpets, 3 trombones, tympani, triangle, bass drum, cymbals, harp, strings. Written in score between January 1st and March 26th, 1874.—The third movement first performed in Prague on May 25th, 1874, and conducted by Bedřich *Smetana*, the whole symphony in Prague on March 6th 1892, with the composer conducting. Score, parts and a four-handed arrangement for piano (Vilém *Zemánek*), published by Simrock, Berlin, in 1912. Duration: 41 minutes.

Just as the third symphony in E flat major, in comparison with the second, testified to a marked advance in Dvořák's compositional technique, so the fourth symphony shows a comparable step forward in the formal command of expressive means and, especially, in the extent to which the composer has thrown off the earlier influence of the neo-Romanticists. Not that even this work is totally devoid of echoes of Wagnerian invention, but they are no more than echoes of very minor importance as compared with the originality of ideas and their treatment and the vigorous strength of national individuality, liberated in part by the example of Smetana's work, in his melodic and rhythmic ideas. As we should expect, this emancipation goes hand in hand with the more highly organised and better proportioned design of the symphony, while the structure of the individual movements, as well as the thematic treatment, show further progress in the direction of greater conciseness and more complete organic assimilation and plasticity. This is well illustrated not only in the opening and closing movements, which are remarkable for their dynamic force and daring constructional inventiveness, especially in their middle and final parts, but also in the slow movement in variation form—the broadly melodic Andante sostenuto, with its deep range of mood, and the original, high-spirited and pawkily gay scherzo. In the orchestration of this work, too, Dvořák shows a clear striving for greater simplicity and transparency, along with richer polyphonic colouring and fuller plasticity of expression. With the exception of the scherzo, in which piccolos are substituted for the two flutes and abundant use is made of the harp and percussion (triangle, bass drum and cymbals), the scoring of this symphony works for the most part with the Beethoven orchestra.

As regards the content of the work, there is no doubt that, except for the calm seriousness of the slow movement, the whole symphony is pervaded by a mood of which the characteristic tone is agitated and emotionally dark in colour. But that tone is never allowed to have the last and decisive word, for, from the first it is held in subjection by the forces of Dvořák's essentially healthy disposition. This, however, gives to the composition its character of impetuous youthful defiance and resolve which, in spite of the most passionate endeavour, is not yet completely successful in the first movement. But after the fervent prayer ending on a note of confidence in the following movement, it proceeds, as if filled with new courage, to refresh itself in the scherzo with a good dose of humour and boisterous spirits, reaching in the logically and artistically convincing consummation of the finale a clarified and balanced view of life.

FIRST MOVEMENT

(*Allegro*, D minor, $^3/_4$)

The mood of the first movement is determined by the nature of the three related themes of the introduction. Above the irregular sinuous movement of the string quartet playing in unison and the sinister halting steps of the bass with which the movement begins pianissimo:

there appears, after four bars, the first and basic theme which, growing out of a simple, rhythmically clear-cut two-bar motif, is at first
darkly restless in expression (2a), but in its further development
quickly clears up and assumes an air of manly resolution:

After a short gradation it opens out into the second theme, in
which a number of clearly differentiated figures are melodically and
rhythmically presented in a passionate and elevated tone:

Immediately following it, almost like a concluding clause, comes
the third theme, bringing out still more emphatically the firm spirit
of resolve embodied in the first:

A short exposition of these themes completes the first section of the movement, for a sudden dynamic descent of theme 4 and a short transitional passage with modulation opens into B flat major, in which the subordinate theme is given out. This new theme, with its soft, supple melodic line and Czech folk-song colouring is an effective contrast to the preceding theme:

Theme 5 is repeated several times, gaining in strength till it reaches a climax in the full orchestra. The concluding part of the exposition, marked by a change into E major, does not introduce any new theme, but again returns to the principal theme, passing its two-bar opening figure (2a) from one instrument to another in a gradual decrescendo. The development works up all the themes so far presented, while its mood is dominated again by the expression of passionate agitation and an energetic fighting spirit.

The recapitulation is chiefly interesting for the way it plunges straight into the passionate theme 3 and boldly develops it in a number of fairly remote keys. The calm entry of the lyric theme 5 and a somewhat listless quotation of theme 2a are only short episodes in a terse and energetic coda.

SECOND MOVEMENT

(Andante e molto cantabile, B flat major, ⁴/₄)

The second movement of this symphony holds a distinctive place in Dvořák's work as being the first example of independent variations. Its great breadth and emotional depth are determined at the outset by the stately, chorale-like character of the principal theme which, despite a certain Wagnerian colouring, is one of the loveliest manifestations of Dvořák's musical thought. The theme consists of two strains—one of ten and the other of eight bars, the latter, however, being derived from the former. The melodic substance of the theme divides up into several independent figures of which the following are the most important:

The statement of the theme itself is entrusted to the wind alone. The mellow, sonorous tones of the clarinets, bassoons, and trombones, joined in the fourth bar by the horns, impart to the theme the character of a solemn, fervently moving supplication. This mood is also maintained in the first two variations which are, in melody and harmony, a regular repetition of the theme, enlivened to some extent by figural embroidery.

The first noticeable deviation comes with the third variation. The theme is broken up into a series of syncopated chords, delivered by the woodwind and horns, which provide what is really the accompaniment to a new melody in the 'cellos, and obviously related to the principal theme:

A further variation begins with a canon at the fifth, divided between the oboes and the violins. At first fairly calm, its expression is very soon enlivened by a bustling imitation of the theme, taken up by one instrument after another, its undercurrent of excitement disturbing not a little the broadly-phrased cantabile of the other instruments:

The excitement grows and leads to a sharp outburst, but calm is again restored, while the fifth variation gives to the violins and woodwind a broad melody derived from the principal theme, into the concluding phrase of which there is woven a faint and dying reminiscence of the above-mentioned diminished theme. Once more the principal theme appears in canon at the fifth as at the beginning of the fourth variation, whereupon its various main elements are reviewed, its diminished version bringing the movement to a close in a mood of calm reconciliation and unclouded confidence.

THIRD MOVEMENT

(Scherzo. *Allegro feroce*, D minor, $^6/_4$)

After the almost religious calm of the preceding movement, the scherzo opens with a startling explosion of almost impish humour. This impression is evoked by an abrupt, uncouth motif, followed by three crashing chords with which the wind, in unison with the strings, opens the movement:

And then the principal theme of the scherzo, at first awkwardly stiff and slow-moving as presented in the tonic minor key, is decidedly grotesque in character.* But the theme, and with it the

8. Allegro feroce

mood of the movement, undergoes a sudden change, acquiring an expression of youthful vigour when, after a new build-up based on the introductory motif (7), it is declaimed in the bright key of D major—this time in unison by wood-wind and horns, above the accompaniment of the rest of the orchestra, in which the harp, here used for the only time in the symphony, has an important say.

The middle part of the scherzo (Trio, *L'istesso tempo*, C major, $^2/_4$) retains no trace of the uncouth primitiveness of the first section. It is in the march-rhythm of a holiday crowd of simple, honest, good-humoured people which, as if coming from a distance, steadily grows in force and volume till it reaches a full-bodied climax and then diminishes, as if receding again into the distance. Its theme is half a humorous grimace and half an expression of proud defiance (with faint reminiscences of the tailors' motif in the last scene of Wagner's "Meistersinger"):

9. L'istesso tempo

The third part of the scherzo is a faithful replica of the first part up to the entry of the key of D major, at which point, instead of a

* Dvořák used this theme later for the middle part of the characteristic piece "In Troublous Times", in the cycle entitled "From the Bohemian Forest", piano duets, op. 68.

repetition of the main theme (8), the humorous theme of the trio
(9) bursts out in the full orchestra. Here follows an interesting episode: into the calm marching step of the horns the violins suddenly
interpolate a motif from the beginning of the scherzo (7a), with a
quotation of the main theme of the first movement (2a), below which
the 'cellos and double-basses weave the supporting motif of the
introduction (1a). It is as if the composer wished once more to
cast a backward glance at the passionate agitation of the starting-
point from which the work had run its course. A sudden clash of the
themes cited brings new life into the movement which, in accelerated tempo, leads to a coda ushered in by the strings in unison, with
echoes of the theme of the Trio (9), and winds up with a vigorous
final quotation of the introductory theme (7a).

FOURTH MOVEMENT

(Finale. *Allegro con brio*, D minor, $^2/_4$)

The last movement of the symphony is in expression and mood
the very essence of courage and confidence. Here, too, the marching-
step is the basic rhythmic element, but how different from the heavy,
good-humoured tread of the trio in the preceding movement!
The principal theme steps out with youthful buoyancy, while the
broad smoothly-phrased lyrical theme of the second subject, though
quieter in movement, in no way holds up the swinging pace set by
the character of the principal theme. In form the movement is a
rondo with two themes and a tendency to digress into sonata form.
The first of the themes restricts itself to two short double bars, of
which the first pair is interrogatory and the second pair a response.

10a Allegro con brio

In its continuation, howerer, it evolves into a melodically, rhythmically and harmonically much softer and slower-moving variant
in the key of F major:

The subordinate theme contrasts with the first in its more tranquil and broader melodic stream (it spreads over 40 bars) and in its
strong cmotional intensity. Here are three of its most significant melodic figures:

An interesting detail appears at the very close of its second exposition: the viola and horn intone a motif whose characteristic trill
and rhythmic effect recall the motif from the Trio of the scherzo (9):

A strongly agitated development, richly varied in modulations,
leads to the lively recapitulation section. On this is grafted an expansive coda, which then rushes with gathering speed to a triumphant and joyful conclusion.

SYMPHONY IN F MAJOR, OP. 76

Instrumentation: 2 flutes, 2 oboes, 2 clarinets, bass clarinet, 2 bassoons, 4 horns, 2 trumpets, 3 trombones, tympani, triangle, strings.

Written in score between June 15th and July 23rd, 1875 in Prague. Performed for the first time in Prague on March 25th, 1879, by the orchestra of the Czech Theatre conducted by Adolf *Čech.*—Published in score, parts and four-handed arrangement for piano (Josef *Zubatý*) by Simrock, Berlin, 1888.—Duration: 34 minutes.

The F major symphony for long held a peculiar position among Dvořák's symphonic works. It was generally known and also designated in print as the *"third"*, not, however, as being the third in order of composition, for it was in fact the *fifth*, but according to the order of publication, after the later (!) symphonies in D major, op. 60 and in D minor, op. 70. It was an intentional deception for which the Berlin publisher Simrock was responsible, for the F major symphony was written in score five years before the *"first"* symphony in D major and almost ten years before the *"second"* in D minor, its opus number being originally 24, the opus number 76 having been given it on publication and against the express wish of the composer.* Before publication Dvořák carried out a revision of the score in which he made some alterations in the instrumentation, several small abridgements, and added considerably to the dynamic indications. The symphony was dedicated to the conductor, Hans von *Bülow*, a sincerely enthusiastic and energetic propagator of Dvořák's works who, shortly before, had described Dvořák in a letter as *"along with Brahms, the most gifted composer of the present day"*.

The misleading numbering of the symphony was the reason why musical opinion, especially abroad, not being informed of the facts

* The same fate overtook a number of Dvořák's other work published at the same time; the string quintet with double-bass, op. 77 (originally op. no. 18), the Symphonic Variations, op. 78 (originally op. 40), "Psalm 149", op. 79 (op. 52) and the Quartet in E major, op. 80 (op. 27).

in passing jugment on the work, did the composer less than justice. It was quite understandable. After the D major and especially the D minor, op. 70, this symphony could not mark an advance either technically or in the individuality and strength of its expression; on the contrary, it could not be looked upon but as a step back. The work, however, appears in quite a different light and its evaluation is very different if it is given its proper place in the composer's creative development. Then we see it as yet another link in that transitional process which carries Dvořák forward from the period of strongest creative ferment, under the influence of the neo-Romanticists, to the period in which, with his return to the tradition of the great classical masters, he achieved complete creative stability and clarity of aim; that is, from the E flat major symphony of 1873, by way of the D minor symphony (1874) and the F major symphony, to the later D major, with which he made his world début as a symphonist. Thus, if we view the works in their proper chronological order, we realize that the F major symphony is not a composition of such pronounced individuality, nor in its form and content so balanced and unified a work of art as the following in D major, but that, compared with the preceding D minor symphony of 1874, it shows a new advance in purity, concentration and neatness of design, as well as in the greater number of musical and constructional strokes of a specifically Dvořák character. And if, in the first three movements, it does not surpass the preceding work, the interest and boldness of musical thought and form, the swift flow, the powerful structure and the beauty of expression of the last movement raise it far above its predecessor.

This last-mentioned inequality between the first three movements and the finale is determined in great part by the content of the work. It is true that the whole symphony in F major, although written in the composer's thirty-fourth year, still breathes the spirit of *youth* (even if it is youth in a more thoughtful mood), which, having passed through an acute personal and artistic crisis, has retained its vigour in its courageous struggle to win through them. Youthful is the bucolic simplicity which, alternating between the sunny smile of a soul at peace and the expression of joyful resolve, radiates from the content of the first movement. Youthful in feeling is the melancholy longing and fervent bliss of the Andante, as is also the moderately gay dancing mood of the Scherzo, which follows it without a break; and it is again the surging vitality of youth which carries the last movement through its dynamic development to the orgy of jubilation with which it closes. And yet one cannot help feeling that the first three movements of the symphony arose in a different emotional climate and mood from the last movement. The former, except for certain passages in the opening movement, are as if enveloped in a veil of shy reticence. This impression is strongest in the two middle movements in which the emotional intensity and the lyric breadth of the Andante are as unmistakably muted as are the joyful outbursts in the following Scherzo. The finale, on the contrary, is quite devoid of any such chamber-music intimacy of tone, being strikingly symphonic in scale and conception, both as regards the character of its musical throughts, their inner thematic treatment and its general architectonic outlines. But, above all, the content is surprisingly different from the rest of the symphony in its urgency and in the way its swift, and in places stormy, emotional current sweeps it forward to the full and unrestrained expression of victorious jubilation at its climax.

In the expressive means employed there is, in the F major symphony, no longer any trace of neo-Romanticist influence. Rather do Dvořák's original affinities with Beethoven again make themselves felt, partly in the first movement, but mainly in the mood of the slow movement. And here we are also put in mind of Schumann's symphonies in the way certain principal themes appear in other movements in the form of reminiscences. Otherwise all foreign influences in this work are in retreat before the steadily consolidating personal and national individuality of the composer. As regards

1. Bedřich Smetana, the first conductor of the symphony in E flat major.

2. Hans Bülow acknowledges the dedication of the F major symphony.

orchestration, it is possible to note, as compared with the D minor symphony, a further step forward towards simplification (the harp, formerly so important, is now omitted), but by no means at the sacrifice of variety and beauty of tone-colouring, the purity and plasticity of which shows Dvořák's growing mastery of the art of instrumentation.

FIRST MOVEMENT

(Allegro ma non troppo, F major, $^2/_4$)

The general character of the opening movement is one of idyllic freshness, and this is the spirit animating the principal theme with which the movement opens without preamble.

It is a theme expressing the dew-fresh fragrance of a spring morning, being based on the simple breaking up of a major triad, but comprising three rhythmically dissimilar figures (*a*, *b*, *c*), each of which is then independently and differently developed in the course of the movement.

The second theme, reminiscent of Beethoven both in its melodic contours and in the agitated bass, is marked *Grandioso* and differs from the mild opening theme in its proud and energetic expression, with a sharply accented Furiant-like syncope in the third bar:

2. Grandioso

This syncope plays an important role in the development of the theme, which, in a transition passage restless in mood and modulations, leads to the entry of the subordinate theme. The syncope already referred to appears here in these two forms:

Figure 2*b*, at the same time, foreshadows the subordinate theme,

3. *dolce*

which is delivered by the violins in D major. It is a calmly phrased and, in spite of its chromatic core, a melodically simple theme with limited possibilities, nor does Dvořák try to develop it in any way, but only repeats it in different figural and harmonic guises, filling in the gaps between its entries now with the characteristically undulating movement of the triplet figure (4*a*), now with the diatonic rise and fall of figure 4*b*, the individual paragraphs being punctuated with massive two-bar entries in the full orchestra.

The final theme, in B minor, then enters in the strings and wood-wind with firm, resolute step,

but, in the process of being tossed from one instrument to another, loses some of its angularity of expression.

The development works mainly with the principal theme (1), alluding only in passing to themes 3 and 2. The recapitulation differs from the exposition in the somewhat broader development of theme 2 in the form, as it were, of miniature variations, and in presenting in the full orchestra and in contrapuntal combination, the principal theme (1) in place of the final theme. This appears in the violins and wood wind, while, below it, the subordinate theme (3) is given to the trombones and lower strings. This, too, proves to be the last climax of the movement, for it is followed by a rapid diminution in strength, the movement ending in as idyllic an atmosphere as that in which it began.

SECOND MOVEMENT

(Andante con moto, A minor, $^3/_8$)

The second movement of the symphony is one of those moderately discursive "lyrically melodic intermezzos" with smaller-scale rhythmic patterns and predominantly melancholy mood such as Felix *Weingartner* describes in his study *"Die Symphonie nach Beethoven"*, examples of which are the Allegretto in Beethoven's Seventh Symphony, the Andante in the Razumovský Quartet, op. 59, No. 2, or the slow movement in some of Schubert's and Schumann's sym-

phonies. In Dvořák's work the movement is of interest as containing, like the slow movement of the somewhat later E major
quartet, the germ of the composer's *Dumkas*, with the as yet undevel-
oped contrast in mood and movement between the two sections
which is a typical feature of the form. In the simple outlines of the
three-part rondo form, this movement is a kind of serenade, the
melancholy cast of which is disturbed only in the middle section
by a short flaring-up of passion. The first part, with its expression
of plaintive longing, is really a three-fold variation of the softly lyrical theme:

It is first given out by the 'cellos with a quiet pizzicato accompaniment in the violas and basses. It is then taken over, after ten
bars, by the violins, supported by the rest of the strings, and later
also by the bassoons and horns, and given room to display itself in a
further twenty bars. On its third entry the theme is assigned to the
flute and bassoon together, this time with increased emotional tension and a counterpoint of bird-like trills and fragments of song in
the clarinet over a more fluid accompaniment of the strings, an
important element being the restless figure in the violas and violoncellos derived from a diminution of the introductory motif *a* and
from the above-quoted theme 6. A short development of this figure
brings the first section of the movement to a diminuendo close.

Like a ray of sunshine lighting up the darkness of a soul sick with
longing, so the mood of the movement brightens with the opening of the middle section *(Un pochettino più mosso*, A major) when,
above the light thrumming of a pizzicato accompaniment, the

wood-wind bring in their own theme—a simple four-bar figure charmingly playful in character:

At first it passes shyly from one instrument to another, but when, finally, the violins carry it up to a higher register together with the flutes, and the 'cellos and oboe add a motif from the preceding section (6), the theme becomes more pathetic in expression. Then the whole section is repeated, now in the key of C major, but with greater breadth and deeper emotional colouring.

The third section of the movement returns to the first theme (6), developing it in new variations in which the flute and oboe or the 'cellos and violins are in the foreground of interest. At first there is a rise in the emotional level which then, however, subsides into the original expression of pensive meditation.

THIRD MOVEMENT

(*Allegro scherzando*, B flat major, ³/₈)

The third movement of the F major symphony links up directly with the preceding movement not only in the marginal note "*only a very short pause and then straight on*", but because the new movement is preceded by a short introduction (*Andante con moto, quasi l'istesso tempo*), which is actually a sequel to the last bars of the second movement. First the wood-wind develop the same rhythm as the last bar of the Andante. This time in the chord of the dominant seventh from B flat major, whereupon the 'cellos introduce a short recitative developed from theme 6, picturing as it were the not very easy transtition from pensive day-dreaming to a gay dancing mood. Then only a few calm chords in the string quartet, a short pause, and the scherzo proper enters with its dancing theme. The form is symmetrically three-part, the first part being built up on a single eight-bar motif of mildly playful and rhythmically jig-like character:

In the course of the section the theme is richly developed, both as a single unit and in its individual figures (especially *a* and *b*), with a wealth of harmonic and orchestral colouring, which is particularly charming in the presentation of the wood-wind, while its gay entry in the full orchestra is boldly announced by a fanfare of four horns in unison underlined by nimble passages in the strings and wood-wind. In the coda the theme seems to recede into the distance, partnered by one instrument after another, till it runs off into a light flirtation in the violins and flute and has a final flourish in the wood-wind, whereupon two shattering chords on the dominant and on the tonic bring this gay dance to a quick, incisive conclusion.

A short modulating passage in the violins leads to the middle section (Trio, *Tempo primo*, D flat major). The playful tone is maintained, but the general expression is of a livelier and more skipping, yet by no means wild character. The theme has a strongly humorous tinge, especially on its first appearance in jocular dialogue between the wood-wind and the strings:

Both groups of instruments continue the teasing conversation, with typically Dvořák ingenuousness and fun (here we are reminded of the later "Slavonic Dances"), right into the middle of the trio, where they join in a sprightly dance in A flat major. Then the mood becomes quieter and the theme, concentrated always in one group of instruments at a time, more flexible. After a short crescendo, the trio resumes the jig-like rhythm of the first section, of which the third is a regular repetition.

FOURTH MOVEMENT

(Finale. *Allegro molto*, F major, $^4/_4$)

It has already been indicated in the introduction that the last movement of the symphony surpasses to a marked extent the level of the three preceding movements. Not only that it wholly emancipates itself from their idyllically restrained mood, substituting for it bustle and movement, strength of passion, élan and joyous rapture, but, above all, in its internal structure, boldness and concentration of design, and also in the character of the themes which are, in this movement, remarkably expressive, richly developed and effectively contrasted, thus differing noticeably from the simplicity, in both content and form, of the previous themes. These qualities entitle it to a place among the composer's most powerful and distinguished symphonic movements. A striking feature is that the tonic key of F major is not allowed to assume the leading role as a matter of course, but has to wage a stubborn struggle with the key of A minor, the outcome not being decided in its favour till the very end of the movement. This tonal antagonism underlines, too, the very different moods in which the principal theme appears in the course of the movement. The expression of firm, almost stubborn determina-

tion (10*a*) and a proud, triumphant fanfare of happy exultation
(10*c*, *d*) being the two poles between which they move.

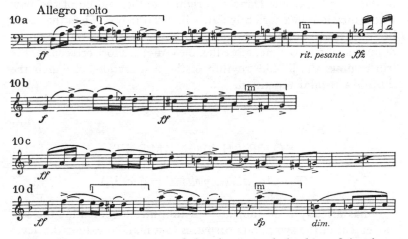

The first two statements of the theme and the key of A minor,
which holds the field for a full 54 bars, give to the beginning of the
movement an almost dramatically tense character. Only after the
development of these themes does a short dynamic rise based on
10*b* lead into the tonic (F major), in which the third version of the
theme makes a triumphal entry (10*c*), followed immediately by the
fourth (10*d*). Towards the close of the last-cited theme (figure *m*)
there is a decline in tension providing the transition to the subordinate theme.

As compared with the fighting resolve and wild happiness of the
preceding motifs, this new theme is calm, broad and leisurely,
with a passionately ardent melodic line.

First it appears in the key of D flat major, in the form of a dialogue between the clarinet and violin, whereupon it is repeated by a flute, oboe and violins in G flat major, closing into the final theme, which is actually its sequel, with an expression of softly expiring, angelic bliss:

This final theme is also the transition to the development, which follows without any repetition of the exposition, from which it is marked off by the sudden, rhythmic and strongly accented entry of the horns with the first two bars of the second theme (11). They are joined by the trumpets, blaring out a noisy fanfare from the principal theme (10a, first bar), some despairing interpolations in the full orchestra leading the movement on to the thematically varied and ingenious involutions of the three basic ideas. In the course of this procedure, there stands out a passage of great beauty—in thought and polyphonic colouring inimitably Dvořák—the episode in A flat major in which the clarinets weave their liquid melody as an inner part above the gently undulating triplets of arpeggio chords and below the high silvery pedal point of the violins:

An allusion to the final theme (12) provides this episode with a delightful close, which dies away until the horns, and after them the trumpets, with the same insistent invitation as at the beginning of the development, start that inward whirl of thoughts and emotions through which the author wins his way back to an unimpaired joy in life and living.

As if pausing to gather new strength and to cast one last reflective look into the past, the strongly dynamic current of the movement is held up for a moment in a $^6/_4$ chord of A minor, struck by the horns, with the oboe above them, whereupon the bass clarinet (above the trombones) declaims with elegiac retrospectiveness the opening of the principal theme (10a). The contrast with the powerful upsurge of the preceding climax is not lacking in dramatic effect. There is a return to *Tempo primo* (i. e *Allegro molto*) and the recapitulation is marked by the entry of theme 10a. This section is quite regular in its repetition of the exposition in the key of A minor, in the short crescendo passage working up the motifs 10a, 10b and a crotchet augmentation of figure *(m)*. With the entry of theme 10c, the key of F major finally gains the upper hand, and in this key the melodiously lyrical subordinate theme is given out (11), in richer polyphony and freer development, as well as the calm final theme (12). This, surprisingly, but quite naturally, opens out into the final figure c of the principal theme of the first movement (1), as if intending to lead back the finale of the work to the idyllic calm of its beginning. This supposition is effectively invalidated, however, by the coda in which the one and only source drawn upon is the gaily youthful theme 10d, which, beginning quietly, rapidly builds up its core in rising sequences to a climax which blossoms out into a broad manifestation of joy and jubilation. Nor does this manifestation come unheralded or unprepared, for the modest germ from which it springs is embedded in the very beginning of the work, as is conclusively proved at the culmination of this great festival of rejoicing, when the trombones burst into the glittering fanfares of trumpets with the main theme from the first movement (1), thus providing the keystone to the arch that spans the whole symphony and gives the work its essential unity of thought and design.

SYMPHONY IN D MAJOR, OP. 60

Instrumentation: piccolo, 2 flutes, 2 oboes, 2 clarinets, 2 bassoons, 4 horns, 2 trumpets, 3 trombones, tuba, tympani, strings.

Sketch completed between August 27th and September 20th, written in score between September 27th and October 13th, 1880 in Prague.—First performance on March 25th, 1881, in Prague, by the Czech Theatre Orchestra conducted by Adolf *Čech.*—Score, parts and four-handed piano arrangement (Josef *Zubatý*) published by Simrock, Berlin, in 1882.—Duration: 40 minutes.

The D major symphony, in reality Dvořák's *sixth* symphony was the first to be published and introduced to the musical world, and even today it is often incorrectly designated his *"first"* Symphony. Dvořák wrote this work shortly after he had earned success and recognition with his "Moravian Duets", "Slavonic Dances", "Slavonic Rhapsodies" and a number of chamber music works. The outside impulse, though not the deeper motive which gave rise to this work, was the wish expressed by the Vienna Philharmonic and especially their conductor, Hans Richter, on the occasion of Dvořák's first introduction to the Viennese public with the performance, on November 16th, 1879, of his third Slavonic Rhapsody, that he should write a new symphony for them. This symphony was also dedicated to Richter, and what pleasure the dedication gave him can be judged from the following extract from a letter written to Dvořák in January 1882 in acknowledgment of the honour: *"On my return from London I find your splendid work awaiting me, whose dedication makes me truly proud. Words do not suffice to express my thanks; a performance worthy of this noble work must prove to you how highly I value it and the honour of the dedication."* And after the rehearsal for the first performance of the work in London (May 15th, 1882), he wrote again: *"This morning we had the first rehearsal of your splendid work. I am proud of the dedication. The orchestra is enthusiastic."**

---

* Quoted from "Dvořák: Letters and Reminiscences" by O. Šourek. Artia, Prague.

The D major symphony, while in close chronological connection with that period of Dvořák's work which saw the first awakening of interest abroad in the as yet unknown Czech composer, belongs to it, in its substance and character, only in part. This period, generally known as "the Slavonic", from a number of works dating from it and bearing this designation, is characterized by its close links, both as regards content and expression, with the rich sources of Czech folk-music as well as by the endeavour to incorporate in traditional art-musical forms the stylization of distinctive types of this song and dance music. The D major symphony embodies the second of these tendencies by replacing, for the first time in the history of the symphony, the usual Scherzo movement with the typical Czech dance known as the *Furiant*. On the other hand, the connection between Dvořák's musical thought and the expressive means of folk music is no longer so direct, for, where a ray does appear from this richly illuminating source, it has first been refracted through the fine prism of the composer's abundantly inventive personality. Thus the process of idealisation is here one of considerable complexity, and, sustained by an individually mature art, has produced fruit which, while neither denying nor wishing to deny the soil in which it has its roots, at the same time bears the marks of new individual cultivation and refinement.

Of the connection of the content of the D major symphony with the period of Dvořák's first successes abroad, there can, however, be no doubt. The feeling of intense happiness with which the recognition of his art and the material improvement it implied filled Dvořák's whole being, after the long years of cold-shouldering, neglect and material hardship, are reflected in this work as unmistakably as in the "Slavonic Dances", the A major Sextet, the E flat major Quartet or the Violin Concerto. Indeed, in this respect, the symphony is a specially characteristic and revealing document. Each movement embodies a masterly stylization of living optimism, courage, rejoicing and good spirits. And, at the same time, it is in mood and expression one of his most thoroughly Czech works. It draws its strength from the Czech countyside, the composer's love for his native environment and his own people giving a warmth of colouring to every thought and, indeed, to every bar of the composition. In this symphony, the humour and pride, the optimism and passion of the Czech people come to life, and in it there breathes the sweet fragrance and unspoiled beauty of Czech woods and meadows. Here the sun shines from a clear and cloudless sky. And just as the mood is one of serenity and unclouded happiness, so, too, the composition is unburdened by any complicated musical problems of form or structure. In the very personal tone of its mood and expression, Dvořák's D major symphony differs very considerably from Brahms's preceding second symphony (with which it has the key in common as well as a similarity of mood at the beginning of the last movement). In its undeniable individuality and originality, in its greater conformity of inward and outward clarification, it rises above Dvořák's own earlier symphonies and mark yet another substantial advance in the composer's creative development. Its expression is throughout clear and unforced, the form correspondingly simple in outline and transparent in texture, yet at the same time rich and attractive in thematic treatment, the instrumentation still further simplified and remarkably plastic, the tone-colouring gay, varied and fresh. A spirit of masterly maturity and classical simplicity permeates the whole work, giving it a truly symphonic nobility of content and design.

FIRST MOVEMENT

(Allegro non tanto, D major, ³/₄)

The first movement of the D major symphony would seem to open up before us the sunny Czech countryside in which everything is blossoming, singing, fragrant and full of happy, contented fulfilment. The lyric and expressive melodiousness of the themes, the rhythmic vitality, the purity and gaiety of the harmonic colouring, the bustling animation of the imitation and the lively alternations of mood, from the softest whisperings to the most splendid dynamic climaxes, all vibrate in the full daylight of Czech life and feeling. And more—behind it we sense the creative imagination of the artist rejoicing in being able to give tangible expression to the beauty around him and to the happiness it evokes within him, giving him the strength and resolution to go on to new work and new tasks. The three basic themes and the important transitional material are all happy in character, but sharply differentiated in mood, so that the movement is not lacking in liveliness and contrasts. The most significant is the main theme which, on its entry, immediately floods the work with light, as it develops charmingly and yet firmly, in the melody and in the bass imitation, from its germinal core:

The descending figure *a* at the close of the above-quoted motif then plays an important role in the movement, not only because it is made considerable use of in the thematic structure, but because it appears as an important element in all the other themes. Immediately following the statement of the first theme, when the melody is taken over by the bass, the flutes reply with a slight modification of this figure (1*b*), while the first thought of the transition, which follows, with an acceleration of pace, the twenty bar exposition of the main theme, is also derived from it (1*c*):

Energetic imitations of motif 1*c*, to which the bass then adds the rhythm of the main theme (1), carry the transition forward through a wide modulation of keys to a new entry of the main theme, given out this time in full strength by the whole orchestra. The closing figure *a*, gaily repeated several times, is worked up into steeply rising and falling sequences in preparation for the new transitional section in which the principal motif is a playful inversion of theme 1*b*:

This section, too, proceeding from the key of B minor, passes through a number of modulations and opens out, after a dynamic crescendo, into F sharp major, when the rising sequences are broken off by a sudden diminuendo of the rhythmically skipping movement of motif 3. This motif then paves the way for the entry of the subordinate theme (4), accompanying it with gay, fluttering figures:

The subordinate theme (figure *a*, theme 1, in the fourth bar) comprises only a small episode of 12 bars, but nevertheless contributes materially to the basic character of the movement, with its typically national colouring and—in spite of its soft minor key—its gay dancing rhythm and playful figural embroidery. All the richer, on the other hand, is the development of the idyllic final-theme, which follows close on the preceding theme, and, though quieter in mood, is delightfully fresh and smiling (a kind of motif *a* from theme 1 is contained in its opening):

5.

Appearing first in the key of B major, in the soft tones of the oboe, supported by the violins and imitated by the bassoon, it opens out, after eight bars, into A flat major when it is taken over by the first violins above an accompaniment of rich figural embroidery. A long and dynamically swelling passage, growing out of the second bar of the theme, of which an energetic variant deserves quotation,

leads to the return in powerful and almost festive tones of the closing theme in B major (5), the melody of which is repeated by the oboe and trombone in canon with a time-lag of one bar. Thereupon the dynamic tension slackens and a quiet echo of this theme in B minor concludes the expositional section, an arpeggiated dominant chord in the third bar leading straight into the development.*

* The repeat marks at the end of the first section should be disregarded in accordance with the composer's intentions, which are clear from a marginal note in his own handwriting in the manuscript score preserved in the archives of the Czech Philharmonic Society (today the Czech Philharmonic): "*once and for all, without repeats*".

The middle section is laid out on a considerable scale and the ingenuity and natural beauty of the thematic design bear eloquent witness to Dvořák's compositional mastery. The focal nerve of this part is the main theme (1), along with the individual element of which it is comprised, and the transitional idea (2) which is employed in particularly attractive variants. The development proceeds calmly for some time. First the clarinet and then the bassoon overlay delicately, almost shyly, the harmonic pedals of the trombones and tuba and the gently undulating motion of the strings, with the introductory figure of the main theme. Then the concluding figure *a* asserts itself, moving calmly from one group of instruments to another, rising and falling till it comes to rest on a delicately oscillating C major tremolo. And again there arises the main theme with various imitations and developing its last bar in tersely dramatic rising sequences. The mood is enlivened by a bustling imitation combining fragments of theme 2 with figure 3:

This is very soon interrupted by a short, charmingly idyllic intermezzo derived from the transitional thought (2) in G major and A major:

But very soon the expression again becomes lively and agitated, working up to the first climax in which the opening of the main theme (1) is delivered in firm tones by the brass, while the strings continue the figural development of the basic element of motif 2. The swirling stream of sound is gathered up into a diminished chord (*b-d-f-a flat*), whereupon the strings proceed in unison to deal with

the last-quoted figure, which passes over by way of augmentation
to energetic crotchet sequences:

2 c

These carry the movement forward with stiff and resolute step
from F minor through the keys of A flat major, B major and D major
to the remote key of C sharp major, and a new climax to the last
part of the development (the opening bars of theme 1), from which
an abrupt transition over the dominant seventh chord brings it
back to the main key of D major and so to the recapitulation.

This section is perfectly regular, both in structure and in the pattern of modulations, with the one exception that the second entry
of the main theme (1) is omitted after the first transition so that
themes 1c and 2 immediately follow. Grafted on to the concluding
section is a broadly designed coda whose gaiety is underlined by
peculiarly exciting rhythmic accents. It grows out of the last immensely powerful return of the final theme (5) and begins by combining
the latter with Ex. 2 in free counterpoint. The momentum of the
movement increases till it suddenly breaks off in a diminished chord
and, as at the close of the development, the strings come forward
with an energetic augmentation of theme 2 (2c), which advances resolutely to the climax of the movement, when the principal theme is declaimed in the jubilant tones of the trumpets and then in canon in
the horns and trombones. Thereupon, with the descending figure *a*,
the stream subsides both in volume and pace, finally dying away
in softly melting D major chords in the wood-wind. The powerful
unison entry of the final theme 5 then brings the movement to a
sudden and impressive close.*

* This whole coda has many points of resemblance with No. 3 (or, in the piano
edition, No. 6) of the "Slavonic Dances", op. 46 (also in the key of D major)

SECOND MOVEMENT

(*Adagio*, B flat major, ²/₄)

In this work of gay good humour and cheerfulness, the second movement has the quality of a softly yearning nocturne and of an ardently passionate intermezzo. Its mood evokes the poetic magic of a warm summer night and perhaps the dialogue of two simple souls sharing with each other the sweet bliss of mutual passion which fills their hearts with happy ecstasy, while, from a distance the muted sound of village music falls upon their ears *(Poco più mosso)*. The movement is designed on broad Beethovenesque lines, with a Slav softness and ardency of expression. It is written in three-part rondo form, the main section alternating three times with the second part, then with the development of its own theme, with the second part again, and finally itself concluding the movement in a typical *a b a c a b a* scheme. The first theme, with its characteristic and recurring interval of a fourth, is tranquil yet warmly lyrical in feeling:

Above a gently rocking accompaniment, it passes from one instrument to another (the score makes no use of trombone or tuba), until it closes into a short and more mobile motif:

This modulates to a broadly spread ⁶/₄ chord in D major, repeated in the soft tone-colouring of the wood-wind and horns and punctuating, in the violins and 'cellos, the imitation in canon of the sub-ordinate theme (8), at first mild and melting like a lover's sighs, but in the course of its development (with the entry of the clarinet in E flat major) assuming a deeper tone of passionate agitation:

On the return of the principal theme (6), its entry gradually pre-pared by the introduction of its own figures and enriched by lyrical arabesques in the violins and flutes, there follows, as already in-dicated, a kind of development, employing the opening figure of the theme in the form of an energetic imitation above the agitated tre-molo of the violas, violoncellos and the firm steps of the double-basses, and also in the form of spacious augmentations or faster-moving diminutions. For the third time, the main theme enters in the high registers of the violins, full of longing and desire, but yield-ing this time to the subordinate theme (8), now in the key of G major, in the contrasted colourings of a dialogue between oboes and clar-inets and with responses in the horn and 'cello over which the flute draws a fine fluid line of melody. The sequel of the movement grows out of the vibratingly sensuous and increasingly passionate develop-ment of the subordinate theme (8), whereupon the movement closes with allusions to the principal theme in the delicately varied co-louring of alternating groups of instruments and in a mood of poetic tenderness and sweet tranquility.

THIRD MOVEMENT

(Scherzo. Furiant. *Presto*, D minor, $^3/_4$)

For Dvořák the character of the scherzo emanated from the general mood of the work. And even if the composer had not, shortly before, been in the most intimate contact with folk-music, taking a special delight in introducing the various types of Czech folk-dances into his cyclic compositions, then in this work, which is the artistic embodiment of folk-gaiety and high spirits, he could not have failed to choose for his scherzo the most characteristic and rhythmically most vivacious type of Czech dance—the *Furiant*. In it the stylistic unity of the work found its most emphatic manifestation, and with it the form of the Czech symphony was enriched for the first time by an element of the same originality as first Smetana and then Dvořák had given to Czech chamber music. The two identical sections of the Furiant are one giddy, breath-taking, high-spirited whirl of sharply accented rhythms, alternately in duple and triple time, which give their character to the two themes which are as merry and expressive as they are specifically Czech. The first of them (9) into which the full orchestra plunges,* after an introductory four bars of rhythmically conform empty fifths in the strings, is a free rhythmical paraphrase of a Czech a folk-song:

* The score of this movement is without trombones and tuba.

This provides the content of the first part, rhythmically full of fire, of which the first part is repeated. The subordinate theme, which opens the second repeat section (10), contrasts with the first not only in the brighter key in which it is set (F major), but also in its fluid cantabile, which is at first disturbed by its sharply accented four-bar apodosis *(a)* :

10.

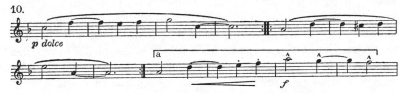

The theme, whose mood is underlined by a rhythmical derivative of the principal theme (9) in counterpoint, is stated twice: first by the violins and then by the horn. The movement then seizes on the concluding strain already referred to (10*a*) and repeats it a number of times in different tone-colourings and in contrapuntal combination with a diatonically descending jig-like figure rounded off by the rhythmic element from the main theme (9). The latter leads to a new colourfully modulated gradation which, at its climax, closes into the repetition of the first high-spirited introductory part.

The Scherzo of this symphony is often ranked along with Dvořák's "Slavonic Dances"—and among the most effective and original of them all. And truly, the melodic invention, the rhythmic variety and vitality and the rich colour-harmonies which distinguish the "Slavonic Dances" are all features it shares with them in a notable degree. Proof that Dvořák's aim was not merely to insert a similar dance into the symphony, but that what he sought was something that would constitute an important part of an organic whole, to which it would conform both in respect of content and form, is provided by the Trio (*Poco meno mosso*, D major). With the sudden change to calm, free, rocking rhythms and long-drawn phrases, it contrasts strikingly with the mood of the scherzo, as if in the intoxicating whirl of the dance the tired body should suddenly come to rest and yield to the sweet delight of feeling the wildly coursing blood subside and flood through every vein. Its melodic core is again derived from the principal theme of the scherzo (9). It begins rather diffidently and then continues in rising sequences, allotted alternately to the flute and oboe, till it opens out into the first inversion of a G major chord of the seventh, above which there pokes up the grotesque little melody of the piccolo:

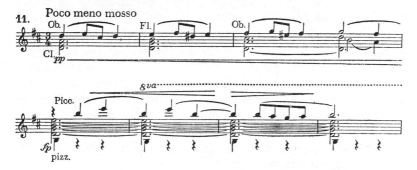

It is an episode as characteristic for the mood of the Trio as the tired, relaxed melody given out by the strings in counter-motion over a dominant pedal. This passage is then repeated in new combinations of instruments, while a new, warmly lyrical thought is introduced in the high registers of the violins.

And then, just as the movement seems to be rocking itself gently to sleep, it is suddenly startled into life again by the principal motif of the Trio. The strings mark out, in sharply descending steps, the

basic rhythm of the Furiant, and again the wild dance of the scherzo
is in full swing in a regular repetition of the first section, except for
a few closing bars which wind up the movement in a final flourish
and with still greater fire and tempo.

FOURTH MOVEMENT

(Finale. *Allegro con spirito*, D major, ²/₂)

The last movement sets the crown on the happy mood of the symphony, not only in the character of the themes but also in the way
they are worked up, for their counterpoint and high-spirited imitations (especially in the bass) dance and frolic and sing out of a
sheer overflow of happiness and good humour. The first entry of
the principal theme, with which the movement opens straight away,
and which is composed of the same notes as the principal theme of
the first movement—only in a different melodic arrangement—is
still gentle and calm in expression:

Given first to the strings, it is transposed after eight bars into
the dominant in which it is re-stated by the wood-wind. When,
however, the strings again take it over, after four bars in a figural
development of what is really a diminished version of the theme, the
character of the movement rapidly gains in vivacity (here the
rhythm of the second bar makes a notable contribution) and the
stormily agitated transition passage, again with animated, figural
work, leads us to the return of the original theme in a powerful fortissimo. The exposition is very easy to follow: it limits itself to a
unison of flutes, oboes and violins contrasting with clarinets, bassoons

and the lower strings, which continue in thirds their wild quaver acrobatics so typical of the whole movement. The theme is rapidly worked up to a steeply dynamic passage, performed by the strings in unison, leading to the dominant, in which key it subsides and gives way to the subordinate theme (Ex. 14).

This proves to be a simple, youthfully sportive theme with strongly marked rhythms, which the composer does not fail to make good use of in the course of the movement.

14.

In fact, the continuation of the theme repeats the first bar several times, while below it the 'cellos and double-basses, bar about, stamp out the rhythm of the second bar, the whole phrase then ending in a new idea which steps out vigorously above the bustling figural work in the lower-pitched instruments:

15.

After two repetitions of this whole episode the movement immediately proceeds to the closing theme which has obvious affinities with the principal theme (13):

16.

The jubilant proclamation of this theme in the full orchestra brings the exposition to a close.

The development, which follows without any noticeable transition, works for some time with the subordinate theme (14), now in its full presentation, now in a lively game of ingenious imitations and

modulations. Not till this playfully teasing game with the subordinate theme has become thoroughly noisy does the principal theme
(13), which has so far made only one shy appearance, storm in
with great determination in the threatening key of B flat minor as
if wanting to quell the exuberance of that boisterous dancing motif.
It appears in canon, in imitation typical also for the rest of the development, in which this theme holds the field unchallenged.

The recapitulation runs a regular course with the usual trans-
positions of the subordinate theme into the tonic key. A notable
deviation, confined however to the instrumentation, appears at the
very end of the finale: the final-theme (16) is taken over by the trombones and tuba, which carry it up in a short, powerful gradation to
a crashing dominant seventh chord in the full orchestra, from which
the violins detach themselves to make a steeply gliding descent to
the beginning of a truly *presto* coda. In it the mood of the work
mounts to heights of unrestrained merriment and jollification. It
begins with the breaking up of the rhythm of the principal theme
(13) into this skipping variant:

which is then seized on by different groups of instruments and gradually transformed into swift flights of quaver-figures of increasing
nimbleness and intricacy. It then takes up the original rhythmic
version of the theme (also in augmentation), and, combining it with
the exultant final-theme (15), builds up to a hymn of joyous ecstacy
at the climax of which the principal theme (13) is twice proudly
declaimed with great power, in festively solemn augmentation and
splendid orchestral colouring.

SYMPHONY IN D MINOR, OP. 70

Instrumentation: piccolo, 2 flutes, 2 oboes, 2 clarinets, 2 bassoons, 4 horns, 2 trumpets, 3 trombones, tympani, strings.
Sketch and score completed between January 13th and March 17th, 1885, in Prague.—First performance in London at a concert of the London Philharmonic Society on March 22nd, 1885, and conducted by the composer.—Published in score, parts and a four-handed arrangement (composer and Josef *Zubatý*) by Simrock, Berlin, in 1885, as Symphony No. 2. Duration: 43 minutes.

The D minor symphony, op. 70, the seventh in the series of Dvořák's nine symphonies, would seem to have arisen as the result of an outside impulse. In June 1884, the London Philharmonic Society nominated Dvořák an honorary member and, at the same time, asked him to write a new symphony for them. A short while before, Dvořák had reaped his first personal successes in England, thus confirming the reputation he had enjoyed there for five years as a composer, and made contact with the Philharmonic Society as a conductor of his own works. Dvořák felt honoured by the distinction shown him and the request accompanying it which, in any case, he would have been anxious to comply with. Nor did it find him inwardly unprepared, for the new symphony had been long maturing in his consciousness, especially since he became acquainted with Brahms's third symphony (in F major), the first performance of which, at the end of 1883, had made such a strong impression as to awaken in him the ambition to come forward with a work of similar achievement and value. Thus the request made by the London Philharmonic provided a welcome pretext for the early realization of a work which, sooner or later, would have had to be written.

Shortly after its first performance in London, the symphony found its way into the programmes of German orchestras under the patronage of three outstanding conductors: Hans *Richter*, Hans von *Bülow* and the highly promising young conductor, Arthur *Nikisch*.

It was first performed on the Continent by Richter with the Vienna Philharmonic on January 16th, 1887. Here it did not meet with the reception it merited to judge from the letter Richter himself wrote to Dvořák dated March 31st of the same year, in which he describes the work as "a favourite of his, perhaps the greatest", and one which "*only a dramatically trained conductor—a Wagnerian (Hans Bülow will forgive me!) can do full justice to*", but remarks that the symphony had not such a reception as he had hoped for "*after what was a really first-class performance by the Vienna Philharmonic*". Whereupon he adds by way of explanation: "*Our Philharmonic audiences are often—well, let us say, queer. I shan't, however, let that put me off...*" Nor did it prevent Hans von Bülow from winning a great triumph for the work at two performances given by the Philharmonic orchestra in Berlin. On October 27th and 28th, 1889, Dvořák was present at both concerts and received hearty ovations from the audience.* Arthur Nikisch then included this symphony in the repertoire for his concert tour of American cities in the spring of 1891 and gave no less than three successive performances of it in Boston.

Dvořák worked at the D minor symphony with passionate concentration and in the conscious endeavour to create a work of noble proportions and content which should surpass not only all that he had so far produced in the field of symphonic composition, but which was also designed to occupy an important place in world music. At the end of December, 1884, he writes to his friend, Antonín Rus, Councillor of Justice in Písek:—"*Now I am occupied with my new symphony (for London), and whereever I go I have nothing else in mind but my work, which must be such as to make a stir in the world and God grant that it may!*" In February he then writes to his publisher, Simrock: "*... I have been occupied with the new symphony for a long, long time; after all it must be something really worth while, for I do not wish Brahms's words*

* An indication of how Dvořák valued this Berlin success is the likeness of Hans Bülow pasted on to the title-page of the manuscript of the symphony and beneath it the enthusiastic note: "*Glory be to you! You brought this work to life!*"

*to me: I imagine your symphony quite different from this one (i. e. the pre-
ceding D major symphony) to remain unfulfilled...*"

Thus it is evident that Dvořák's artistic ambition was nourished
simultaneously from a number of sources. It was his wish to
present to the English public, which had meted out to him an ever
greater measure of recognition, a work that would document his
achievement as a symphonist not less emphatically than his success
as a composer of oratorios. The circumstance that he was writing a
work for a highly distinguished artistic institution, for which the
great composers of the past had written their works and for whom
Beethoven had once created his Ninth Symphony, must also undoubtedly have stimulated him to the highest exertion of his powers. At
the same time it was Dvořák's wish that this new symphony should
not fall short in significance and beauty of Brahms's Third Symphony,
which represented in his mind the highest achievement in modern
symphonic composition and whose value as a work of art he looked
upon as a measure by which to gauge his own work. But it was also
his wish, as the above quotation testifies, to earn the personal com-
mendation of Brahms, his sincere friend and adviser. And finally,
as in all his creative endeavour, this time, too, he wished to enrich
Czech art with a work that would add new laurels to its fame. Touchingly convincing proof of this is to be found again in a letter addres-
sed on Old Year's Day, 1884, by Dvořák to a friend of old standing,
Alois *Göbl*, manager of the Rohan estates in Sychrov, near Turnov,
in which he writes: "*Today I have just finished the second movement —
Andante — of my new Symphony, and am again as happy and contented in
my work as I have always been and, God grant, may always be, for my
slogan is and always shall be: God, Love and Country! And that alone can
lead to a happy goal...*"

Dvořák's endeavour was indeed crowned with enviable success.
In the power and scale of symphonic conception and the form in
which it finds expression, his art in this symphony reaches heights
such as he had never achieved before, and which, in point of nobility,

dignity and coherence of musical thought, he was never to achieve again. The individual themes are sustained by a truly symphonic sense, which determines their expressiveness and force and gives them the qualities allowing of rich and free harmonic treatment. The thematic work shows an outstanding feeling for beauty and articulation of line, for transparency of texture and plasticity of form, and for the organic coherence of the thought content. The boldness and originality of the harmonic combinations bring out the remarkably plastic expressiveness of the melodic ideas, keeping pace with their development, combination and culmination. The spirit of a great symphonist-architect emanates in full glory from the work as a whole, and from each movement, from each section and, indeed, from each bar, building up before us a composition of monumental proportions, unified in all its parts, bold in design, of material without flaw or fracture, a composition which is one of the greatest and most significant symphonic works since Beethoven.

The design of the D minor symphony is, and rightly so, strongly affected by the character of its matter. The work is the closing and also the culminating expression of that creative period in which Dvořák's inner being was torn by the passionate struggle of an artist's deep and sincere love of his country with strong ambition and desire for world recognition and success. After the première of the opera "Dimitri" at the Prague National Theatre, Dvořák had begun to cherish the wish to make a name for himself abroad in the field of dramatic music. His friends abroad did not, however, support this work in the measure that he had expected. But what they did do was to try to induce him to make a bid for recognition by composing a new opera based on an original German text. Dvořák was at the parting of the ways. His strongly developed national feeling would not permit him to set a foreign-language libretto to music. On the other hand, a certain bitterness towards the theatre management in connection with the negotiations for the production of "Dimitri", as well as the wish to gain outside recognition for his work, laid upon him a constraint to avoid in his new operatic work material so exclusively Czech as to be an obstacle to its production abroad. Of the outcome of this inward struggle there could be no doubt: it ended with Dvořák setting to music such purely Czech material as—"The Jacobin". Nevertheless, the seriousness and intensity of the spiritual struggle it involved is witnessed to in a number of important works mirroring the pent-up and conflicting emotions which strove in him for the mastery: the feeling of smouldering anger, of Promethean defiance and passionate doubts, of numb pain and of resignation to his Fate, and in the end the feeling of inward satisfaction at a victorious decision. These find strongest expression where Dvořák's musical thought is not bound by any secondary considerations—in absolute music. The path leading from the Piano Trio in F minor by way of the "Scherzo capriccioso" and the "Hussite" overture to the D minor symphony is an eloquent record of the individual phases of struggle waged by Dvořák to a happy conclusion.

The D minor symphony, as has already been observed, marks the last and culminating phase of this period of inward strife. In it defiance surges up more strongly and resolutely than in any other of the works cited; in it the passionate longing for a firm and worthy resolve stirs his soul to its very depths and lays bare its spiritual wounds; the finale of the work, however, does not end on a note of passive resignation, but rises to a glorious climax of manly, honourable and triumphant resolve. The whole symphony has thus the character of the stern confession of a mind in which the subconscious strength of age-old Czech stubbornness, of painful inward strife and firm moral resolution, as in the preceding "Hussite" overture of which, as the analysis will show, there are echoes in the D minor symphony, as well as certain affinities in the thematic ideas.

It is interesting to observe how the stubborn defiance and stern resolve which permeates the expression of the whole symphony is also transmitted to the orchestration, curbing to some extent the

customary rich profusion of Dvořák's tone-palette. Especially the
scoring of the first movement is unusually austere and quite like
Beethoven in its sober simplicity. The second movement shows a
warming up of tone in the frequent use by the composer of romantic-
ally-coloured cantilena passages for horn. The first and last part of
the Scherzo—more than the Trio—has the tone-colouring of the
classical orchestra (the movement is written without trombones),
individualizing whole groups of instruments rather than single
instruments. Not till the last movement does the composer proceed
to employ a more daring scale of colour-values, and, especially in
the development, we meet again with passages which are inimitably
Dvořák in their glorious colour-harmonies.

FIRST MOVEMENT

(Allegro maestoso, D minor, ⁶/₈)

The content of the first movement is determined by the two basic
moods of the work: the predominating expression of stubborn defiance with occasional outbursts of passionate anguish and longing. Heavy as a black cloud hanging low on the horizon and threatening a terrible storm is the principal theme, drawn over an ominous
deep tonic pedal, its first strain proceeding in monotonous quavers
moving melodically within a narrow compass, while the concluding
phrase rises uneasily to a diminished chord:

The unrest concealed in the rhythm of the second strain of the theme quickly grows as the theme is given out for the second time in the clarinets and leads to the building up of a strongly agitated transition section, which combines a number of themes rhythmically related. The first of these (2a) actually grows out of the closing figure of the main theme:

2a

and its firm dynamically expressive movement and unusual harmonic connection are as characteristic of this period of Dvořák's composition as is the theme immediately following (2b), whose origin points to the same mood of unyielding defiance as that which gave rise to the main allegro theme of the "Hussite" overture.*

2b

The rhythm of the semiquaver figure in theme 2b develops into two further transitional motifs, of which the one is energetic and stubborn (2c), while the other is in delicately passionate two-part counterpoint (2d):

* The theme from the "Hussite" overture:

Allegro con brio

In a short dynamic gradation based on the rhythmic figure *a* of the principal theme (1), the transitional section gathers up for a new entry of this theme, first in the tonic (D) and below a high tremolo, and then in the full orchestra with a terrifying volume of sound, harsh and stern as mountain giants thrusting up their peaks through the thickly gathering storm-clouds. The accumulated tension, however, is not yet ready to discharge. The force of the explosion is caught in a dissonant chord and the expression subsides by way of a short transition into the delicate cantilena of the second theme in which the soul seems to be seeking peace and reconciliation:

This theme is tenderly delivered by the flute and clarinet, accompanied by the delicate hum of the violins and violas and supported by the pizzicato of the violoncellos. But in the fourth bar its melodic calm is disturbed by a rhythmic semiquaver figure which, like the persistent return to the subdominant (E flat), so tellingly conveys that undercurrent of passionate sensibility which the first restoration to calm vainly tried to cover up. The theme is repeated, its colouring strengthened by the first violins, but this time the sixth bar is followed by a four-bar unit of descending sequences opening straight into the final theme (4), in which passionate agitation rises to a cry of anguish as the closing phrase modulates into the bitter key of B flat minor, in which the horn plaintively interpolates fragments of the principal theme (1):

The concluding section of the exposition, in which the mood is, in places, tragically impassioned, does not introduce any new thematic material.

The development, which is relatively short, is designed on firm, expressive lines. It begins with shy reminiscences of the subordinate theme (3), to which the key of B minor gives a tinge of melancholy. The soul, which seemed for a moment to have caught a glimpse of salvation, is assailed by new doubts and vainly seeks a vanished phantom. But not for long. The expression again becomes more animated, and the principal theme (1) now definitely assumes the leading role in the development. Its main figure is taken up by one instrument after another and, having passed through a number of contrasting moods and wide modulations, the development concludes with a new and culminating climax of tone as the full orchestra bursts out with the original version of the principal theme.

This marks the beginning of the recapitulation, which is on the same lines as the exposition, but more concise in structure, in as far as it omits the transitional section (2a—d), while expanding the last part through the addition of an impassioned coda. In it defiance gathers its forces for a final victory: the two main themes (1 and 2b) rise in broad sweeping sequences, and it seems to have reached its goal with the triumphant delivery of the principal theme in F major by the trumpets and horns and its repetition with overpowering force in the full orchestra in the tonic key of D minor. But for the last time. Now theme 2*b* again asserts itself, sharp harmonically discordant discussion arises between the violins and woodwind, the horns break in wildly with theme 2*c*, and bold descending chords relentlessly drag down the theme of defiance from its height of apparent triumph into the abyss of the darkly despairing key of D. Above its pedal, the movement ends in a mood of dark resignation, from which delicate allusions to 2*a* and 2*b* fail to rouse it, while the principal theme proceeds listlessly and sorrowfully, dying away at last in the horns and violoncellos.

SECOND MOVEMENT

(*Poco adagio*, F major, ⁴/₄)

With manly resolution, the composer had endeavoured to achieve a state of spiritual equilibrium. The first movement of the symphony tells of the anguish which this struggle cost him and how his spirit, tempest-tossed on the sea of his own emotions, sought peace and sought it in vain. The close of the movement shows that, in spite of a glimpse of victory, the struggle has not yet been resolved, and, exhausted, his spirit once more withdraws into the darkness of the opening mood. The second movement goes on to tell of how, as yet unable to rally his forces for a renewal of the combat, he pours out his impassioned longing and desire for inward peace and serenity, its widely ramified thoughts building up—as is now the rule in Dvořák's slow movements—to great musical paragraphs of rare depth of feeling and remarkable nobility and beauty of expression. Here is the theme which, like a prayer bringing peace and consolation, is the framework in which the whole movement is set:

5. Poco adagio

It becomes, however, the intimate and passionate confession of a soul consumed with longing to be delivered from torturing doubts and uncertainties and giving full vent to its grief and anguish. Like hands raised to Heaven in supplication, the main theme, whose kinship with the introductory theme (5) is clear, is given impassioned utterance and borne on a restless wavy accompaniment in the strings,

while the auxiliary theme, similar in mood, is steadied by deep anchoring chords in the trombones:

Here, the chromatically descending sequences, there, the steep sevenths and sixths, give an indication of the profound anguish out of which the author's longing is born. And if that pain is still muted and only half-conscious, then it finds free and unrestrained outlet in the lovely theme with which the horn, as through a mist of tears, opens the middle section of the movement, its closing bar overlapping with the clarinet's pathetic answer to the softly murmuring accompaniment of the violins and flutes:

The expression becomes increasingly impassioned as the full orchestra builds up a short paragraph on this stormy figure

and again subsides, whereupon a new expressive theme rises in passionate dialogue between the clarinet and horn (D flat major), later the flute and bassoon (E major), in which longing and anguish find expression and relief:

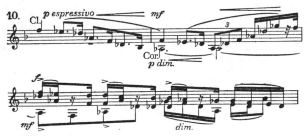

This last theme is underlaid by a delicate tremolo in the violas, while the 'cellos enter half a bar later with a scale-like figure of which the rhythmic pattern, as also that of figure *a* of theme 9, plays an important part in the design of the movement:

The richly varied modulations in the middle section of the movement skilfully underline the character of the moods and the expression. The third section—completing the symmetrical structure of the rondo form—is similar in thought-content to the first, but is presented in new orchestral colours and with the employment of the full range of polyphonic resources. An agitated crescendo leads to the climax of the movement, with a powerful F major in the full orchestra, which gradually dies down to make way for theme 9 taken over by the strings and now rhythmically diminished and punctuated by bright fanfares in the trumpets and horns.

The dark cloud has lifted. The anguish that weighed upon his soul has lightened and the simple prayer with which the movement opened is again evoked: in the oboe, above the scarcely perceptible tremolo of the violins, the introductory theme (5) rises with warm fervency, its second element (bracketed) leading gradually up to theme 10 which now, clear and calm, without trace of passion or of pain, concludes the movement in a mood of inward tenderness.

THIRD MOVEMENT

(Scherzo. *Vivace*. D minor, $^6/_4$)

The passionate outpourings of long pent-up emotions have brought relief and the principal theme of the scherzo, like a gleam of sunshine breaking through the calm and purified atmosphere, enters in the gravely dancing rhythm of the violins and violas. But in its dark key there is the intimation that all is not yet well. Scarcely has the theme begun before it is joined by the violoncello and the bassoon, the slow rise and fall of whose countermelody acts draggingly on the light-footed melody above it.

Thus from the first the expression of a gayer, lighter mood is not allowed to have its way and renewed frustration calls forth new defiance, which finds expression in the continuation of the principal theme in the course of a broad, fully articulated period to which vigorous rhythms almost give the effect of syncopation:

11b

The plaintive, questioning countermelody from Ex. 11a gains in intensity on the repetition of the theme, thereby provoking answering defiance, reflected not only in the hammered rhythms of the principal theme as it storms above wild passages in the violoncellos and double-basses, but also in the secondary theme:

12.

The repetition of this whole section, with new melodic counterpoint in the first violins and rapid figural passages, fails to effect any tranquilisation of mood and so the close of this section (and also of the movement, the third being only a repetition with small divergences of the first) is a wild, unhappy dance in hard, syncopated, sforzando rhythms and dark orchestral colouring, in which the expression of wrathful defiance flares up with no less fury than in the opening movement.

As if awakening from the ugliness of a dream which we brush from our eyelids to find ourselves nestling in the lap of Nature and surrounded by all her charms, our being filled with a sense of rare and complete oneness with the world around us and our hearts vibrating in sympathy with the harmonies of the Universe: such is the mood of the Trio (*Poco meno mosso*, G major), which develops from a motif of delightful freshness and charm, worked out, for the most part, in canonic imitation:

Now it sounds cheerful as the song of birds, now like the distant echoes of a huntsman's horn, again like a tender pastorale, as the soft trills of a new auxiliary theme are given out in dialogue between the violins and the flute:

or then like the expression of a lover's passionate yearning. The wide modulations through which the main theme (13) of the trio is passed and the fine tracery of delicate contrapuntal and figural embroidery heighten still further the extraordinary beauty of the middle section of the movement.

It is, however, only a short, gentle intermezzo like some lovely but fleeting vision soon to be dispelled by an abrupt return to reality. The first part of the scherzo is repeated, the only divergence being the interpolation before its close of an emotionally coloured episode based on the secondary theme (12), broken up into soft sighs, in contrast with which a tersely worked-up climax seals the movement all the more decisively with the imprint of its basic mood.

FOURTH MOVEMENT

(Finale. *Allegro*, D minor, $^2/_2$)

We may say of the fourth movement of the symphony that it is one splendid manifestation of elemental strength in which unyielding defiance unites with the firm will to gain the victory over all inward difficulties and conflicts. The thematic material is so arranged

that it no longer admits of any compromise of mood or any return
to the expression of wounded sensibilities and spiritual suffering
with which the preceding movements were interwoven. The principal theme, characterized by an almost harsh stubbornness and
tenacity of purpose, declaimed by the horns and violoncellos, opens
the movement without further introduction:

The first three notes are actually a melodic variant of the above-
mentioned theme from the "Hussite" overture and of the auxiliary
theme (2b) from the first movement, in which the rising feeling of
defiance is so expressively embodied. The obstinate hard-headed-
ness of the south Bohemian peasant is reflected in the strength and
uncompromising mood of these themes, in which a German critic
justly sees a significant pointer to the national individuality of the
work, which otherwise has no obvious affinities in its thought content with Czech folk music. The sequel to the above-quoted theme,
which grows out of the last three bars, also possesses an interesting
connection with the thematic material of the "Hussite", not only
retaining the rhythm of the subordinate theme of its allegro section
but also its characteristic descending sequences:*

15b

* The theme from the "Hussite" overture:

A dynamic gradation leads to the re-entry of the principal theme, the original leap of an octave to the altered subdominant now taking the form of an impulsive triplet figure which is subsequently made frequent use of in the thematic structure of the movement:

The transitional section, too, which is signalled by the stiff staccato rhythms of a statement of the theme by the strings in unison, is presented in unequivocal terms and bristles with fighting defiance:

16.

At the close of the paragraph there appears yet another short chromatic motif which makes an important contribution to the dynamic and contrapuntal climaxes in the development and coda:

17.

With his subordinate theme Dvořák aimed at introducing an effective contrast and was extraordinarily successful because—now that he is certain of the victorious outcome of the struggle—he does not hesitate to strike a happier note, and so, for the first time in this work, chooses a melody with national colouring:

18.

Its continuation in a theme of almost jubilant triumph is declaimed by the violins above the agitated semi-quaver tremolo of the wind instruments,

19a

and is then taken up by the full orchestra (19*b*). The expressive Schubert rhythm is enlivened by the typically Dvořák cross-accents of the horns:

19b

A short transition leads to the development in which the strings in unison give a calmer version of the stormy figure in theme 19*a*, accompanied in the wind instruments by a rising and descending passage based on an arpeggiated diminished chord (contained in the second bar of the principal theme and of considerable importance in the harmonic structure of the moment). The actual development begins with a variant of the principal theme (15*a*), with a mysterious Beethoven-like pizzicato unison in the strings, first stated in A minor and then in B flat minor:

At the third chromatic rise into B minor, the theme is restated by the violins in its original form, opening a bustling section whose interest is enhanced by rich polyphonic imitation. The rhythmic accentuation of the latter becomes increasingly agitated, especially when the principal theme—the living nerve of the development—is joined by the transition theme (16), the rising chromatic motif (17) and the dotted rhythm of the final theme (19). If the previous exposition of the themes showed a masterly command of contrapuntal resources and great strength of expression, here in their daring combinations, alternations and melodic modifications, in their expansive augmentations and grotesque diminutions, in the seemingly inexhaustible figural and contrapuntal invention with which their constituent elements are worked up, a movement of monumental proportions and great dramatic power takes shape. It is designed to contain two climaxes, both of great emotional intensity, the second leading straight into the powerful recapitulation of the principal theme. Similarly, as in the first movement, the recapitulation of the finale omits the transition material and proceeds to prepare for a magnificently effective and highly dramatic coda. The D major, to which Dvořák has fought his way with indomitable courage and strength of will, sounds forth in a great closing chord in solemn proclamation of a decisive and hard-won victory.

SYMPHONY IN G MAJOR, OP. 88

Instrumentation: piccolo, 2 flutes, 2 oboes, cor anglais, 2 clarinets, 2 bassoons, 4 horns, 2 trumpets, 3 trombones, tuba, tympani, strings.

Sketch written between September 6th and 23rd, 1889, at Vysoká in Bohemia, score completed on November 8th of the same year in Prague.—First performed by the National Theatre Orchestra in Prague on February 2nd, 1890, then in London by the Philharmonic Society on April 24th, and in Frankfurt-on-Main on November 7th of the same year, the composer conducting on all three occasions. The score, parts and the composer's four-handed pianoforte arrangement were published as Symphony No. 4 by Novello in London, in 1892, and by the Musikwissenschaftlicher Verlag in Leipzig, 1941. Duration: 38 minutes.

Just as the preceding Symphony in D minor, op. 70, was the culminating expression of the passionate unrest and stubborn struggle which convulsed Dvořák's inner being in the period between the opera "Dimitri" and the oratorio "Saint Ludmilla", so the G major symphony, the *eighth* in Dvořák's production, was a work whose content reflects the succeeding period of the composer's spiritual tranquilisation and clarification. After a severe spiritual conflict in which the victory was not easily won, and after the exhausting labour demanded by several monumental works (in addition to the D minor symphony, "The Spectre's Bride" and "Saint Ludmilla"), Dvořák slowly recovered, and, going into himself, sought relaxation and refreshment in small works of lyrical intimacy (the second series of "Slavonic Dances", the Piano Quintet in A major, op. 81, a number of songs etc.) and in personal reminiscences reaching back to his early youth ("Love Songs", the revision of old, almost forgotten manuscripts, the opera "Jacobin"). Permanent clarity of outlook and at the same time a new upsurging of his creative powers were the valuable gains which close contact with Nature brought him in this period of introspection and solitary contemplation. His own garden in Vysoká, which he loved *"like the divine art itself"*, and the fields and woods through which he wandered, were at that time more than ever a welcome refuge, bringing him not only peace and fresh vigour of mind, but happy inspiration for new creative work. In communion with Nature, in the harmony of its voices and the pulsating rhythms of its life, in the beauty of its changing moods and aspects, his thoughts came more freely to a mind that was at that time quite unusually receptive to experiences. Here he absorbed poetical impressions and moods, here he rejoiced in life and grieved at its inevitable decay, here he indulged in philosophical reflections on the substance and meaning of the interrelation between Nature and life. All these feelings, moods and reflections then found their fullest expression in the three-part cycle of overtures: "Nature, Life and Love"; individual facets are, however, already mirrored, whether directly or indirectly, in the series of compositions which arose between "The Jacobin" and Dvořák's departure for America, and include the "Poetic Tone-Pictures", the Piano Quartet in E flat major, the G major Symphony, the "Dumky" Piano Trio, as well as the "Requiem" and "Te Deum".

The G major symphony is one of the group of works which, in the above-quoted list, has no fixed programme, although in certain passages it is not without traces of poetic reflection. In this respect it differs from the F major symphony with which, in its thought content, it is most nearly akin, but from which it is separated by the sum of all those signs of creative development which mark the advance between what was properly his twenty-seventh and his eighty-eighth work. Nor is there any vestige of the youthful explosions of passion or of the stern and painful conflict which make up the content of the D minor symphony. In the G major symphony there reigns a spirit of happy tranquility as if, raised above the bustle of daily existence and proud of the high aims he has set himself, the author was now enjoying the happiness and satisfaction which is art's own reward and the delightful impressions which loving and intimate intercourse with Nature awakened within him. And he does so in the full strength of his creative powers and with the courage openly to acknowledge his kinskip with the simple folk environment from which he sprang and in which he grew up. Two characteristic qualities give to this work the authentic hallmark of Dvořák creation. Above all, the variety of mood and the emotional eruptiveness which were so typical of Dvořák's human and artistic personality, and which are not to be denied in this symphony, even though, as in the preceding Piano Quartet in E flat major, the dominating expression is one of healthy, proud man- liness. This, especially in the first and last movements, gives them a youthfully animated and happy, spritely character, while in both middle movements it is muted by an undertone of poetic meditation. Besides this, however, in the G major symphony perhaps more completely than in any other of Dvořák's symphonies, there are manifested the composer's Slav origins, without which he could not have created the second series of the "Slavonic Dances", the various "dumkas" and "Legends", nor even "Dimitri" or "The Water- Goblin". In the symphony we feel these basic affinities, not merely in the folk-character of certain melodic ideas, but above all in a number of important harmonic and rhythmic features, at times even in the instrumentation.

In its formal aspect, too, the G major symphony ranks among Dvořák's most independent and original symphonic works, a fact of which the composer was well aware, for he himself declared that in this work he wished to create a symphony different from the others and showing a different treatment of certain musical ideas. In its main outlines, however, he keeps here, too, to the traditional form of the classical symphony, with its movements designed in sonata and rondo form, yet permitting himself important deviations such as we do not commonly find in his creative production and especially not in the works of his creative maturity. This is true mainly of the opening and closing movements which, in spite of the general coherence and artistic unity of the whole, are distinguished by an abundance of interesting structural detail, testifying convincingly to the remarkable degree of mastery Dvořák had achieved in the organic integration of his artistic material. The middle movements keep much more to the beaten path although, for instance, the close of the scherzo is far from being conventional. What is important, however, is that in the whole structural design there is nothing either fortuitous or forced, but that all the original details in the design of the work grow naturally out of its content and out of its altogether individual temper and emotional atmosphere.

FIRST MOVEMENT

(Allegro con brio, G major, $^4/_4$)

As if to stress the solemnity of the moment when Man makes his entry into the world of Nature, the first movement opens with a festively grave theme of chorale-like character, which the violon-

3. Adolf Čech, the first conductor of the symphonies in B flat, F and D major, Piano Concerto, String Serenade and some of the Slavonic Dances.

4. Facsimile of a page form the sketch for the symphony "From the New World".

cellos and wind instruments draw over the calm time-beats of the pizzicato of the basses in a broad 17-bar period beginning as follows:

This introductory theme is itself an altogether untraditional element, for it stands like a motto at the beginning of each of the three main sections of the movement (exposition, development and recapitulation) and always in the same version, only on its third appearance with changes in the scoring, nor does it play any further role in the thematic design of the movement. Alone a characteristic figure from its middle part (indicated by brackets)

1a

is made use of later in the movement as an important structural element mainly in combination with the principal theme (see 2a and 2b). The mood of the theme, whose character and key (G minor) contrast strongly with the basic, proudly joyful expression of the movement, only then brightens with its entry into the key of G major. Here, above the clear tonic triad of the violins, the flute gives out the principal theme based on the arpeggiated chord of the triad:

Its expression is of still calm with a touch of playfulness, but in the course of the movement it undergoes considerable modification as it passes through a wide range of mood, reaching triumphant heights of happiness and manly pride. Most often the transformation is effected by substituting for the rhythmic skipping movement of the second bar the gravely resolute step of the two bars from motif 1*a* and combinations such as the following:

In the exposition, too, before it gives way to the subordinate theme, the first subject, with the help of new auxiliary motifs, grows into a fairly long sub-section displaying a great variety of mood and a steep rise of dynamic tension. And this represents a new structural feature in the movement, though it is not the only instance of its kind in Dvořák's work. Let us follow its scheme: as the first statement of the principal theme (2) in the flute is concluded, the piccolo takes up the last note and continues it in a long high whistle like the almost supersonic atmospheric vibration of a hot summer day. Below it, in the strings, there is still an echo of the closing interval of a third, narrowed then to a second,

which later is employed in the introduction of the subordinate theme (see Ex. 5). The high sustained piccolo is then joined by the pedal of low *d* in the tympani. In the wide compass between them, there rises in rapid crescendo a lively auxiliary motif whose gay fanfares would seem to be an invitation to some rural festivity (the alternating D major and C major of this passage is typical of this symphony, underlining with its Mixolydian colouring the ethnical origins of its expresssion):

3.

At the dynamic climax of these sequences, crowned harmonically by a dominant seventh chord, the principal theme storms through the deep-pitched instruments, whereupon a rapid passage works up in the strings to the dominant *d* which, for a moment, holds the stream suspended in mid-motion. Theme 2*a* is then taken up by the violas and 'cellos, its initially serious expression very soon losing itself in the frolicking counterpoint of the violins (theme 3) and of the flute (bar 2, theme 2), whereupon it is joined by a new melodic motif which seems suddenly to have broken into a dancing measure out of sheer *joie de vivre:*

4.

An agitated dynamic and rhythmic build-up leads finally to the jubilant return of the principal theme (2) in the original G major and in massive scoring for the full orchestra.

Herewith ends this section of the exposition, for, with the close of the principal theme, there is a sudden falling off in tone and a simultaneous abrupt change of key to B minor; after a short harmonically delightful idea, whose expressive rising seconds were foreshadowed at the beginning of the exposition (2*c*),

5.

there rises in the flutes and clarinets, above the restless rise and
fall of the triplets in the violins and 'cellos, a simple but original
subordinate theme tinged with melancholy and accepting the suggested key of B minor:

Supported by the heavy tread of octaves in the trombones and
double-basses, this works up again to a climax which again breaks off
at its height, whereupon there follows without further delay the
final theme, raising the movement to the brighter key of B major:

This theme, quiet at first, quickly assumes a more agitated expression, leading by way of effective bass imitations of the last bar
to a climax of rejoicing (B major), the trumpets and trombones
solemnly declaring theme 2*b* and the lower strings immediately
following with an imitation of the rhythm in canon. The tide of
dynamic tension rapidly rises, but again subsides, the brightness of
B major is dimmed to B minor (theme 2*b* is pensively repeated in
the horn), then a further modulation follows through the G minor
dominant seventh chord, while the muted trumpets and horns intone
the rhythm of the same theme, thus carrying the movement forward
to the development.

    The middle section of the movement opens in the same way as
the beginning: first the introductory theme (1) is restated in its original reading and instrumentation and then the principal theme (2)
is delivered, as on its first presentation, by the flute over the tremolo
of a G major chord in the violins. It does not conclude so simply, however, but repeats its close in mounting sequences, with canon imita-

tion in the oboe and reaching a climax in the massive entry of the
third inversion of a B flat major chord of the seventh. From this
point the movement runs its course with fairly sharp alternations
of mood. First a strongly accented version of the principal theme (2)
combined with the rhythmic figure of motif 3. This quietens down
to a charmingly playful pastorale in which theme 2*a*, with folk-
music colouring, is uttered in ardent tones over a droning bagpipe
fifth, while above it are gay running bird-like figures and trills in the
flute and then in the violins (a double episode in F sharp major and
A flat major). Thereupon a diminished version of theme 2*a* again
appears in bustling imitation in the wind, rising to a shrill diminished chord *(c—eflat—fsharp—a)*, following which a powerful E minor
combines the principal theme (2) in the violins with a diminished derivative of 2*a* in the lower-pitched instruments, and, after a new gradation, still shriller exclamations in the violins, the wood-wind and
the horns, the trumpets interpose into the wildly whirling figures
of the violins, over the firm steps of the trombones and tuba, the
chorale-like introductory theme (1) orchestrated to bring out its
grave beauty and noble simplicity.

   The entry of this theme marks the beginning of the recapitulation. The closing chord of G major, in which the theme culminates,
shows a sudden falling off in strength, while the principal theme (2),
at a slower pace and not without a certain meditativeness, rises in
the cor anglais and is taken over, always an octave higher, first by
the clarinet and then by the flute. A short modulating episode based
on the figure from the second bar of the same theme provides the
transition to the subordinate theme (G minor), in place of the long
transitional section at the beginning of the exposition, and through
it to the final-theme (G major). On to which is grafted a lively coda
in which the rhythmical skipping element from the principal theme
(2) plays the leading role.

SECOND MOVEMENT

(Adagio, C minor, $^2/_4$)

The second movement of the symphony might very aptly bear
the title of one of Dvořák's "Poetic Tone-Pictures" (a cycle composed about the same time as the symphony): "*In the Old Castle*". Its
mood is probably of the same origin but its poetic content is developed more broadly. It is as if the composer were resting at the foot
of some old ruin whose blurred outlines rise against a sky from which
daylight is rapidly fading, calling forth that strange melancholy
which the contemplation of deserted human habitation and even
the shadow of past glory raises in our breast. The basic mood of the
movement is well expressed in the dark, gloomy first theme dis-
played in a short paragraph delivered by the quartet:

The triplet run-up covering the interval of a fourth (indicated
by brackets) is made important use of throughout the movement.
Out of it there immediately grows a short auxiliary motif combined with the principal theme as follows:

In paragraphs of a similar plan to that on which the two themes
are based, the exposition then runs its course, now stealthily making
its way through the gloaming, now proudly advancing with head
erect. Having opened out into C major and spanned with quiet
little steps the basic interval of a fourth in the 'cellos and basses, it

makes way for the development section in which, above the delicate staccato accompaniment of the strings, the flute and oboe deliver a

calm and spacious melody (embodying the rising triplet of the first theme), warmly emotional in colouring and full of a yearning wistfulness:

A new picture rises before the mind's eye: as if some courtly knight of old should serenade his lady in the gathering twilight. The dreamy yearning grows in intensity as the solo violin develops the melody in G major above the delicate rustling of the violins and the staccato accompaniment now taken over by the wood-wind.

Then the splendour of past glory takes shape as the waves of the orchestra swell with the gradation of the scale-like motif (9), till it is crowned by the majestic entry of the principal theme (8), this time in the festive key of C major, punctuated by bright fanfares in the trumpets.* Only twice, however, is the theme presented in this festive garb: the noisy C of the trumpet abruptly breaks off, as if realizing the tactlessness of its intrusion, and themes 8a and 8b continue delicately and dreamily as in the exposition. The vision fades and another takes its place: the middle part of the movement is filled with recollections of storms and fierce battles in rugged

---

* It is interesting to note how the theme at this point approaches in expression the noble solemnity of the principal motif from the free introduction to the "Hussite" overture.

imitations of the opening theme (8), accompanied by the agitated tremolo of the strings and the sharp, challenging calls of the trumpets. The storm dies down in the heavy descent of the 'cellos and double-basses, there is a short moment of reflection—and then the mind turns once more to pleasanter thoughts. The love theme (10) appears again, this time in the violins to the staccato accompaniment (9) of the flutes, clarinets and bassoons. And, finally, as if enveloping the dreamer and his vision in the beauty of a calm night, the scale-like figure of theme 9 descends at a slower pace and there rises from the depth to meet it, in semiquaver sequences, the opening bars of theme 8, while between the two, first the flute and clarinet, and then the bassoon, weave a delicate new motif:

Once more the violins give out the principal theme and, over the first inversion of an F minor chord of the seventh, the movement returns at last to the key of C major in which the motif 8*a* in the quiet dusk of even gradually dies away in the trumpets like the distant fanfares of the castle watch. And so ends the movement, intimate in character, but rich in its variety and eloquence of mood.

THIRD MOVEMENT

(*Allegretto grazioso*, G minor, ³/₈)

Intimacy of content and form is also characteristic of the third movement of the symphony, the scherzo, which is, however, much simpler as regards mood. The composer, rambling through the fields and woods on a fresh summer morning, here gives expression to the thoughts which rise to the surface of his consciousness—without sharp outbursts of joy, without the accents of passion and agitation. The violins open the movement with a graceful, slightly melancholy dancing measure over a wavy accompaniment in the woodwinds:

It is the only thematic element in the whole first section and from it are later derived two chromatic variants:

The same calm but even more delicate and rather brighter mood characterizes the middle section of the movement (G major) in which the composer, whether unconsciously or in association with a personal recollection, revives Toník's song from his opera "The Pigheaded Ones": *"So young the maiden, so old the man"*:

Thus the whole movement runs its course in a unity of mood and pace, the third part being a regular repetition of the first. An acceleration of tempo, however, marks the short coda in which the theme of the middle section (13) is transformed into a lively dance in duple time combined with a new contrapuntal idea in the violins and trumpets:

This moderately gay little dance concludes an original and neatly constructed movement in which the quality of the mood is matched by the refinement of the thoughts and the delicate texture of the instrumentation (the orchestra is without trombones).

FOURTH MOVEMENT

(Finale. *Allegro ma non troppo*, G major, $^2/_4$)

The last movement of the symphony sings from a heart full of joyful pride, freely and unashamedly acknowledging the folk origins of its inspiration. Along with the first, the finale is the most complex and the most attractive in form, for, while retaining the general outlines of a sonata movement, in the exposition and recapitulation it is enriched by a variation development of the principal theme (similar in procedure to the finale in Beethoven's "Eroica"). The principal theme itself is a rhythmically vigorous and folk-coloured two-strain motif of twice eight bars, beginning with the same arpeggiated triad on the tonic as the first movement (2):

Before presenting it, however, the composer permits himself a structural divergence by opening with a gay fanfare of solo trumpets

baseb on a rhythmic derivative of bar 3 of the principal theme which
ingeniously forecasts the mood of the movement:

Only when the fanfare has died away, followed by a few rhythmical drum-beats, does the principal theme (15) make its entry first
in the 'cellos, as cited above, with broad good-humoured self-posses-
sion, its rhythm imitated in canon in the bassoons and double-
basses. In the first variation the lower strings swing the theme forward at a resolute pace, the imitation then being taken over by the
violins and violas. The second variation shows a sharp quickening
of the pace and sets the whole orchestra dancing, the basic rhythm
of the theme being effectively contrasted with gay semiquaver passages. The third variation shows no slackening of movement and is
entrusted to the solo flute, which lightly draws a line of dialogue
over a soft tremolo in the violins and violas, while by an original
stroke the inner part contains a pianissimo version of the opening
fanfares (15a):

The fourth variation is a regular repetition of the second, only
expanded at the close by the resolute steps of the strings in unisons
which provide the transition to the subordinate theme (C minor).
It is actually again a variant of the main theme, for it retains its
rhythm and only assumes a different melodic guise:

16a Ob.Cl.

The comparative primitiveness of the expression and the monotonous harmony and rhythm would seem to point anew to Dvořák's
affinities with the musical sources of Eastern Slav peoples.

The theme is quiet and curiously melancholy and preserves this
character in its new modification, intoned by the flute in rising sequences above the softly sinuous movement of the violins and 'cellos:

16b Fl.

This slightly grotesque meditation is soon, however, interrupted
by the massed entry of the same variant (16*b*) in deep octaves in the
'cellos, bassoons and basses, combined with imitation in canon in
the clear tones of the trumpets. It proves to be a short modulating
passage leading from F major to C minor, in which themes 16*a* and
16*b* resound in rude force and with a kind of barbaric pomp.

The movement then passes straight on to a short, animated development working up the expressive elements of the principal
theme (15). At its height, effectively prepared above the pedal of D,
the trumpets and horns sound the introductory fanfare (15*a*), first
in festive triads, sharply alternating simple D and C major, and then
in a massive unison several octaves deep.

The volume of sound diminishes from this point, the expression
becomes more composed and the 'cellos bring back once again the
principal theme in its quiet, original form (15). This marks the
beginning of the recapitulation, which is shortened by the omission
of the subordinate theme (16) and its accessories, and is in fact a
new series of variations on the principal theme. These variations are
of particular beauty, both in expression and mood as well as in

harmonic colouring and instrumentation. As if in the composer's soul the meditative chord had once more begun to vibrate, the theme, assuming an ever more dream-like quality, is clothed in wonderfully soft warm colours and with the Brahmsian purity and delicacy of workmanship in the development of the variations which had long since distinguished Dvořák's highly original "Symphonic Variations", op. 78. The return of the theme itself, in which only the second eight-bar strain is somewhat modified, is followed first by a variation in the strings, the theme proceeding in delicate octaves in the 'cellos and basses, while the violins and violas embroider it harmonically with independent contrapuntal parts. A further variation is given out by the clarinet, supported by the calm harmonic tones of the bassoons and horns, while an airy tremolo hovers high above it in the violins and violas. The final and not altogether complete variation is taken over by the string quartet along with the bassoon, while the theme is delivered by the first violins, which develop it into a cadence of deeply reflective expression. Above the quietly descending scale-like passages and the retarding tread of the basses, and above a soft tremolo in the second violins and violas, the flute and the oboe in leisurely fashion bring back the interrogatory opening figure of the principal theme (and in the same time as the first movement, Ex. 2), the violins answering in a development of the third bar of the same theme (15a):

Suddenly, however, the theme bursts out into a quick, wildly merry variation from the exposition, to which a short coda is tacked on in still gayer harmonies and tone-colours. This brings the work to a spontaneous and jubilant conclusion.

SYMPHONY IN E MINOR

"FROM THE NEW WORLD, OP. 95"

Instrumentation: piccolo, 2 flutes, 2 oboes, cor anglais, 2 clarinets, 2 bassoons, 4 horns, 2 trumpets, 3 trombones, tuba, tympani, triangle, cymbals, strings.

Sketch completed between January 10th and May 12th; scored between February 9th and May 24th, 1893, all in New York. First performance at the concert of the Philharmonic Society in New York on December 16th, 1893, conducted by Anton *Seidl;* in Europe, by the Spa Orchestra in Karlovy Vary on July 20th, 1894, conducted by August *Labitzky;* in Prague, on October 13th, 1894 by the National Theatre Orchestra, with the composer conducting. Score, parts and the composer's four-handed piano arrangement published by Simrock, Berlin in 1894 (as the "Fifth Symphony"). — Duration: 40 minutes.

The Symphony in E minor, known as "From the New World", is the *ninth* and last in the series of Antonín Dvořák's symphonies. It was the first of those works which arose altogether on American soil, in the period of three years, from October 1892 till the spring of 1895, in which Dvořák held the post of director of the National Conservatory of Music in New York. It was in the Carnegie Hall in New York, too, that it had its famous première which, perhaps, set the crown on all Dvořák's triumphs up to that time. The audience, well prepared by detailed preliminary articles and analyses, published along with musical quotations in the leading New York dailies, overwhelmed Dvořák with seemingly unending ovations and the critics were unanimous in their judgment of the work for which they had only words of the warmest admiration. These expressions of general acclamation were shared by the National Conservatory, which awarded Dvořák the prize of 300 dollars for the "*most original symphony*" in a nation-wide contest. The high justification for the symphony's first success was splendidly confirmed by its later destiny. The symphony has become not only one of Dvořák's most frequently performed works, overshadowing, almost regrettably, interest in his other symphonies, but one of the most played symphonies in world music.

The symphony "From the New World", moreover, occupies a special place among Dvořák's symphonies, not only because of the special circumstances which accompanied its composition, but above all for its quite special character in respect of expression, construction and content. In both these connections, those features are important which were determined by the impressions made on the composer by his stay in America and which he himself aptly sums up in a letter written to Bohemia during the composition of the symphony when he says: *"I should never have written the symphony like I have, if I hadn't seen America"*.

As regards the expressive material of the symphony, its special character is determined in the first place by the melodic, harmonic and rhythmic qualities of the themes with which Dvořák became acquainted in Negro and Indian folksongs (or in their echoes in the works of certain American composers) and which colour almost all his American production. These qualities may be generally formulated as follows: the melody shows a predilection for the so-called pentatonic scale i. e. major scale in which the fourth and seventh degrees are omitted (as: *c, d, e, g, a*). In the minor mode a natural minor seventh is common, and this gives the melody its characteristic colouring; in addition, the sixth degree is often omitted. Noticeable, too, is the persistent return to a certain note, most often to the tonic or dominant, which underlines the melancholy expression of the theme. Typical of the harmonic character is the pedal point on the tonic or dominant or the bagpipe combination of both, such as is common in primitive music still unaffected by art forms. From the point of view of rhythm the most striking feature of these themes are their frequent punctuations and syncopations, and then, especially, their alternating use in the same theme! This, however, is all that is "American" in the themes of the E minor symphony. It is, therefore, a great mistake to say that Dvořák made use of the melodies of Negro folksongs in his work. He, himself, protested against such a view in connection with the first performance of the symphony and declared: *"I did not make use of one of these melodies. I wrote my own themes embodying in them the qualities of Indian music and using these themes as subjects. I developed them with all the resources of modern rhythm, harmonisation, counterpoint and orchestral colouring."* (New York Herald, December 12th, 1893). In the spirit of these songs (as he expresses himself elsewhere) Dvořák created, in fact, his own motifs which had, it is true, a specific new flavouring, but which, in spite of their novelty, are pure Dvořák and, combined and alternated with the composer's "Czech" themes, coalesce or mutually enhance each other with remarkably good effect.

The structure of the symphony, "From the New World", was determined to a considerable extent by the character of the thematic material. The short four or, at most, eight-bar themes are, especially in the first three movements, arranged in strict accordance with the traditional symphonic scheme and give to the movements their classical simplicity and clarity of form. This plasticity of design and cogency of expression is maintained also in the last movement, though it differs from the preceding movements in its remarkably complex and altogether unschematic structure, whose originality and boldness of construction substantially contribute to the imposing culmination of the work for which it provides the finale. An important feature of the thematic design, underlining at the same time the organic coherence and expressiveness of the movement, is also the systematic repetition and summarizing of the principal themes of the individual movements at culminating or otherwise important points in each of the following movements—a structural principle of the Romantic symphonies which Dvořák had applied in certain earlier symphonies, but never so systematically or with such effect as here.

As for the content of the work, the E minor symphony takes its place among those works which solve no complicated problems connected with either a musical or ideological programme, being only the simple, direct communication of impressions, moods and feelings with which the composer's mind was filled. It is natural that the impressions and moods evoked by new and very different surroundings might, because of their inner relation to America, truly entitle us to call this symphony, as also the other works which arose there, "American", certainly with much greater justification than for the characteristic colouring and form of its themes. The most lively and immediate impressions to be reflected in the symphony are those made on Dvořák by New York in the first period of his stay in America and in the period in which the symphony arose. The life and bustle of the city on the Hudson, in which Dvořák was caught up for a relatively long time and by which he was daily surrounded; the rush and hurry at the harbour landing-places and wharves, with ships arriving from and departing to the most distant parts of the globe, whose movements he followed with the same intense interest as he used to watch the trains in Prague from above the Vinohrady tunnel; that immense ant hill of nationalities of every kind, of which the Negroes perhaps interested him most, awakening in him, as a simple man of the people, a feeling of sympathy and a deeply human interest in their fate: all this affected him very powerfully, and the picture that had formed in his consciousness could not fail to find its artistic outlet in the work which first began to crystallize in New York, or to engrave itself in it with the same spontaneity as originally called it forth. This picture is presented mainly in the opening and closing movements of the symphony, with their swift flow and surging rhythms, their stormy dynamic movement, their swiftly changing impressions and moods, soaring at times to heights of impressive grandeur.

But that other America, the quieter, more poetical, more idyllic America, did not remain without its influence on this first of Dvořák's works to be composed in the New World, though it did not arise from personal experience, as in later works, but from the workings of an imagination nourished by reading and reflection. There is no doubt that in this connection the most important role

was played by Longfellow's "Song of Hiawatha" with which Dvořák had long been acquainted in a Czech translation and which he
re-read in America with such interest that for long he considered
setting it to music. According to his own statement, the two middle
movements were written under the impression evoked by Longfellow's poem and provide very clear testimony (especially the free
movement) of the deep and powerful effect of the solemn beauty
of the American prairies and virgin forests which the poem exercised on the composer's imagination.

It was not, however, only American impressions which determined the content of the symphony. As in all Dvořák's American
works, here, too, these impressions contrast and merge with moods
to which the composer's frequent recollections of his native country
and still more frequent longings for home gave rise. The whole time
that Dvořák spent beyond the ocean he never ceased to think of his
homeland, and the longer he was away from it the greater was his
desire to see it again. This homesickness is thus another important
factor affecting the content of the symphony and, even though it
does not make itself felt as strongly as in later compositions, its
presence can be sensed, especially in the middle movements.

Such is, in rough outline, the formal and internal character of the
work which ranks among the most powerful, most attractive and
most original manifestations of Dvořák's creative spirit, and also
among the most outstanding and most successful symphonies in musical history.

FIRST MOVEMENT

(E minor, *Adagio* $^4/_8$, *Allegro molto*, $^2/_4$)

The first movement in this symphony is preceded, contrary to
Dvořák's custom, by a slow introduction, thus bringing it all
the more strikingly into conformance with classical symphonic

form.* It is as if he were experiencing once again the emotions that filled him as he stood on the deck of the ship anchoring before the harbour and wondering, when he first glimpsed the new land to which he had come, what the future held in store for him. A quiet melody tinged with melancholy is delivered by the 'cellos of which the syncopation in the very first bar immediately evokes the setting in which the symphony was born:**

Suddenly, as if roughly awakened from day-dreaming to reality, the fragment *a* storms forth in all the strings, followed by hard drumbeats and the shrill shrieks of the wind instruments. Then the 'cellos and basses, with measured step, modulate suggestively into the key of B flat major, while above them the flutes and oboes dance in the rhythmic syncopation of the opening theme until, with a diminished chord in the horns, violas and 'cellos, an energetic motif is first announced which constitutes the main theme of the movement (2), as if a great gust of that new atmosphere shortly to be embraced should surge out to meet him. A short gradation developed out of motif *a* of the introductory theme (1) ends with a wild beating of drums and, against the delicate tremolo background of the violins, the horn enters with the principal theme (2), thus opening the allegro section.

* In a letter to the conductor, Oskar Nedbal, in 1900, Dvořák gives his instruction that duction for the introduction should be *"as leisurely as possible"*.
** This theme is related, both in rhythm and melody, to that on which the variations are based in the later String Quartet in E flat major, op. 97.

The 4-bar theme (2*a*) has a 4-bar sequel (2*b*) whose playful hopping rhythm contrasts with the resolute rhythmic expression of the theme proper.* On its repetition in the oboe, the theme modulates to G major and when the second figure (2*b*) opens with a deceptive cadence into B major, motif 2*a* rears its head challengingly in the massed strings, its individual elements providing the steps of a steep dynamic ascent till it sounds forth majestically in the lower wind and strings and then is taken up by the full orchestra. This marks the climax of its first appearance, for figure 2*b* this time develops in a longer melodically and dynamically falling sequence, which provides a gradual transition to the subordinate theme (3).

This transition is a stroke of genius and a striking demonstration of Dvořák's mastery of organic thematic construction. Intimations of the subordinate theme (3), which has its germ in figure 2*b*, appear in the violas and 'cellos in the transitional section so that, on its actual entry, it rises organically and almost imperceptibly from the melodic current of the movement. The theme itself is unmistakably "American" in character, and we can hardly err in supposing that there, in his mind's eye, the composer saw before him the Negroes of the New World. The nostalgic melancholy of the theme, underlined by the small melodic compass and the persistent return to the tonic, the characteristic Doric mode with the lowered seventh degree, the smothered effect of the lower range of the flutes and oboes, the long-drawn-out harmonics of the violins, the monotonous interpolation of the horn and, on the repetition of the theme, the similarly monotonous repetition of the fifth *g-d* in the 'cellos: all this is as new and unaccustomed in Dvořák's work as was the picture present to his mind in the creative art of composition. This is well illustrated by the following example:

---

* The main melodic element of this sequence (an ascending interval of a third) is important, for it recurs, as we shall see, in several further themes in the symphony. (See Exs. 3, 6, 10.)

But it is only the theme which is exotic. In the course of its further exposition by the double-basses, below the imitations in the violins, and when it is taken up by the violins themselves, it is again pure Dvořák, who has assimilated this unusual phenomenon and is able to discourse and reflect on it in his own Czech way. Equally familiar, too, is the new transitional theme (4) which breaks into the above-mentioned exposition of the second subject, its first more robust section being given to the 'cellos and basses, and the second section, in broad cantabile, to the flutes and clarinets, which had punctuated the first section with the gay rhythms of the quail's call (no doubt a sudden recollection of home!)

The softly lyrical expression of this transition theme paves the way for the final theme (5) and, as first given out by the solo flute above an arpeggiated chord in the violins, sounds equally soft and melting. This becomes somewhat gayer in the violins against the characteristic syncopated accompaniment of clarinets and bassoons, and finally sounds forth in festive splendour in the trombones and lower strings, achieving a climax that concludes the actual exposition, which is then repeated.

In the development all the kaleidoscopic first impressions seem to converge, alternate rapidly, melt into and impinge sharply on one other. Figure 5a, followed by the alternation of an arpeggiated triad, begins energetically, is joined by a delicate allusion to theme 5 in the horn, flute and trumpet successively; the oboes introduce the motif 2b, whereupon the dance begins with a grotesque diminution of theme 5 divided between the cellos and flutes:

The first bar of this diminution, persistently repeated, is the throbbing nerve of the rest of the development in which the movement rises uniformly, the wind bringing in themes 5 and 2a alternately as the firm and expressive points in a pell-mell of thoughts. From A major this section modulates through A minor, F major, F sharp minor, E flat minor and E minor, in which key the violins again set motif 2b dancing, till its somewhat wild whirlings are suddenly cut short by a diminished chord.

A short transition in which the oboe and then the flute give a calm citation of the principal theme (2a), into which the violins only very timidly interpolate the first bar of motif 5b, leads to the recapitulation. As compared with the exposition there is only one notable divergence—the setting of the subordinate and final themes (3, 5) a semitone higher, i. e. in G sharp minor and in A flat major, the movement closing with a fully and massively orchestrated coda in which themes 2a and 5 dominate in the victorious tones of the trumpets and trombones.

SECOND MOVEMENT

(*Largo*, D flat major, $^4/_4$)

As indicated above, the second movement was inspired, as Dvořák is said himself to have acknowledged, by Longfellow's "Song of Hiawatha", and more especially by the scene, "Funeral in the Forest"*. Perhaps Dvořák had here in mind those verses of the poem in which the death and burial of Hiawatha's spouse, the lovely Minnehaha of the tribe of the Dakotas are described. The great breadth of the movement and the high serenity which informs it would seem to testify to Dvořák's intention of portraying in tone the picture called up by those parts of the poem which depict, in charmingly animated and poetical colours, the natural beauties of the American interior, with its wide uninhabited plains, its deep forests and broad rivers. The tone of lamentation in the middle appears to refer directly to the pathos of the burial scene, and this is confirmed by the sketch, in which this movement bears the title "*Legend*". However, we are equally justified in supposing that the truly moving depth and expressiveness of feeling which characterizes this movement was conditioned not only by literary reminiscences but, above all, by the emotions awakened in Dvořák by the recollection of his distant home, of the melancholy, wide expanses of the South Bohemian countryside, of his garden refuge at Vysoká, of the deep solemn soughing of the pine forests, and the broad, fragrant fields in which, not long before, the G major symphony and the Overture "In Nature's Realm" had been born, of the "feathered choir" whose gay song, as he willingly confessed, had inspired so many lovely melodic thoughts. These are the memories sung in the slow movement

* The affirmation that the movement originated in a sketch for a cantata or musical drama based on Longfellow's poem does not seem to be likely, as the themes of the movement are sketched among the other first motifs dated December 20th, 1892.

of the E minor symphony, in which is also expressed the desire and deep nostalgia for what inspired them.

The series of grave, long-sustained and majestic chords of E major, B flat (6) major, E major, D flat major, B double flat major, G flat minor, D flat major in the brass, clarinets and bassoons, opens the movement like the drawing back of a curtain revealing the scene to the spectators' gaze. The muted strings, in a passage marked *ppp*, alternate with the wind instruments, while above their long-drawn-out and muffled chords, the cor anglais begins to sing its soft broadly-phrased song with its lovely expression of pensive melancholy, the opening notes of which again contain the melodic element of theme 2b:

The first part of the song is then followed by the repetition of the introductory chords in the wood wind, while the strings continue it in a kind of middle section, the three-part form being rounded off by the cor anglais with a return to the opening melody, a pair of muted horns concluding the song with a distant echo of the first bar of theme 6. The whole of this first part of the movement breathes the glorious calm and noble simplicity of Nature. Then, as if a soft breeze should ruffle the surface of the broad acres of ripening grain above the delicate rustling of the violins and violas, there is set in motion a short undulating section (*Un poco più mosso*, C sharp minor) the melody of which, delivered by the flute and oboe, contains the typical minor seventh indicative of its American origin.

This phrase runs its course only twice and then the slow pace of the movement is resumed. Above the monotonous pizzicato steps in the basses and the delicate oscillations of isolated tremolos in the violins, the clarinet weaves its sadly moving lament:

The whole of this section is repeated with some divergencies, whereupon the concluding part brightens from C sharp minor to C sharp major, in which the flutes, oboes and clarinets develop a short, cheerful dialogue as of bird voices with a variation of the basic theme (6):

The voices multiply as the movement rises by way of a short six-bar gradation to the crashing entry of a chord of the sixth in A major, in which key the orchestra gives out three themes simultaneously: while the lower strings maintain the sextolet movement of the six semiquavers of motif 6a, the grave introductory theme (6) is festively given out in the trumpets, the trombones deliver in victorious tones the opening rise of the principal theme of the first movement (2a), and the violins and horns together share with the wood winds the final cadence motif phrase of the same movement (5).

From this height there is a rapid dynamic decline, the key of A major being persistently maintained till, with a sudden change to D flat major, the movement returns to the great melody of the cor anglais (6). Four bars later its theme is taken over by the strings, whose song, as it dies away, is interrupted by three long pauses, and then, reduced to a solo violin and violoncello, concludes in an elaborate cadenza in the first violin. The grave opening chords in the horns, trombones and bassoons, a rising passage in the violins and, finally, a mysterious pianissimo chord of four divided double basses close the movement which, with its profundity of thought, poetry of mood and musical beauty, is undeniably one of the loveliest movements in the whole of symphonic literature.

THIRD MOVEMENT

(Scherzo. *Molto vivace*, E minor, $^3/_4$)

For this movement, too, Dvořák is said to have found the inspiration in "*Hiawatha's Wedding Feast, in which the Indians dance*". If that is so, he could only have had in mind that scene in which the handsome Pau-Puk-Keewis, called the Storm-Fool, "began his mystic dances", as described in the following verse of the poem:

> First he danced a solemn measure,
> Very slow in step and gesture,
> In and out among the pine-trees,
> Through the shadows and the sunshine,

Treading softly like a panther.
Then more swiftly and still swifter,
Whirling, spinning round in circles,
Leaping o'er the guests assembled,
Eddying round and round the wigwam,
Till the leaves went whirling with him,
Till the dust and wind together
Swept in eddies round about him.

The expression and mood of the first and third section of the
scherzo would confirm such an assumption. The principal theme
is rapped out first in the wind instruments, with the persistently re-
current fourth from the rhythmic figure of its first bar, and is continued in free canonic imitation in the tympani accompanied by the
gay tremolo of the triangle. Then the double-basses repeat that interval and, keeping to the same rhythm, the strings progressively
build up the ambiguous chord of *e-g-b-d*. Above their crotcheted
movement the theme itself begins the dance (9) in typical canon:

At first it moves nimbly but delicately in the flute and oboe, imitated in the clarinet. Then it appears in the grotesque combination
of first violin and tympani, while the clarinet keeps bursting in
with the tonic. Finally a short gradation in the strings, on an augmented triad, leads to a wild whirling dance in which the whole
orchestra joins,* the horns and later the wood wind complicating
the rhythm of the theme with a measured syncopation in duple time.

Then the dance suddenly subsides, a fragment *a* of the principal
theme is carried over from the strings to the bassoons, the tempo
slows down *(Poco sostenuto)*, the mood brightens into E major and,

* The scoring of the movement excludes trombones.

above a rocking waltz-rhythm, a supple, softly flowing cantilena passage is repeated several times in the first bar of which we again meet with the frequently mentioned element from theme 2*b* of the first movement:

This delicately lyrical but short intermezzo is interrupted by the entry of the principal theme (9), and, with a short dynamic rise, in the last bar of which the horns, violoncellos and double basses give a caricature of the melody of the principal theme of the third movement (2*a*), the movement opens out into a new mad whirl with the principal theme of the scherzo, in rhythmic and sound effect wilder and more fiery than before. This ends the first section of the scherzo.

In the short transition to the Trio the two-bar motif 9 swings lightly from one group of strings to another above the delicate tremolo of the kettle drums and the sustained chord of the clarinets and bassoons, till brought to rest by a new quotation of the principle theme from the first movement (2*a*) in the melodic form quoted under 2*c*.

It seems that the author' s eyes have torn themselves away from the picture that fascinated them, its contours fade and the spirit involuntarily sinks into reflection till, carried on the wings of thought, it finds itself contemplating a new picture incomparably more fascinating than the first. The last section of 2*c* is taken up by the flute, as indicated in Ex. 2, and, having modulated into C major, passes it onto the violins which develop it into a rocking accompaniment to the dancing theme of the Trio performed by the wood winds.

11a

The shape of this theme has nothing in the least American about it; on the contrary, it is one of Dvořák's melodic thoughts born out of direct contact with Czech folk dance song and not without a flavouring of Schubertian melodic invention. Suddenly the composer forgets the Indian wedding and its wild dance and his spirit is far beyond the ocean in the peaceful meadows of southern Bohemia. And as the theme proceeds in a light tripping movement, against a background of delicate trills in the violins and wood-winds, all at once it seems that there falls upon his ears the cooing of his beloved pigeons in Vysoká:

11b

This part of the movement having ended with a more richly orchestrated repetition of its theme 11a, the first part of the scherzo is repeated and finished off with an effective coda. This contains a dialogue between the principal themes of the first (2a) and third (9) movements, which mounts in passion through several modulations and is capped by an immensely massive chord in E major, from which the trumpets disengage themselves to deliver the final motif from the first movement (5). The movement seems to be dying away in a diminuendo of the first two bars from motif 9 when, instead, it concludes with a crashing E minor chord in full fortissimo.

FOURTH MOVEMENT

(Allegro con fuoco, E minor, ⁴/₄)

In a critical evaluation of the last movement of the New World symphony, it must be borne in mind that, between the conclusion of the sketch of the preceding movements and this, there was a pause of at least three months. During this time Dvořák decided not to return to Bohemia for the summer, as he originally intended, but to spend it in the Czech settlement of Spillville in the state of Iowa and in getting to know something of the American countryside. When he set to work on the score of this movement, his children had already set out out on the journey to America and arrived shortly after its completion. The composer's recollections of the homeland do not, therefore, intrude so much into the foreground, but where they do appear they are no longer tinged with that special melancholy, yearning quality; the longing for his native land yields to joy at the thought of reunion with his family and curiosity as to what new scenes and experiences await him in the as yet unvisited regions of America. That whirl of impressions with which the first movement is filled returns, therefore, in the fourth movement in still greater strength and is intensified to a festive tumult which, at the close of the work, triumphs over all the other feelings which warred within him during his sojourn in America. It is doubtless due to the quality of the content that the movement rises in expression to such imposing heights and that it bursts the narrow, formal bands of the strictly classical form in which the other movements are confined, that its thematic work overflows with an inventive wealth of melodic, structural, variational and contrapuntal ideas, and that the inner structure is so bold and truly monumental.

With steps quickened as it were by impatience, the strings, after a few introductory bars, usher in the principal theme:

12. Allegro con fuoco

It is an expressive theme, full of resolution and fighting élan. Taken as a whole it forms the two parts of a marching song: its first part presented twice in the trumpets and horns (the second time in double octaves), while the rest of the orchestra accompanies them with firm accentuation of the strong beats; the first strain of the second part, given to the strings alone, maintains the melodic line of the theme, but transposes it to the upper dominant, in four-part harmony and supported by firm steps in the double basses; the closing section repeats the original theme in a unison statement by the wood wind and violins, while the violins and violas weave in and out between the powerful time-beats in the rest of the orchestra. This complete exposition of the theme is followed, without any break in movement or strength, by a transitional thought which is really a diminished variation of the basic theme:

12a

Both in rhythm and tone quality, this theme, with its expression of bustling activity, provides a sharp contrast to the determined and measured character of the original theme. With the figure *n*, of its second bar, it comes finally to rest on the diminished chord of the seventh of *C sharp-E-G-B flat*, over which there rises in the clarinet a secondary theme modulating at once regularly into G major.

13. Cl.

Having extricated himself for a while from the jig-saw of American impressions, the composer finds himself in spirit again in his native Bohemia. Hence the longing and deep yearning of theme 13, hence its powerful sweep and its convincingly Czech-Dvořák character. And this character is underlined in the immediately following final theme which, is pure Czech folk-song in mood and tone.

However, the gay sound of the trumpets and the persistent drumbeats do not allow this song from home (in which the binary form is retained) to melt the heart. On the contrary, listening to it the expression brightens, a smile steals into the eye, and, before you are aware, the composer has seized on the last bar of the main section of motif 14, and, repeating it with stubborn insistence, ornaments it now above, now below, with humorous variations, somewhat in the manner of a *chaconne*. And then, in descending sequences of the same bar, plunges straight into the development.

Here the American impressions dominate, putting to flight memories of home, and all the important themes of the symphony are marshalled for review. It opens with a jubilant citation of the principal theme (12), and works for the most part with its lively diminution, accompanied by the contrapuntal allusions to the main themes from the slow movement (6) and the scherzo (9). Then the main theme of the finale (12) again takes the field, all the brilliance of the brass being employed to provide a climax to the development. This climax then marks the beginning of the recapitulation, which diverges from the exposition only in omitting the transitional passage of variations and proceeding straight to the principal theme.

5. Anton Seidl, the first conductor of the symphony "From the New World".

6. Carnegie Hall in New York,
where the symphony "From the New World" was performed for the first time.

This principal theme, given out in the full force of three trombones in unison against a background of rhythmic beats in the rest of the orchestra, suddenly loses strength and is repeated in the oboes and horns, whereupon the violins immediately proceed to the lyrical subordinate theme (13) now in the key of E major. But, strange to say, the recollection of home seems this time to have gripped the heart! The final theme (14) has lost its first cheerfulness and emotional ardour, in the flutes and clarinets it is tinged again with wistful longing, while on reaching its middle section the bassoon unexpectedly hums a nationally coloured tune in a melancholy bass:

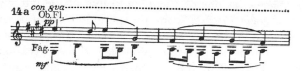

But a return must be made to present reality. As the final theme quietly dies away, the horn enters with the cadential phrase from motif 2a, spanning a compass of four octaves and announcing with gay fanfares its earlier lively mood which dominates the broad coda with a series of magnificent climaxes. The principal themes of all three preceding movements (2, 6 and 9) are once more reviewed, and even the chorale-like series of chords from the introduction and the close of the largo are brought in by the full orchestra in majestic procession until the wood wind and strings direct the stream of the movement into E major. In this key the theme of the finale (12) again loyally consorts with theme 2a of the opening movement until their dialogue is cut short by a storm of simple chords in the whole orchestra. The work, however, does not close with these, but dies away in a delicate, long-sustained and pianissimo E major chord in the wind, without trombones.

II

CONCERTOS FOR SOLO INSTRUMENT AND ORCHESTRA

Most closely related to Antonín Dvořák's symphonies in scale and organic structure are the concertos for solo instrument and orchestra. They are three in number, each dating from a different period of creative production: the *Piano Concerto* from the period preceding that of a fully crystallized national character and at the same time of world-wide success, the so-called "Slavonic" period; the *Violin Concerto*, as one of the high points of the latter period; and the *Violoncello Concerto* from the period of Dvořák's stay in America.* None of these concertos arose altogether spontaneously in the sense that inward necessity alone led to their creation; each was dictated above all by the wish to express personal gratitude by dedicating a major concert work to an artist to whom Dvořák felt himself under an obligation. The Piano Concerto was written for the celebrated Czech pianist, Karel *Slavkovský*, the Violin Concerto for Joseph *Joachim* in Berlin, and the Violoncello Concerto for Hanuš *Wihan*, an outstanding virtuoso and member of the Bohemian Quartet.

All the more praiseworthy, then, is the fact that Dvořák's three concertos are each an organic part of his life's work, that they are not merely compositions written to show off with the greatest effect the soloist's virtuosity, but are the expression of a true spiritual experience forming the core of the *musical content*. In the interpretation of this content, the solo instrument and the orchestra participate in equal measure in the thematic and general structure of the work. Each of these is essentially a *symphonic* composition,

---

* Dvořák wrote another violoncello concert in A major at the beginning of his career as a composer (1865), but only with piano accompaniment, for which reason it is not included in this group (it was published by Breitkopf and Härtel, Leipzig, in 1929, and arranged for orchestra by Rafael Günther).

in fact, three-movement symphonies, in which the solo instrument is subordinated to the organism as a whole. And even though the solo part in other respects retains the leading role, it is thematically in uninterrupted contact with the symphonical build-up of the individual movements, and keeps within its framework in even the technically most brilliant and showy passages. Thus Dvořák gave convincing proof of the seriousness and also, for his time, of the new sensibility with which he grasped and carried out his creative mission no less in compositions of this character. It is certain that this circumstance, too, has contributed in no small measure to giving these three concertos, all bearing the hallmark of the composer's inspired genius, a rare vitality, so that they continue to enjoy now, as they have always done, great favour among the music-loving public. Nor is this fact affected by the knowledge that recognition was accorded from the first only to the violin and violoncello concertos, whereas the Piano Concerto, with its equally high artistic values, was not given due acknowledgment until later.

In form, all three concertos are similar in their main outlines: between two quick movements of sonata or rondo form a slow movement is inserted. They vary substantially, however, in the inner construction of the various movements, which is different in each work, but freest and most original in the Violin Concerto. The old cadenza before the close of the first movement is retained only in the earliest of the group—the Concerto for Pianoforte. The main difference, however, is in the character of the content, which naturally dictates the form, a middle position being held between the broad pathos of the Piano Concerto and the Romantic imaginativeness and passionate, emotional yearning of the Violoncello Concerto by the lyrical, richly melodic and happy Violin Concerto. The orchestra is limited in the Piano Concerto and Violin Concerto to the small classical ensemble which, alone in the Violoncello Concerto, is supplemented by trombones and tuba.

1. CONCERTO FOR PIANO AND ORCHESTRA IN G MINOR, OP. 33

Orchestra: 2 flutes, 2 oboes, 2 clarinets, 2 bassoons, 2 horns, 2 trumpets, tympani and strings.

Written towards the end of summer 1876 and finished on September 14th of the same year. First performance by Karel *Slavkovský* with the orchestra of the Czech Interim Theatre, conducted by Adolf *Čech*, on March 24th, 1878, in Prague. Score, parts, and accompaniment by a second piano (arrangement by Josef *Zubatý*), published by Julius Hainauer, Wroclaw, (Breslau), 1883. Duration: 35 minutes.

Dvořák wrote the first of his concertos when he had already completed a considerable number of original works which later proved to be of lasting value, but of which he had heard very few performed. Public success was still a rarity for him, even at home. It is not surprising, therefore, that for his first concerto he should choose the instrument of a master who had shown the greatest interest in Czech composers, and also in a number of Dvořák's own works. The artist in question was Karel *Slavkovský* (1846—1919), a musician of outstanding abilities and sensitive intelligence who founded a school of piano-playing in Prague at the beginning of the 'seventies, and, at the same time, took an active part in Prague concert life, both as a soloist and in chamber ensembles. With him in mind, Dvořák wrote his first concerto, its content reflecting the contemporary spiritual moods which lead from the sketch for "Stabat Mater" (spring 1876), by way of the "Moravian Duets" (summer of the same year) to the score of "The Peasant A Rogue" (first half of 1877).

This Concerto, which in style and instrumentation still remains very close to the Beethoven concertos, remained long overshadowed by the success of the two later concertos, because of the relative thanklessness of the solo part as compared with its demands on technique and interpretation. This neglect has, however, lately been made good to a considerable extent (thanks mainly to the revision of the solo part carried out by the late Professor of the Master Class of the Prague Conservatory, Vilém *Kurz*), and rightly so, for in it Dvořák has created a work of unusual beauty of thought, individually balanced structure and intense emotional power. A special feature of its musical content is the dynamism which carries it from the proud pathos of the first movement through the deeply ardent intimacy of the middle movement on to the high-spirited jollity of the finale.

The first movement (*Allegro agitato*, G minor, ⁴/₄), is written in broad and richly embroidered sonata form, based on three principal themes. The first of these themes, and the one to which the greatest prominence is given, is imbued with the dignity of expression of an antique hero, and appears for the most part in the original broad version (1), agitated by the rhythmic motif 1*a* either following or combined with it, and in places passing into the diminished variant 1*b*:

The second and subordinate theme, which provides a striking contrast to the first, is smilingly lyrical in mood, in expression strongly coloured by Czech folk music and fascinating in the unfolding of its melodic line.

Quite different again is the shape of the third and final theme, which alternates a broad phrase of chorale-like gravity in the strings with three bars of playful jig-like figurations in the piano (3a) followed by a leisurely sweet melodic variation (3b):

The movement is so constructed that the sonata exposition is preceded by a special introduction in which the orchestra presents first the principal theme (1), along with its rhythmically energetic cadence-phrase 1a and variant 1b with which the solo piano makes its entry, and then, gathering up fragments of the principal theme, modulates through A flat minor into F major till it reaches the actral exposition.

In the principal theme much play is made with the progressive re-petition of its second and third bar, a lightly accented variant of which is soon made use of by the piano as material for the transition to the entry of the subordinate theme (2 in the relative major key of B flat). The elaboration of this theme, presented successively by the strings, the solo instrument and, finally,—with an energetic leap from the key of B flat major to that of D major—by the wind in-struments, is relatively short and dies away in a delicate chromatic passage in the piano, closing into a calm entry of the final theme (3), whose variational strain (3b) is threaded in and out of the melodic line of the flutes, oboes and violins by the piano, with bell-like figu-rations or pearly runs.

In its first half, the spaciously planned development (one of the longest in Dvořák's sonata movements) works up elements of the sec-ondary theme (2). These, accompanied by consistently impassioned passages in the piano, are tossed from one instrument to another till a powerfully built-up gradation leads to the second half. The section is completely dominated by the principal theme (1), which begins *grandioso* in its original shape, its various figures being then developed in the course of a long and expressively flexible process. The movement ends with a regular recapitulation and a beautiful, expansive cadenza in the solo instrument based on the principal theme, which imparts its manly nobility to the coda with which the movement comes to an effective close.

The second movement (*Andante sostenuto*, D major, $^4/_4$), after the spirited display of the first, is marked by a complete tranquillization of expression and remarkable warmth of feeling. It grows into a three-part pattern with two main themes, of which the first is calm and melodically vocal (4), while the other undulates more flexibly and shows an increasing richness of melodic embroidery (5):

In the first part of the movement the two themes alternate with a still more yearning thought, otherwise not made use of, but forming the continuation to the second.

The middle part of the movement limits itself to a discussion of the second theme (5), whereupon the last part resumes the first theme (4), which rises from a calm broad flow of melody, figurally embroidered by the piano in a sharply rhythmic variant, to a *grandioso* in the full orchestra, the volume of sound then falling off till the movement finally expires in a sigh.

The third movement (*Allegro con fuoco*, G minor, $^2/_4$) has, in the main, the character of a *capriccio*. Structurally it combines the sonata with the rondo form, working alternately with three themes, of which the first two brighten the content of the composition with a spice of lively humour. The first theme, in stiff, sharp rhythms, their angularity increased by chromatic alteration, produces the effect of playful stubbornness:

6.   Allegro con fuoco

The second theme, however, is strongly humorous, both in its rhythmic hopping melodic line and later, again, in the pizzicato accompaniment of the strings:

7.

An element of contrast is introduced into the movement with the third theme, of which the melodic line sweetly vibrates with passionate yearning, the phrase closing with a languishing air.

8.

This theme, appearing first in the key of B major and then in B flat major, creates oases of lyrical repose without unduly holding up its forward surge. The middle of the movement broadens out into an ample development of the second theme (7), with a great display of rhythmic resource and inventiveness, combining, in places, with the first theme (6). The yoking of the two themes then brings the composition to a cheerful end in the brightly optimistic key of G major.

2. CONCERTO IN A MINOR FOR VIOLIN AND ORCHESTRA, OP. 53

Orchestra: 2 flutes, 2 oboes, 2 clarinets, 2 bassoons, 4 horns, 2 trumpets, tympani, strings.

Written in summer 1879, first revision completed by May 25th, 1880, and the second in summer 1882. First performed with the orchestra of the National Theatre, with Mořic *Anger* conducting, at a violin concert by František *Ondříček* on October 14th, 1883 in Prague. Score, parts and piano accompaniment (arrangement by Josef *Zubatý*) published in 1883 by Simrock, Berlin. Duration: 29 minutes.

Dvořák's Violin Concerto, which belongs to the time of the artist's first successes abroad (and only a year after the first series of "Slavonic Dances"), is, in its wealth of melody and musical charm, one of the most affecting manifestations of the composer's musical lyricism—that lyricism of the people in which there are blended, with remarkable harmony, melancholy, unaffected warmth of feeling and youthful gaiety. Its mood is that which characterizes folk song and dance, and there is no doubt that is why Dvořák specially modified and limited the compass of the first movement, which closes without a break into the middle Adagio,* in order to give the flow of melody all the more room to broaden out in this

---

* Dvořák considered the continuity here to be of no small importance, as is apparent from his letter to Simrock (16th December, 1882), in which he rejected the suggestion that the first two movements of the concerto should be separated.

lovely slow movement and thereby heighten the contrast with the wild whirl of furiant rhythm let loose in the last movement. Because of the content of the composition, he was able, with a light heart, to forego the effect of brilliant solo cadenzas, showing in this respect too, the good taste and courage of an artist of modern perceptions. Thus he created a powerful work, highly successful both for the characteristic beauty of the musical subject-matter and for the great attractiveness of the solo part—a work which can worthily take its place beside the concertos of Beethoven and Brahms, and is a permanent part of the repertoire of every great violonist. (In the definitive stylisation of the violin part, the composer had the benefit of the valuable advice of Joseph *Joachim* to whom the work is dedicated.)

The first movement of the concerto (*Allegro ma non troppo*, A minor, $^4/_4$) is, as already mentioned above, far from traditional in its form. It does not begin with the usual orchestral exposition of the themes but, combining features of the sonata form with those of the rondo, creates the impression of a daring but well-thought-out and constructively disciplined improvisation. Its main theme consists of two parts, the orchestra opening the work with the first rhythmically well defined part (1*a*), while the solo instrument continues, after four bars, with the second part, which is slower in movement and somewhat meditative in mood (1*b*):

After a short development, concluded with an energetic unison, the orchestra introduces a new theme in a calm, smoothly-phrased cantabile (2*a*), of which a sweet, brightly luminous variant (2*b*) is entrusted—after the return to the introductory theme (1*a*)—to the solo violin:

There is some further enlargement of theme 1*b*, a return is made to motif 2*a*, and then the solo violin presents the third theme in C major, with its warm Czech folk-music colouring (actually the subordinate theme):

A kind of development of the principal theme (1*a* and 1*b*) follows and is energetically built up to a climax, whereupon the movement, shortened by the omission of the sonata recapitulation, passes with a calm quotation of theme 1*b* straight on into the second movement (*Adagio ma non troppo*, F major, $^3/_8$). In this movement, the lyric element in the work culminates in an outpouring of sweet, tender melody while the thematic elements all seem to have their roots deep in the soil of Czech national music. The solo violin opens the movement with a broad cantabile in which both thematic ideas, linked together, vibrate with the passion of a lovers' embrace.

The next paragraph, in slightly quicker tempo (*Poco più mosso*), makes a new contribution with a theme in a minor key (5) and an agitated rhythm, the contrast being underlined by a quiet, softly reflective accessory (6):

Again the expression of the movement is permeated by a happy sweetness of desire when the strings, in the dominant of F major, begin to weave a lovely new folk-coloured melody, above which the clear trills in passages of the solo violin soar singing like a lark above the flowery fragrance of Bohemian meadows:

The solo instrument then repeats this melody in the key of E major, having developed it into a new entry of the motif 4*b* (in C major), and, after a short energetic gradation in the orchestra based on motif 5, returns to it again, this time developing it broadly in the keys of A flat, F and A major. The movement then comes to a close with quiet allusions to both parts of the principal theme.

The third movement (*Allegro giocoso, ma non troppo*, A major, $^3/_8$) supplements the lyrical character of the concerto with one of Dvořák's most delightful and most ingenious art stylisations of Czech folk-dance. It is written in the form of a freely arranged rondo of which the gay main theme, which dominates the movement and is presented every time in a new combination of instruments, is in three-part song form. The opening and closing periods comprise a theme of ten bars with syncopated "furiant" rhythm in the bright tone-colour of the high registers of the violins, the solo violin on top (8a), while the middle period is in pure triple time (8b):

After the broad presentation in rondo style of these two ideas, the winds, with a sudden swerve into F major, introduce a new humorously orchestrated motif of typically *"furiant"* character (8c). Out of it there develops a strongly rhythmic variant of 8b which stamps its way vigorously through several keys (8d):

Syncopated rhythm is also a feature of the first of two subordinate themes (9) following close on one another, while the second jigs above it, always finishing with an energetic final stamp in the relative minor mode (10):

A further enlargement of the second of these themes is followed by a return of the whole main theme (8*aba*), the first part of which is sung by the violins above a droning bagpipe fifth, with the kettle-drums good-humouredly thumping out the rhythm.

A song section is set with charming originality in the middle of the movement, the contrasting rhythms of its duple time and the faint melancholy with which it is tinged being strongly reminiscent of Dvořák's characteristic *dumka* movements. It develops from a theme in two sections, which has again the delightful simplicity of typical folk-song melody:

The beginning of this theme is worked up in agitated imitation until it again yields to the main theme (8*aba*), the first part of which is given to the G string of the solo violin, while the rest of the violins and violas weave a counter-melody about it. The theme continues as at the beginning, with the auxiliary motifs 8*c* and 8*d* as before, followed by themes 9 and 10 (both in A major) presented by the solo flute in three descending sequences; this gives way once more to a short citation of the dumka theme 11, now decidedly cheerful and briging the composition to a fierce and fiery conclusion.

3. CONCERTO IN B MINOR FOR VIOLON-
CELLO AND ORCHESTRA, OP. 104

Orchestra: piccolo, 2 flutes, 2 oboes, 2 clarinets, 2 bassoons, 3 horns, 2 trumpets, 3 trombones, tuba, tympani, triangle, strings.
Written between November 8th, 1894, and February, 9th 1895, in New York. The coda of the last movement rewritten after the author's return to Bohemia and completed in Písek on June 11th, 1895.—Dedicated to Hanuš *Wihan.*—First performed at a Dvořák concert in London, on March 19th, 1896, with the composer conducting and Leo *Stern* as soloist. First performed in Prague with the same soloist and the composer again conducting at a concert of the Czech Philharmonic (National Theatre Orchestra) on April 11th, 1896. Score, parts and the composer's piano accompaniment published by Simrock, Berlin 1896.—Duration: 36 minutes.

The Concerto for violoncello and orchestra is the last work composed by Dvořák during his three years' sojourn in America (1892—95). Along with the E minor symphony, which opened this phase in the master's creative work, it is his most widely known symphonic work. If the symphony was inspired, above all, by the first impact of new impressions with which the busy life of New York flooded Dvořák's being, and only in part also by the expression of the artist's distant homeland, the Concerto in its emotional content is nourished by longing for home and by memories of his own country and people. Its character is, as compared with the two preceding concertos, highly romantic, and this to some extent explains not only the choice of the manly, full-bodied and resonant tone of the 'cello for the warmly emotional solo part, but also the richly coloured orchestral palette. Unlike the other two concertos, the composer works here with a full Romanticist orchestra, stresses the role of the brass, gives the horns independent melodies, introduces brilliant fanfares in the trumpets at dynamic climaxes, and writes festive, grave and soft organ-like passages for the trombones and tubas. The work is particularly prolific in musical ideas, possesses great variety

and flexibility of expression, is richly melodic and deeply felt and
contains, on the whole, only very occasional allusions to those typical features of American original or imitated folk-song which
characterized the preceding compositions of Dvořák's American
period.* If the Violoncello Concerto returns, after the altogether
original Violin Concerto, to the traditional form of three independent movements in which the Piano Concerto in written, it still
renounces any indulgence in brilliant solo cadenzas.**

---

* See the lowered seventh in the minor key in theme 1 and the pentatonic
scale in themes 2 and 5.

** When Simrock mentioned to Dvořák that Professor Wihan suggested add-
ing an independent cadenza written by himself to the third movement (the
manuscript is in the Prague Antonín Dvořák Museum), Dvořák reacted very
sharply in these words. "*I must insist on my work being printed as I have written it…
I shall only then give you the work if you promise not to allow anyone to make changes —
Friend Wihan not excepted—without my knowledge and consent—and also not the cadenza
which Wihan has added to the last movement… There is no cadenza in the last movement, either in the score or in the piano arrangement. I told Wihan straight away when
he showed it me, that it was impossible to stick such a bit on. The finale closes gradually diminuendo—like a sigh—with reminiscences of the I. and II. movements—the solo dies away
topp —then swells again—the last bars are taken up by the orchestra and the whole concludes
in stormy mood.—That was my idea and I cannot depart from it.*"—We can understand
Dvořák's standpoint if we realize that he had his own special reasons. Wihan's
cadenza would have interfered with that closing section of the concerto which
he rewrote after his return from America, and in which he paid a tribute to the
memory of his sister-in-law, Josefina *Kaunic*, née *Čermák* (d. May 27th, 1895),
whom he highly esteemed not only as a dear friend, but also as the charming
young actress who, long years ago, when he was still a viola-player in the orchestra of the Interim Theatre, had awakened in him a secret passion (the
expression of this unrequited love was his first cycle of songs entitled "The Cypresses", 1865. See also p. 181). With the thought of her in mind, he had already
introduced into the second movement of the concerto a theme (see 8*a*) which is
a paraphrase of his well-known song "Leave me Alone", from "Four Songs"
op. 82, of which Josefa *Kaunic* was particularly fond, and then, under the impression caused by her death, there appears a fragment of this melody at the
close of the work, as it is described in the letter quoted above, and which explains why he was so firmly set against interference with its conception.

7. František Ondříček, the first soloist of the Violin Concerto.

8. *Facsimile of a page from the manuscript score of the Violoncello Concerto (Second movement).*

The first movement (*Allegro*, B minor, $^4/_4$) has two different expositions of the main themes. The first of them is, in accordance with older usage, attributed to the orchestra without the solo instrument, its mood forecasting accurately the general character of the whole work. With a grave and almost heroically sublime pathos of expression, which is yet romantic in tone, the principal theme (1), is presented in which the American hint in the lowered seventh of the second bar disappears quickly in the firmly descending steps of the following pair of bars, but appears again in the course of the movement in the melodically expanded form *b*:

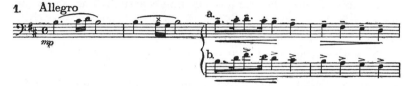

In the exposition of the theme another characteristic element is combined—a descending second (*m*), which is employed fairly frequently later in the movement:

If it is possible to sense a strong emotional tension in the principal theme, in spite of all its manliness, it is much more evident in the subordinate theme delivered here in the introduction by the solo horn (2). In its first eight bars it seems to be almost an echo of some popular American songs, but, as it continues in its broad flow of melody, the moving fervency of Dvořák's nationally unalloyed temper *(b)* makes itself ever more strongly felt:

Dvořák himself came very near defining the essential quality of the theme when he wrote, in a letter from America to one of his friends, that whenever he played it, his whole being was moved.

The close of the orchestral introduction is actually only the transition to the real exposition which the solo violoncello opens with a resolute presentation of the main theme (1), now broadly developed and with its constituent figures fully worked out. The theme itself is given in its original form, later in its characteristic combination with the above-mentioned descending second *m* (1*c* in the tonic), and, finally, in a rhythmical diminution (1*d*). In adidtion, some prominence is given to a thematic motif, while the wood-wind performs a gay accompaniment above the sustained line of melody in the cello (3), as also to the somewhat expanded, expressively insistent and passionately tinged descending second *m* (1*e*):

In lovely contrast to the rhythmically varied and active character of this part is the warm lyrical fervour of the secondary theme (2)

which, in its continuation, is somewhat disturbed by lively figurations and altered harmonies;

while its passionate intensity increases in the two themes of the closing section of the exposition, both of which sound the romantic note of the composer's native land:

The development in the first movement is very short, confining itself to working up the materials of theme 1, which rises to a passionate climax, making the beginning of the recapitulation all the more effective with its anguished augmented motif in the key of A flat minor, whose peculiar charm is underlined by a dreamy countermelody developed by the solo flute into a new and independent thought:

But for the fact that theme 2 is first solemnly declaimed and repeated by the full orchestra, the recapitulation is perfectly regular.
The solemn pathos of certain parts is extended to the coda, which
brings the movement to a close with the principal theme (1) in a
brilliant *grandioso*, the splendour of chivalry and romance combining
with a tone of happy and agitated expectancy.

The second movement (*Adagio ma non troppo*, G major, $^3/_4$) is
undoubtedly the crown of the whole work and one of the most moving manifestations of Dvořák's lyrical genius. In simple, three-part
rondo form, it is a hymn of deepest spirituality and amazing beauty.
The melody wells up with a fervency that stirs the innermost being
and yet has nothing of sentimentality about it. In its calm breadth
and profound feeling there is some affinity with the mood of the
Largo of the E minor symphony and also with the sublime pathos
of the "Biblical Songs".

The melodic line of the first section is built up of several thematic
paragraphs which follow one another in rising gradations of expressive intensity. The movement opens with the calm and gentle
introductory theme (7a) delivered by the oboes and bassoons and
followed by the solo violoncello.

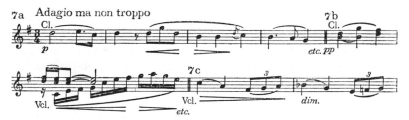

The wonderful tenderness of the theme pervades its continuation,
but the soft dreamy expression of the melody sung by the clarinets
above the grave chords of the trombones is agitated by the passionate urgency of a lead-up in semiquavers in the cellos to another
paragraph on a still higher level of emotional intensity (7c). This

reaches- its climax below the lightly arched phrases of the solo flute, in the sighs of descending semitone intervals already noted in the first movement *(m)*.

The section dies down with a quotation of the introductory theme *(7a)*, whereupon the full orchestra opens the middle section with a four-bar motif in which the solo instrument sings a melody *(8a)*, of which the beginning is a very literal paraphrase of the middle section of Dvořák's song "Leave Me Alone", from the cycle of "Four Songs" op. 82, as can be seen from a comparison of the two melodies transposed into the same key:

Mention has already been made in the note on p. 176 of what led Dvořák to allude to this song. The thought, however, is also from a purely musical standpoint a very happy one, for it fits in perfectly with the mood of the movement, growing organically out of its melodic substance like the lovely embodiment of a powerful longing for something very dear and very remote. This is true not only of the theme itself, but also of its development, embodied in an intimate dialogue between the cello, flute and oboe, and opening out into a passionate final clause (with characteristic sighs *m* in the solo part):

The whole paragraph is then repeated in the same form except for some changes in the orchestration.

The third part of the Adagio is analogous to the first, only elaborated at the beginning and at the end. The introductory theme *7a* is first presented by three horns, whose grave invocation restores tranquillity of mood, whereupon the violoncello works up the theme into a kind of cadenza, whose expressive fervency is communicated, on their return, to the motifs 7b and 7c and culminates at the close of the movement in the palpitating harmonies of the violoncello and orchestra of thrilling tenderness and beauty.

A passage in the solo instrument raises an arch of melody to a trill trembling as it were on the brink of tears, and, as it dies away, the movement concludes with the same expression of profound calm with which it began.

The third movement of the Concerto (*Allegro moderato*, B minor, $^2/_4$) is altogether infused with the tone of happy anticipation of the composer's early return to his own country and of its happy fulfilment. The principal theme is in a minor key, but immediately following its appearance in three horns above the strong marching steps of the violoncellos and double basses, and after a rapid dynamic rise characteristically coloured with the gay tinkling of the triangle, it makes a resolute entry in the solo instrument and strikes a new note of happy excitement.

Its energetic swing is confirmed by a second thought in the bright key of D major, in sprightly rhythms (10), while a third motif makes great play with the rhythmic and dynamic energy of the first theme, both in the terse form of the orchestral intermezzo (11*a*) and in the freer melodic line of the solo instrument (11*b*):

Out of the rhythm of this last motif there grows another theme, softer in expression in the same degree as it is warmer and more sweetly tender in feeling:

The last theme of this first part of the movement, delivered by the clarinet and violoncello in two-part counterpoint, holds up the lively flow of the movement for a while, imparting to it, at the same time, a slight tinge of melancholy:

The second section of the finale opens with a theme which breathes a moving warmth of feeling, utterly Czech in tone and with a Smetana-like colouring in its cadence-figure:

The tone of quivering tenderness which permeates this whole theme is strengthened when, after passing through several modulations, it reaches the key of B major in which the solo violin and cello sing a duet of intoxicating beauty and irresistable emotional ardour. From now on the key of B major dominates the movement. Theme 9 has the leading role, first in its proud original form, then in a festively grave enlargement delivered by the wood wind, and finally, in a romantic, meditative colouring, when the flutes, clarinets and especially the muted trumpets allow it to expire into a mystic pedal of warm pastel-tinted chords.* A quotation of the principal theme from the first movement (1), followed by that of the second theme from the Adagio (8a), which, in the key of B major, is now a literal quotation of the opening phrase of "Leave Me Alone", and a new allusion to theme 1, brings this sensitive part of the movement to a close. The composition ends with a short, rapid gradation, in which the trombones, to the gay accompaniment of the trumpets, declaim once more a solemn broadening-out of the main theme of the finale (9).

* The rest of the composition was written by Dvořák after his return to Bohemia. See note on p. 176.

III

SERENADES AND SUITES

In Dvořák's production of absolute as opposed to programe music, there is another and last group of cyclic compositions for orchestra with a firmly integrated and fuctionally organised content and structure—the Serenades and Suites. These works, too, revive an old form of composition of several movements, such as are symphonies and 'concertos, but differ from these mainly in their simpler, more intimate character, both as regards content and form as well as in their almost chamber-music instrumentation. Serenades—as compositions written originally for the wind band—were meant for evening performance in the open air (the word *serenata* in Italian means evenings music) and only later developed into compositions for concert performance with the addition of the strings, while the Suites were an early form of composition consisting of a number of small dance movements extended later to include quieter movements based on poetic moods.

Dvořák created two examples in each of these two kinds of cyclic compositions: one serenade for strings, another mainly for wind instruments; and while the first of the two suites is written for a small orchestra, consisting of a variety of combinations of wind instruments with strings, the second, originally a piano suite, which originated in Dvořák's American period, is rewritten for a large orchestra. All four of these compositions are among the most attractive and original manifestations of Dvořák's creative art, their national character in the serenade for wind instruments and the first suite, designedly entitled "Czech", being underlined by the fact that the dance movements are wonderfully effective art idealizations of characteristic types of Czech folk dances.

1. SERENADE IN E MAJOR FOR STRING ORCHESTRA, OP. 22

Written in score between May 3rd and 14th, 1875.—First performed by the Prague Philharmonic (the combined orchestras of the Czech and German Theatres), conducted by Adolf Čech, on December 10th, 1876. The composer's piano arrangement for four hands was published in 1877 by Starý, Prague, the score and parts in 1879 by Bote and Bock, Berlin.—Duration: 25 minutes.

The Serenade for string orchestra is mainly cast in a poetic mood, with an overtone of ardent longing, yet not altogether devoid of a certain cheerful gaiety, which is the note on which it ends. The work consists of five smal lmovements, including two scherzos and a slow movement in the middle. They are for the most part in ternary rondo form, and an indication of the character of the theme is the way in which it lends itself to canonic imitation.

The first movement (*Moderato*, E major, $^4/_4$) creates the setting for the atmosphere of the whole serenade. Its opening and closing sections grow out of a calm, gently undulating and softly melting theme (1*a*), the continuation of which is rhythmically somewhat more animated (1*b*), while the ardency of expression is further underlined by the interpolated element *m* introduced on its repetition.

The theme of the middle section, with its impulsive rhythms, is much livelier (2*a*), but it combines, too, on repetition, with a calmly phrased counter-subject (2*b*) maintaining the same atmosphere of twilight and sweet desire.

Lovely in the poetry of its mood is the conclusion of the movement, where the violins respond to the principal theme in the 'cellos and double-basses, with a modification of a peculiarly beautiful harmonic colouring.

The second movement (*Tempo di Valse*, C sharp minor, $^3/_4$) is really a fully developed scherzo, though not indicated as such. Two identical sections, based on a waltz and symmetrically divided into three parts, are separated by a quieter Trio. The opening figure (3*a*) of the middle repetition of these sections alternates with the same motif in mazurka rhythm (3*b*):

The middle section of the movement is in the key of D flat major and deals mainly with a broadly phrased lyrical theme of warm sensibility (4). As it proceeds, it is agitated by a very sharply accented variant of figure *n* from the walz-theme (3*c*):

In spite of its dancing movement, the mood of the whole is strongly permeated with tender passion.

The third movement (*Vivace*, F major, $^2/_4$) is also a scherzo and is indicated as such. In contrast to the yearning dreaminess of mood of the preceding movement, it is gay to the point of abandon in the spirit of its first theme (5). This is again in canonic imitation, and opens out later into a bustling semiquaver passage:

The second theme (6*a*), however, brings tranquillity and warmth into the movement, especially when its opening phrase develops into a pleasingly lyrical clause not unrelated to theme 5:

The middle section of the movement, transposed into a minor key a semitone higher, is strongly erotic in mood and colouring:

After this broadly developed middle section (actually a Trio), the first section is repeated with considerable abridgement of the individual paragraphs, and with short allusions to the theme of the Trio (7) in the conclusion.

The basic mood of smouldering passion completely dominates the slow fourth movement (*Larghetto*, A major, $^2/_4$), the loveliest and most deeply expressive of all. It develops out of a grave, broadly lyrical and throbbing theme (8), the miniature intermezzo with its livelier middle motif (9) only stressing by contrast the prevailing mood, as if a light breeze were to ruffle the surface of the deep tranquillity of night.

It is a movement with a spaciously phrased melodic line, a true Nocturne, singing of the strength, beauty and ennobling power of love.

The fifth and last movement, in sharp contrast to those preceding, concludes the work in a mood of mettlesome high spirits (*Allegro vivace*, E major, $^2/_4$). In its form and thematic treatment, it is relatively the most complex and interesting, being a kind of daringly individual conception of sonata form. Unusual, too, is the fact that the first of the three themes, which after a resolute fortissimo entry storms through canonic imitations and ends with unabated vigour and decision, seldom appears in the tonic key, which the secondary theme, passionate and broadly phrased, seems equally anxious to avoid:

The tonic key of E major is first thoroughly established with the third theme (12), whose spirited rhythm and alternating major and minor mode are strongly reminiscent of the much later "Slavonic Dances":

A not less surprising stroke is when, at the point where some kind of development might be expected, there is a sudden falling away in tone without, however, any slowing down of the momentum maintained by the persistent repetition of the rhythmic figure from the preceding theme, while the violoncello—as if in tender reminiscence—enters here with theme 8 from the slow movement; or when, at the conclusion of the recapitulation of the first part of the movement, with its rich development of theme 11, the musical flow of the movement is held up by a return to the calm of the beginning of the movement (theme 1), thus bringing the whole serenade, which concludes in a whirl of boisterous high spirits, within the framework of a single artistic unity of mood.

2. SERENADE IN D MINOR FOR WIND INSTRUMENTS, VIOLONCELLO AND DOUBLE-BASS, OP. 44

Instrumentation: 2 oboes, 2 clarinets, 2 bassoons, double bassoon (ad. lib.), 3 horns, violoncello and double bass.

Written in score between the beginning and the 18th of January, 1878.— Dedicated to Louis *Ehlert.*—First performed by members of the Czech orchestra in Prague, with Dvořák conducting, at a concert of his own works on November 17th, 1878. Score, parts and paino arrangement for four hands by Josef *Zubatý*, published by Simrock, Berlin 1879.—Duration: 26 minutes.

The second of Dvořák's serenades is written altogether in the style of old compositions intended for evening performance in the open air by an ensemble of wind-instruments. This determines not only the choice of instruments—a close-knit chamber ensemble, in which the wood-wind band has the leading role while the strings only strengthen and give greater flexibility to the bass. It also determines the whole idea and musical content of the composition, for only one of the four movements is in a vein of calm reflectiveness, while the tone of the others is dominated by old-world, good-humoured cheerfulness. In spirit and expression, on the other hand, it is new even for its time, both in its ideas, effectively and skilfully derived from the specific character of the instruments, and in the originality of thematic treatment. The hallmark of the composer's national individuality is given to the scherzo sections, which are in the spirit of the Czech "*sousedská*", while the middle part is interwoven with "*furiant*" rhythms. Thematically the serenade is interesting in that the principal themes of all four movements employ the interval of an ascending fourth (see the bracketed figure in examples 1, 3—7), while the score reveals in every bar an outstanding mastery of the art of orchestration.

The first movement of the serenade (*Moderato quasi Marcia*, D minor, $^4/_4$), in simple ternary form, has a humorous, march-like character, and it has been aptly suggested that it is rather like the pompous and slightly ludicrous march of village musicians coming to give a performance. The principal theme, with which the first and the last part are mainly taken up, makes slyly good-humoured fun of this naively pompous tendency (1), while the middle section develops rather hesitatingly and self-consciously out of a simple thought (2), and then out of its more decorative variant (2*a*), or combines with a simple little quaver figure (2*b*):

The second movement is a scherzo. The musicians have announced their arrival and now open up with a lively dance tune. Dvořák himself wrote Menuetto above this movement but, as already mentioned, the quieter first and last scherzo sections (*Tempo di Menuetto*, F major, $^3/_4$) have clearly the character of a Czech "*sousedská*" (a slow dance), especially in the folk-music colouring of the theme:

The middle part (*Trio, Presto,* B flat major), of which the lively theme 4 is developed from the semiquaver figure of the preceding theme, has the character of a very quick dance, in parts with typically *furiant* syncopated rhythms:

And now the musicians play a real lover's serenade. In the slow third movement (*Andante con moto,* A major, $^4/_4$), over the calm crotchet progression of the bass and the acquiescing chord interpolation of the three horns, the clarinet and oboe draw a lovely cantilena of delicate melodic charm and great warmth of feeling:

This cantilena is the thematic nerve of the whole movement, supplemented in places by the tenderly palpitating motif 5*a*,

which takes over the ascending intervals of a fourth and fifth from
its own theme and, combining with the latter in the middle of the
movement, works up to a whirl of imitation.

Truly a movement of rare beauty of ideas and strong emotional
content!

At the close of the Serenade, however, there must be a gay rous-
ing piece. So the fourth and last movement of the Serenade
(Finale, *Allegro molto*, D minor, $^2/_4$) is extremely lively and contains,
also in its design, a number of strokes that are both original and
witty. It opens with a unison statement by all the instruments of
a theme which is somehow related to the principal theme of the
first movement (1), but with an unconcealed gaiety of aspect:

It only flashes past, however, and leaves the field to its closing
phrase *m*, of which the ascending fourth gives rise to a new auxiliary
thought in broken rhythm, alternately tossed to the high and low
instruments:

6a

This gaiety of mood reaches a climax with a new variant of the
first theme which, in the double sixths of the clarinets, has a touch of
country simplicity and humour:

This idea is broadly developed, even though it is interspersed with allusions to the closing figure *m* of the original theme, which at length succeeds in quietening the movement down to prepare for a somewhat more serious, but paukily humorous and charming folk-coloured idea, with a polka rhythm in the second pair of bars (in B and D major):

It is, however, only like a short and friendly greeting from her in whose honour the serenade is played, and soon the movement returns to the gaily careering theme 6*b*, surprisingly interspaced with several bars of the march from the beginning of the first movement (1). The musicians, proud at having successfully carried out their task, leave with the same slightly ludicrous solemnity with which they arrived. A *presto* coda based on theme 6*b*, extremely gay in mood and with a final jubilant flourish of trumpets, brings this delightfully spontaneous and original work to a close.

3. CZECH SUITE, OP. 39

Instrumentation: 2 flutes, 2 oboes, cor anglais, 2 clarinets, 2 horns, 1 trumpet, tympani, strings.

Written presumably in April,1879.—First performance by the Czech Theatre-Orchestra in Prague, conducted by Adolf Čech, on May 16th, 1879. Published under the incomplete title "Suite für das Orchester" in score, parts and four-handed arrangement for pianoforte (F. *Brissler* and R. *Niclau*) by Schlesinger, Berlin in 1881. — Duration: 22 minutes.

Dvořák's first suite dates from the so-called "Slavonic" period of the artist's production, very near in time to the first series of the "Slavonic Dances". It is also closely linked with these by the dance character of its five movements, which comprise art idealizations of the same specifically Czech types of folk dance: the polka, the "*sousedská*" and the "*furiant*", which is why the composer entitled the work "Czech Suite". In its intimacy of expression and thematic treatment, and not least in the very delicate and individual character of its musical matter, this suite forms a group with the two serenades, as is also apparent from the interesting circumstance that it crystallized out of the author's original intention to compose another serenade. It is also written for a small orchestra, the strings combining in each of the five movements with a different group of wind instruments, occasionally augmented by the kettle-drums.

The "Czech Suite" opens with a short Preludium of pastoral cast (*Allegro moderato*, D major, $^4/_4$) based on a single, firmly contoured theme, the idyllic character being underlined by a dominant pedal point, an ostinato of a major second *d-e*, and by the orchestral colouring in which the string tone is enriched by a sensitive use of the tone qualities of pairs of oboes, bassoons and horns:

The theme runs through a range of different keys and harmonic colourings, enhanced by rich contrapuntal embroidery, with an endearing unaffectedness and with a fine sense of design, so that the movement develops into a model of the musical lyric.

The second movement is a Polka (*Allegro grazioso*, D minor,

$^2/_4$). The principal theme of the first and third parts is tinged with the same soft melancholy as in the Polka movements of the Dvořák D minor quartet, op. 34 and the Sextet in A major, op. 48.

Here too, however, as in the Polka of the Sextet, the melancholy colouring fades as soon as the theme, in its continuation, switches to the key of F major, and the trill figure, at first in the upper part and later in the bass, sets the movement dancing:

Equally gay is the livelier Trio in D major, of which the theme seesaws in a semi-quaver figure on rising planes (Ex. 3), the movement ending with a regular repetition of the first part.

As the third movement, Dvořák introduced into the "Czech Suite" a delightfully typical "*sousedská*" (*Allegro giusto*, B flat major, $^3/_4$), also based on a single theme (4) of which the development takes the form of canonic imitation (4*a*):

The movement, which steps out in vigorous, stamping rhythms, indulges on its way in gay processes of imitation and modulation, while, in addition to its own theme, use is made of the accessory figure (4*b*), rhythmically derived from the second bar of the theme in the form of a contrapuntal accompaniment:

In the scoring, this movement differs from those preceding in the substitution of flutes and clarinets for oboes and horns.

The fourth movement of this Suite comprises a delicate, beautifully orchestrated Romance *(Andante con moto,* G major, $^9/_8$) poetical in mood, like the introductory pastoral, but with a stronger undercurrent of emotion. The calm cantabile of the theme develops into a dialogue between the flute and the English horn to the triplet accompaniment of the strings,

while the middle part of the movement is coloured with an unmistakable reminiscence of Smetana:

The series of movements finishes up with a rhythmically very fiery Furiant (*Presto*, D minor, $^3/_4$), of all Dvořák's furiants one of the most characteristic and effective. The three-part movement, of which the first and last parts grow out of a syncopated theme, maintains, despite its setting in the soft key of D minor, an expression of gaiety and verve.

6. Presto

In the theme of the middle part of the movement, now in the bright key of D major, Dvořák approaches more closely than in any other of his furiants to the furiant melody of the national song "Peasant, peasant, peasant, and once more peasant" (7), stressing its typically Czech character by adding an equally characteristic five-bar period, interesting as opening with the same ascending and descending fourth out of which is evolved the theme of the preceding Romance (5).

Just as the principal theme in the first and third part of the Furiant, so also the theme of the Trio is worked up to an imposing climax, returning, as an effective high-point, at the end of the last part extended to include a variant of the principal theme (6). The use here of trumpets and kettle-drums, the only place in which they are employed in the whole "Czech Suite", contributes not a little to the youthful élan of the Furiant, and so also to the note of cheerful good spirits with which it ends.

4. SUITE IN A MAJOR, OP. 98b

Instrumentation: Piccola, 2 flutes, 2 oboes, 2 clarinets, 2 bassoons, 4 horns, 2 trumpets, 3 trombones, tuba, kettle drums, big drum, cymbals, triangle and strings.

Sketch for piano written between the 19th and 23rd February, 1894; the fair copy completed between February 24th and March 1st of the same year in New York, where it was also scored after January 19th, 1895. The version for orchestra was first performed by the Czech Philharmonic, conducted by Karel *Kovařovic,* on March 1st, 1910, in Prague. Score, parts and piano arrangement for four hands (Roman *Veselý*) published by Simrock, Berlin 1911.—Duration: 20 minutes.

Dvořák's second suite, written originally for piano, but subsequently orchestrated, arose during the composer's sojourn in America and also embodies in most of its musical ideas the typical features of his American compositions. Like the Czech Suite, this one, too, comprises five movements, the dance movements, however, being this time of cosmopolitan character (polonaise, gavotte). The general tone of the work is one of charming idyllic light-heartedness with a tinge of the romantic longing which is also a typical trait of Dvořák's American compositions.

This latter mood dominates the first movement of the Suite (*Moderato,* A major, $^4/_4$), which is in three-part form, the outer parts tranquil, the middle part more agitated in expression. Thus the first theme proceeds quietly with its smoothly-phrased descent from the sixth degree (1a), but is animated in its continuation, which develops out of the bar (1b):

The theme of the middle part (*Piu mosso*, A minor) has something romantic and passionate about it, in spite of its staccato playfulness, underlined by canonic imitation (2), and in spite of the transposition to the minor mode.

2.   Pochettino più mosso

The second movement (*Molto vivace*, C sharp minor, $^3/_8$) is also in ternary form, the first and third part this time very quick and vigorous, and separated by a quieter middle part. Its wildly whirling first theme (3a), with its persistently repeated single note, gives it a capriccio-like character, which clings to it even in the continuation of the theme (3b), the germ of which is contained in its last two bars:

3a   Molto vivace
3b

The very lovely middle part of the movement, in D flat major, provides a rhythmic and dynamic contrast to the busy activity of the preceding part, an expression of softly tender yearning being embodied in the flexibly-phrased cantabile of the theme of which the development is embroidered with bird-like trills:

4.

The third movement (*Allegretto*, A major, $^3/_4$) is the most complicated in form and variable in mood. It is actually a rondo, of which the principal theme (5) is characterised by the sprightly rhythms of the polonaise step, whereas the other two are either in a tone of passionate regretfulness (6) or of heart-sick reflection (7). And if the former is not a little reminiscent of Schumannesque romanticism, the latter (7) reveals clearly in its narrow melodic range and in the lowering of the seventh degree its American origin.

The fourth movement (*Andante*, A minor, $^4/_4$) is quite the opposite of the preceding movement, being the simplest of all in form, expression and mood. It grows out of a single theme coloured with tender passion (8), which is repeated several times with only small deviations and, in the middle, yielding place for a short time to the accessory motif 9.

The quality of the basic theme, and its recurrence in the manner of a refrain, gives this little movement the character of a tenderly reminiscent lullaby.

The fifth movement (*Allegro*, A minor, $^2/_2$) concludes the suite with a rhythmically animated and delicately accented Gavotte, of which the principal theme in the key of A minor (10a) and its variant in A major (10b) have again a typically American flavour.

Whereas the beginning of the movement rises with the first theme to a passionately stormy gradation, the entry of the second theme, despite all its sportiveness, effects a change of mood with its expression of dreamy desire (especially fascinating is the episode in F sharp major), and out of this mood, as also out of the melodic elements of the theme, indicated in example 10b by brackets, there grows Dvořák's logical conclusion of the suite with a return to the principal theme of the first movement (1a), its broadly impressive re-entry at the end of the Gavotte giving the suite a unity of design similar to that which distinguishes the two serenades.

IV

RHAPSODIES

A rhapsody in instrumental music may be described as a composition of free formal arrangement, usually organised in paragraphs, having a mainly narrative musical content. Dvořák wrote, in all, four such orchestral compositions, the first in 1874 and the others three or four years later. According to contemporary sources, the composer had in mind, from the first, the composition of a cycle of "Slavonic Rhapsodies", after the manner of the well-known "Hungarian Rhapsodies" by Liszt, but at that time restricted himself to one, to which he gave the general title of "Rhapsody", and only when he came to completing the other three, which he wrote in quick succession and grouped under a single opus number, did he realize his original intention, being no doubt suitably disposed for the work by the close chronological proximity of the first series of "Slavonic Dances". In these three "Slavonic Rhapsodies" he already possessed a clear conception of the organic structure of this type of composition, whereas in the first, a work of undoubted individuality and charm, a certain measure of hesitation is apparent, which is also why he did not make this work public.

It should be pointed out that a rhapsody is fundamentally a form of "absolute" music and remains such even though it is possible to associate it with a certain subject. This is true of all four of Dvořák's rhapsodies. And though the author himself gave no indication of having been influenced in his composition by any extra-musical ideas, the character of their musical content, and especially the orientation of their moods, allow us to give them a programme which—and were it of the vaguest kind—would be of value as helping the listener towards a better understanding of the work. For this reason a sketch of the extra-musical background is included here along with the analysis of the individual Rhapsodies.

1. RHAPSODY IN A MINOR FOR LARGE ORCHESTRA (ORIG. OP. 15)

Instrumentation: piccolo, 2 flutes, 2 oboes, cor anglais, 2 bassoons, 4 horns, 2 trumpets, 3 trombones, tuba, kettle drums, cymbals, big drum, triangle, harp and strings.

Written in score at the beginning of September 1874 and finished on the 12th of the same month. First performed by the Czech Philharmonic, with Oskar *Nedbal* as conductor, at Dvořák's posthumous concert held on November 3rd, 1904, in Prague.—Score, parts and piano arrangement for four hands (Roman *Veselý*) published by Simrock, Berlin, 1812.—Duration: 19 minutes.

The first of Dvořák's rhapsodies is in A minor, with a distinct bias towards rondo arrangement, while the basic mood is manifestly h e r o i c, involuntarily calling to mind the composer's last symphonic poem "The Hero's Song", of the year 1897, with the subject matter of which it has much in common. This heroic mood also determines the character of the two main themes, which interpenetrate the whole work, imparting to it a mood of fighting determination and a mournful, contemplative tone, only lit up by occasional shafts of lyrical sunshine, and telling not only of a firm will to fight for the realization of a dream, but also of the intoxication of victory when that dream becomes reality.

The first of the two main themes, both of which appear at the very beginning of the composition *(Allegro moderato,* ⁴/₄*)*, is energetic, bold in its contours and clean-cut rhythms (1), while the other, which follows close upon the first, is gravely chorale-like in tone and, at first, in the colouring of the clarinets and horns, not without a tinge of melancholy (2 in D flat major):

1. Allegro moderato

The themes are twice more presented in alternation and in the most varied nuances of mood, the second then bringing this part of the movement to a festive grand climax in the keys of C and A major, with a powerfully imposing volume of orchestral tone. The vital forces have gone through their first baptism of fire, steeling the will alike to the bitterness of disappointment and to the brightness of high hopes.

It is possible now to relax a little; with theme 1 the musical stream begins to flow more calmly, and in the delicately clear tone of the trumpets a new melodic theme is announced and developed in two variants (*Moderato*, E major):

After a short discussion of theme 1, there is a return of theme 3*b*, in the key of C major, which links up with the second theme in a new variant, 2*a*, with which the second paragraph of the Rhapsody culminates in D flat major.

Some development is made of theme 1, at first again gravely contemplative (*Andante con moto*, C minor), but then becoming increasingly agitated till it is cut short by two delicate quotations of theme 2

and a new exposition of the lyrical theme 3. A short coda carries the composition to the heights of a jubilan and victorious conclusion, the full orchestra blazing out with festive pomp a recapitulation of theme 2 in C major, followed finally by theme 1 in the tonic.

2. THREE SLAVONIC RHAPSODIES OP. 45

Dvořák returned to his design of writing a number of Rhapsodies in a specifically national tone when he had aroused the interest of the Berlin publisher, Simrock, with his "Moravian Duets", and when—seeing some possibility of making a name for himself abroad —he aimed at composing his works in a nationally Czech and so also characteristically Slavonic vein. The three "Slavonic Rhapsodies", which the author grouped under op. 45, and the first series of "Slavonic Dances", op. 46 (see page 214), which arose at the same time, are the most notable and also the most charming and successful products of this creative period. Compared with the first rhapsody of the year 1874, the "Slavonic Rhapsodies" are on a very much higher level, not only in the individual and national originality of their musical content, but also in the greater and more flexible command of the basic rondo form as illustrated by each in a different way. The fine scale of nuances in the formal realization is, however, determined by the quality of the content: three sharply delineated and lively tone-pictures without any expressly defined programme, in which there are mirrored, with the softness and naive earnestness of old woodcuts, the different, characteristic epochs of the Czech past.

"SLAVONIC RHAPSODY" IN D MAJOR, OP. 45 N° 1.

Instrumentation: piccolo, 2 flutes, 2 oboes, 2 clarinets, 2 bassoons, 4 horns, 2 trumpets, 3 trombones, kettle drums, big drum, triangle, strings.

Sketch begun on February 13th, and score written between February 19th and March 17th, 1878.—Dedicated to Baron *Pavel* of Dervies.—First performed by the orchestra of the Czech Interim Theatre, with the composer conducting, on November 17th, 1878, in Prague. Score, parts and piano arrangement for four hands (composer) published by Simrock, Berlin, in 1879. — Duration: 10 minutes.

The first "Slavonic Rhapsody" may be interpreted as a conscious musical idealisation of the earliest period of Czech history. The principal theme is pastoral, and its pleasing melodic line seems to sing the happy idyllic existence of tillers of the land and keepers of flocks in the legendary age of Forefather Čech and Libuše, whether it breathes sweet calm in the wood-winds or sounds forth in monumental gravity of expression in the full orchestra dominated by the brass (1). The grave dignity of the warriors of that age, as well as the love of merry games in the greenness of fertile valleys, are expressed in the second theme with syncopated rhythms and close either with a descent into the relative minor key (2*a*), or with a four-bar period of high-spirited jollity (2*b*):

The first theme, mysterious intimations of the characteristic rhythm of which appear in the solo kettle-drums, is broadly developed in an introductory passage, the whole work being designed in Rondo form (*Allegro con moto*, ⁶/₄).

Another paragraph, transposed to the key of B flat major (*Tempo di marcia*, ²/₄), works up the materials of the second theme (2*a* and 2*b*), developing it with rich invention and running the gamut of a wide range of moods. It proceeds, once with a firm marching step, again at a slow and measured pace, now with solemn dignity, now dancing gaily along, but finally, too, assuming a veiled dreaminess of expression. Having thus reached the transition section, the third part of the movement again opens with the first theme (1), which it develops with lively modulating imitations, whereupon it continues with a gay variant in the key of C major (1*a*):

culminating in its festive declamation in contrapuntal combination with theme 2:

Theme 2 again assumes the dominant role in both its variants, whereupon the first theme closes the composition in its original idyllic and figurally embroidered form, dying away at last in the muted tones of the trumpets and horns.

"SLAVONIC RHAPSODY" IN G MINOR, OP. 45, NO 2

Instrumentation: 2 flutes, 2 oboes, 2 clarinets, 2 bassoons, 4 horns, 2 trumpets, 3 trombones, kettle drums, big drum, triangle, harp and strings.

Written in score between August 26th and September 18th, 1878.—Dedicated to Baron *Pavel* of Dervies.—First performed as "Slavonic Rhapsody" No. 1. Published as for No. 1, except that the piano arrangement for four hands is by Josef *Zubatý.*—Duration: 13 minutes.

In contrast to the idyllically bright and, for the most part, calm character of the first "Slavonic Rhapsody", the second is full of rhythmic movement and bustle, its tone is darker in colouring, in conformity with its basic minor mode and especially with the nature of two of its three main themes. But not even here is there lacking, in places, the lively gaiety of the dance which finally sets its seal on the work, but such passages do not weaken the impression of the stir and movement of battle, of the basically heroic mood in which the whole work is cast. This determines, too, the more complex arrangement of the rondo form than sufficed for the first "Slavonic Rhapsody". Not only are there three themes here instead of two, but the first two, which dominate the composition, are now worked up more closely, being combined, contrasted and merged in a process in which, at its climax, both are again presented in high plastic relief.

The shape of these two themes and their transmutations show, however, considerable divergence. The first, with its sharply accented rhythms, announced at the beginning of the composition by its readily identifiable minor seconds (1*a*), appears then successively in the following main variants (1*b*—1*d*):

1a   Allegro ma non troppo

The second theme is, by contrast, distinguished by a grave and noble pathos of expression (reminiscent in its confirmation of the beginning of the Czech National Anthem: "Kde domov můj?") and restricting itself to its basic one-bar phrase:

These two themes, in rondo alternation, form the substance out of which the first part of the composition develops, the chromatic colouring and sharp rhythms of the first introducing a whirl and eddy of movement, while the expressive breadth of the second plays an important role at the dynamically impressive culminating points. A triple alternation of these themes is followed by a new exposition of variant 1*b*, which is joined by a third theme, softly melodic in its core (3*a*), but passing over, as its rhythmic intensity increases, into the sprightly dance variant 3*b*:

The exposition of this theme, allusions to which occur again before the close of the composition, is, however, only a softly lyrical intermezzo in the otherwise powerfully agitated tone of the rhapsody, which, in its final part, proceeds to new treatment of the two basic themes, this time making much of variants 1*a* and 1*c*, in places clashing aggressively with the solemn motif 2, and winding up in G major with that inner acceleration of movement of which Dvořák had the rare secret.

"SLAVONIC RHAPSODY" IN A FLAT MAJOR, OP. 45, Nº 3

Instrumentation as for "Slavonic Rhapsody" No 2. Completed in sketch on September 22nd, and written in score between then and December 3rd, 1878, with some pauses.—Dedication the same as for Nos 1 and 2.—First performed at a symphonic soireé of the Band of the King's Musicians, conducted by the Court Kapellmeister, Wilhelm *Taubert*, on September 24th, 1879; first performed in Prague, under the composer's baton, on March 29th, 1880.—Published along with the two preceding rhapsodies (four-handed pianoforte arrangement by the composer).—Duration: 14 minutes.

The third of the "Slavonic Rhapsodies" has its own thought and emotional content, which is different again from the other two. In its gay, almost mosaic-like but thematically well integrated section, there comes to life all the romance of medieval chivalry, with its sharply contrasted lights and shades. It sings its glory and splendour, recalls its games and famous tournaments, the hunting of the deer in the royal forests, the chivalrous love of brave knights and fair ladies, and the wholehearted delight in dance and carnival and the jollity of grand festivities. Hence the *capriccioso* character of the work both in form and content; hence, too, its kaleidoscopic changes of movement and mood. The rhapsodic style is immediately established in the introduction (*Andante maestoso*, $^9/_8$) with the exposition of the principal theme in the solo harp:

The serious tone of the theme soon gives way, however, to a very gay, rhythmically accelerated and lively variant 1*b* (*Allegro assai*, $^2/_4$):

The mood of light-hearted jollity to which this variant gives expression is further underlined when its development is followed quite naturally by a no less gay and lively subordinate theme (2*a*):

The two main themes, fresh and vigorous in character, are repeated several times, in a number of modulations. Then there spring up, like little episodes, the softly yearning theme 1*a* in the solo violin or flute, a sudden ceremonious flourish of trumpets (2*b*), an unexpected quiet reminiscence of the grave opening of the composition (1*a*) or maybe a meditative cantilena embodying new variants of the second theme (2*c*):

2b Trb.

ff grandioso

Before the end of the composition the principal theme is declaimed once more, its original gravity and nobility of expression (1*a*)
enhanced by a tone of festive pomp (*Poco andante*). Then, however,
variant 1*b* closes into a short coda, whose breath-taking prestissimo
is unexpectedly cut short at the very close by a delicately pensive
quotation of theme 2*c*.

V

SLAVONIC DANCES

The name of Antonín Dvořák, by an almost inseparable association of ideas, instantly calls to mind the "Slavonic Dances". Nur-
tured from childhood in the atmosphere of the folk-tradition of
village music, and with its bright, vigorous rhythms in his blood,
Dvořák at times took delight in composing dance music as one of its
most typical manifestations—either as independent compositions or
as part of cyclic compositions comprising several movements. In
the two series of "Slavonic Dances", however, he created a work of
quite exceptional quality, a work which not only testified in a
peculiarly convincing way to his creative genius, but one on which,
above all, was founded the world-wide reputation which his art
enjoyed.

The two series of "Slavonic Dances" are separated in time by a
period of eight years (1878—1886), and, in the order of his works,
by the opus numbers between 46 and 72. In two respects, however,
they have a common origin: both series were written in response
to the request of his Berlin publisher, Simrock, and both were originally written as piano duets. Only later were they given the orchestral dress in which they took the whole musical world by storm.
The beauty and unique character of the musical thoughts, as well as
the author's amazing mastery of the compositional art are, however, equally demonstrated in the piano version. And though, as will
be shown in the following detailed analyses, each of the two series
of "Slavonic Dances" has its own, clearly differentiated unity of
mood and expression, conforming to the different stages of the composer's work and life, the works have this in common that both liter-
ally teem with the most delightful melodic and harmonic ideas,
that both are engendered by richly fertile rhythmic invention joined
with inexhaustible vitality and wit, and, that both series are

created with all the artistic resources of a great composer's art.

His own conviction, which he repeatedly impressed on his pupils, that the value of a work of art lies not in the idea but in what the composer makes of it, was never illustrated more forcibly that in the "Slavonic Dances". Not, let it be understood, that the thematic ideas, comprising the core of the musical content, should be thought to lack intrinsic value, for, as has already been pointed out, they, too, have their clearly delineated individuality and uncommonly fresh and peculiar charm. The way, however, in which Dvořák utilizes these ideas, the inexhaustible resource with which he works them up, varying, contrasting, combining and embroidering them, is a manifestation of genius in the truest sense of the word. A simple repetition of the original theme occurs only when the structural or inner logic of the work demands it. For the rest, it is impossible to express too great an admiration for the inventiveness with which Dvořák continually modifies the theme, whether in the form of melodic variations or harmonic and modulating transitions from one key to another, or by shifting it from the higher to the middle or lower registers. And here, too, he reveals extraordinary imaginative gifts in the resourcefulness with which he breaks up a theme and makes independent use of its fragments, which often blossom forth into new themes. The spontaneity of effect is all the greater in that the compositional exuberance which Dvořák here displays has nothing strained, forced or unnatural, that everything pulsates with real life and with the intoxication of movement and rhythm which makes a man express his mood in dance. Nor is it any different when we consider the endless variety of thematic ideas which the composer's imagination brings forth and which link up, alternate and combine without ever producing the impression of merely fortuitous or arbitrary concatenation.

All these outstanding features of the "Slavonic Dances", though present in the original piano version, are brought out with still greater plasticity by orchestration. The whole character of the work demanded it, and it is not surprising that Dvořák was easily induced to set about the instrumentation of the dances even before he had finished the first series in the piano version. The symphonic nature of the dances, inherent in the polyphonic structure of their melody, called for it as did the scope they gave to a wide and highly differentiated scale of tone values, and not least, of course, their symphonic verve and expressiveness. Dvořák's extraordinary feeling for orchestral tone-colour and mastery of the technique of instrumentation enabled him, in translating these pearls of musical composition into terms of the orchestra, to bring out with the utmost plasticity and colourfulness all the most significant elements of their expression and to whip up their sparkling vital rhythms to the height of passion and intensity. If Dvořák could write to the publisher Simrock of the second series of "Slavonic Dances": "Die Tänze werden brillant instrumentiert, es wird alles krachen," ("The Dances will be brilliantly orchestrated, they will bring the place down"), and "sie klingen wie der Teufel" ("they sound like the very Devil"), he could have said the same with equal justice of the first series, even though in this respect, too, each group has its own qualities determined by the content.

All the features described above make of the two series of "Slavonic Dances" a work uniquely lovely and uniquely effective, a work remarkable for the merging of highest inspiration and consummate art, and for the fact that this great art, without being in the least obtrusive, speaks straight to the heart of the widest of audiences, to the heart of the common people out of whose spiritual moods and needs the "Slavonic Dances" were born.

1. THE FIRST SERIES
OF "SLAVONIC DANCES", OP. 46

Written in the original version of piano duets between March 18th and May 7th, 1878, and scored by August 22nd of the same year.—Dances 1., 6. and 3. were first performed on May 16th, 1878, by the orchestra of the Czech Theatre in Prague, conducted by Adolf Čech.—Published in score and parts by Simrock, Berlin, 1878.—Duration of the whole series, with intervals: about 40 minutes.

A request for a cycle of "Slavonic Dances" came to Dvořák from the Berlin publisher Fritz Simrock who, immediately after entering, through Brahms's recommendation, into business contact with him, and knowing his "Moravian Duets", was already in a position to appreciate the outstanding and original gifts of the Czech composer. He thus made a concrete suggestion that Dvořák should write a series of "Slavonic Dances" for piano duet in something like the style of Brahms' "Hungarian Dances" which, at that time, had won great popularity. Dvořák reacted to this suggestion very readily; broke off the composition of the Slavonic Rhapsodies and in a short time the eight "Slavonic Dances" were finished in the piano version as requested. The sketch itself, in which the pen had evidently much ado to keep pace with the birth of ideas, having time to record only the bare melodic lines of the dances, almost without compositional notes (except for an occasional "melody in the bass", "figuration in the left hand" or harmonic indications), is eloquent proof of the miraculous spontaneity with which the whole work came to life. It was certainly the work of not more than a few hours.* And with the same élan as distinguished the realization of the first piano version of the "Slavonic Dances", Dvořák also carried out their orchestration, especially when he realized how entirely suited

* It may be of interest to know that, in this sketch, the A flat major dance is in the third place and the D major in the sixth, as in the orchestral version, whereas the piano version reverses the order.

they were, in conception and feeling, to this medium, which brought into full bloom their rare originality and beauty.

Of the suggestion put forward by the publisher, Dvořák seized on only the basic idea: the creation of art stylizations of characteristic Slavonic dances. He did not, as did Brahms in his "Hungarian Dances", make use of the actual musical material of folk dance and song, but took over only their rhythms as their most significant and expressive element, creating them otherwise from his own new material. Nor did he hesitate to provide greater contrast of expression and form by changing the movement and basic rhythmic elements in the course of the various dances. In the first series of eight dances—with the single exception of the second—he chose characteristic types of *Czech dances*, the *furiant*, the *polka*, the "*sousedská*" and the "*skočná*" (a kind of jig): all dances full of healthy gaiety and youthful vitality, the natural expression of an elemental, unspoiled love of life and living.

An enumeration of the chief compositional features of the first series of "Slavonic Dances" may best be summarized under the following headings:

The form is mainly three-part rondo form, all, however, free in arrangement as the musical content and inner mood of each dance seemed to demand. The main parts are often worked up out of two themes of contrasted expression and mood, while the middle parts in the ternary scheme are developed more broadly and with more varied treatment of the theme.

The themes themselves are regularly periodic, consisting of four or eight-bar sections extended to sixteen-bar paragraphs. Themes in the major mode, as taken over by Dvořák from Moravian folk music and such as he made most frequent use of in his "Slavonic" period, have a tendency to open into a final period in the relative minor mode, just as alternations of the major and minor modes in general, though perhaps in the same key, are employed very effectively and naturally throughout the work.

Variations of the theme, with frequent changes of key and a no less frequent delight in the most varied figural embroidery of the melodic line, are a further characteristic of the "Slavonic Dances" just as striking and irresistable as the typical underlining of the inner parts in the function of counter-melodies. A peculiarly Dvořák trait, and one which lends special charm to the dances, is the highly expressive, lively and fluid line of the bass in which contemporary critic rightly saw the reflection of Dvořák's strong sense of humour.*

And, finally, as regards the orchestration of the "Slavonic Dances", it may be noted that Dvořák uses the full orchestra (without tuba and harp) for the first eight dances, but with that sense of economy which is the mark of genius, along with an uncanny instinct for the effective combination and contrast of tone-colour—in which each group of instruments and each instrument is, according to the inner demand of this or that passage, accorded its essentially appropriate and altogether delightful rôle.

FIRST DANCE IN C MAJOR

Instrumentation: piccolo, 2 flutes, 2 oboes, 2 clarinets, 2 bassoons, 4 horns, 2 trumpets, 3 trombones, kettle drums, big drum, cymbals, triangle and strings. Duration: $3^3/4$ minutes.

The first of the "Slavonic Dances" is a truly festive introduction to the whole group. After a long sustained chord of C major, which sounds forth in the powerful tones of the full orchestra as if giving the signal for the whirl of gaiety to start, a quick and spirited "fu-

---

* The noted German musical scholar and critic, Louis *Ehler* (1825—1884), welcoming enthusiastically the publication of the "Slavonic Dances" in a notice in the Berlin "Die Nationalzeitung", said that "Dvořák writes such jolly and original basses that on hearing them the real musician's heart laughs within him".

riant" in ternary form sets the pace (*Presto*, $^3/_4$). It is the first and, at the same time, one of the most brilliant of Dvořák's idealizations of the Czech dance. This had already won popularity in art stylizations (carried out for the first time in classical form by Bedřich Smetana in the second act of the "Bartered Bride"), and, in addition to its fiery verve, is characterized mainly by the original rhythm alternating (in its first and second, and in its fifth and sixth bars), between the impression of double and triple time. In the first of the "Slavonic Dances", this rhythmic feature is entrusted to the brass and percussion instruments in the theme which dominates the first and third parts of the dance:

The theme develops by simple repetitions into a regular period of sixteen bars (with the typical Dvořák opening out into the relative minor key) and then follows a variety of transformations of a softer character. The first of these is deserving of special attention, coming in on the heels of the main theme in C major with an unexpected modulation to A major delivered with simple charm by the wood-wind:

The same sudden change of key (C major—A major) signals the transition to the middle part of the dance which—though equally gay and nimble—is altogether softer and somehow more playful in character. It grows out of a new theme, light and happy in movement (1*c*) which, nevertheless, with its syncopation in the fourth and eighth bar, as well as its modulation into the relative minor mode of F sharp, retains its affinity with the basic theme (1*a*)—an affinity underlined by its repeated contrapuntal conjunction with new variants of the same theme (1d, 1e):

The third part is a fairly regular repetition of the first except that, at the close, a slight lull is provided by a quotation of the first two bars of the principal theme (1a), followed by two allusions to the theme of the middle part (1c), whereupon, flinging all discretion to the winds, the principal theme ends the dance in one wild breath-taking whirl.

SECOND DANCE IN E MINOR

Instrumentation as for Dance No 1.—Duration: 4¹/₂ minutes.

The second dance in the first series of eight "Slavonic Dances" is an exception in as far as it is not the idealization of a Czech folk-dance, but is an analogy of the Ukrainian "dumka" whose characteristic alternations of mood, meditative moods tinged with melancholy contrasting with moods of wild and elemental gaiety, suited Dvořák's own disposition and so was a particular favourite with the composer. In this dance he expresses these mutations through the rondo form, the individual paragraphs (*Allegretto scherzando* and *Allegro vivo*, ²/₄) developing out of the same basic theme (2a, 2b), for the accessory 2c only develops the last bar of the

semiquaver figuration with which the main theme was interwoven
earlier, and combining all the ideaswith perfect ease and flexibility
in two or three-part harmonies.

2a Allegro scherzando

2b Allegro vivo

2c Allegro vivo

This is one of the "Slavonic Dances" in which refinement of feeling finds as convincing expression as elemental vitality and verve,
and in which the charm of the melodic cantilena is yoked with complete rhythmical spontaneity.

THIRD DANCE IN A FLAT MAJOR

Instrumentation as for Dance No 1.—Duration: 4 minutes.

Third place in the first series of "Slavonic Dances" is taken, in
the orchestrated version and in the sketch, by a Polka which, in the
piano version, is in the sixth place (*Poco Allegro*, $^2/_4$). It is a real
Czech polka with a smilingly attractive folk-coloured theme drawn
over a simple and characteristic polka accompaniment and an
equally characteristic ostinato in the horn, always signalled by a
run-up neatly derived from folk-music:

At times the dance becomes more agitated when, in Rondo fashion, the first theme alternates with a very strongly accented and dynamic second theme:

But the original expression of good-natured playfulness is resumed, underlined by a semiquaver figuration embroidering theme 3a, and this warm mood continues in the next paragraph of the Rondo form set in E major, its pretty theme delivered in a tone of melting desire by two solo trumpets over a quiet accompaniment of triplets in the violas:

There follow, in turn, paragraphs with theme 3b and 3a in new variations and transmutations, whereupon the dance concludes with an accelerated coda, which works up the material of the second pair of bars in theme 3b.

FOURTH DANCE IN F MAJOR

Instrumentation as for Dance No 1.—Duration: 6¹/₄ minutes.

Another type of Czech folk-dance is presented in the Fourth Dance. This time it is the quiet "sousedská" (*Tempo di Menuetto*, ³/₄) written in regular ternary form, with the symmetrical parts

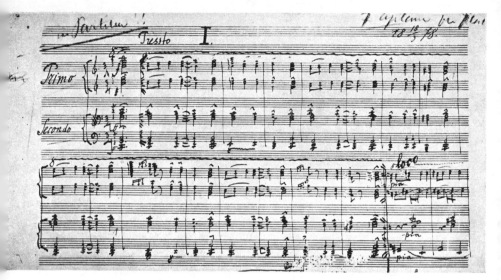

9. *Facsimile of the*
first page the manuscript of the Slavonic Dances.

10. Hans Richter.

rocking along at an easy pace, while the middle part is of a humorous and lively stamping character. The germ of the eight-bar theme of the first and last parts is a fanfare-like arpeggiated common chord (4a) which, in a later imitation, is melodically contracted (4b):

In the middle part, extended, as compared with the piano version by a one-bar violoncello cadenza*, the mood and expression are animated by the character of the new theme (4c), which differs from the first mainly in the delicate precision of the rhythmic pattern, with its typical stress on the first and third beats, the split tonic triad appearing again in its final phrase.

A ten-bar codetta in accelerated tempo based on the final phrase of 4c is grafted on to a strictly regular repetition of the first part (without repeats).

FIFTH DANCE IN A MAJOR

Instrumentation as for Dance No 1. Duration: 3¹/₄ minutes.

The fifth of the "Slavonic Dances" again adds to the number of folk-dance types selected by Dvořák for idealization. This time it is a rollicking, high spirited "skočná" (*Allegro vivace*, ²/₄), a jig-like

* It is the only compositional addition in the whole series made in the process of orchestration.

dance typical of the Bohemian countryside. Its melodic theme (5a), stretching over a complete octave, becomes important and determines the whole character of the dance, not only as the theme of the basic section in rondo form, but by its characteristic interval of a fourth, which becomes the supporting figure of a more smoothly-flowing theme developed in variational style in the second phrase (5b). A similar figure, this time in the interval of an octave, accompanies the gaily abandoned theme of the fourth paragraph from its eighth bar (3c):

The whole dance is lively throughout in movement and expression and closes with a typically Dvořák coda sweeping the dancers off their feet in a final breath-taking prestissimo.

SIXTH DANCE IN D MAJOR

Instrumentation as for Dance No 1., but with one flute only.—Duration: 4¹/₄ minutes.

The sixth Slavonic Dance, in the original piano version the third (*Allegretto scherzando*, ³/₄), revives again the "sousedská" in all its old-world charm with an ingenuousness which is the more telling for the wit, originality and inventive resource with which the whole composition is inwoven. The theme of the symmetrical parts (6a), softly pastoral, part grave, part gay, is, in itself a delightful example of the composer's inspiration:

6a Allegretto scherzando

Not less charming is the theme of the middle part, whether it trips daintily in light staccato (6b) or is stamped out fortissimo and marcatissimo for the most part over the semiquavers of a resolute figuration in the bass (6c). It presents a different aspect in each of its several entries, its tone-volume swelling powerfully and then diminishing, with corresponding changes in the tone-colour and even in the key. Incontestably one of the pearls in the first series of "Slavonic Dances"!

6b

SEVENTH DANCE IN C MINOR

Instrumentation as for Dance No 6.—Duration: $3^1/_4$ minutes.

The seventh of the "Slavonic Dances" may be described as another stylization of the "skočná" in Rondo form (*Allegro assai*, $^2/_4$). It begins with an incisive theme in two-part canon at octave, played by oboe and bassoon, its four-bar continuation being repeated in descending diatonic sequences:

In the next section, the theme—this time in descending thirds—is followed by a more lively thought with a smaller rhythmic pattern, related to the first theme by the motif *n*.

And finally, after repetition of the first section (*7a*), the two-bar phrase *m* breaks into a third theme at a quick vigorous pace—the gayest of all and deeply tinged with the colouring of folk music:

This theme is presented delicately by the violins in A flat major but, immediately following its repetition, it makes a jump to the key of F major and is taken up by the whole orchestra. At its third repetition, it returns in its original key and delicacy, but with figural

embroidery which, in the divided sixth of the trumpets, sounds particularly charming and playful. All three paragraphs are then alternated with new skilful strokes in the handling of the themes, whereupon the dance procedes to its conclusion with steadily rising dynamic force and quickening tempo, and with only a short moment's
respite before the last bars of theme 7c.

EIGHTH DANCE IN G MINOR

Instrumentation as for Dance No 6. — Duration: $3^1/_4$ minutes.

Dvořák ends the first series of "Slavonic Dances" with the same
type of dance as that with which he introduced it: a "furiant" of
breathless tempo and fiery rhythms (*Presto*, $^3/_4$). Only the ideas are
different and differently disposed. The dance is articulated in regular eight-bar periods, mostly repeated, and the basic themes, in
characteristic relative major and minor modes (8a), go through endless transmutations as the mood grows wilder and faster, or suddenly
subsides to relative calm (8b, 8c, 8d):

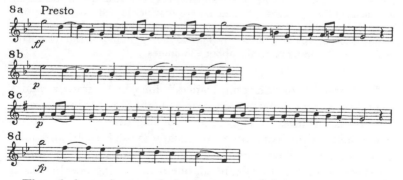

The whole section concludes in a tone of dreamy meditation in
keeping with the character of the tranquil and gently undu-

lating melodic line of the new theme in the clear key of G major, delicately sung by the flutes and oboes over the ostinato of a rhythmic figure derived from the rhythms of the preceding themes:

And now everything is repeated from the beginning up to the presentation of the theme 8*a* in a new modulation, before the entry of the calm cantabile of theme 8*e* is allowed to die away, whereupon the gay, light-hearted dance finishes with the four energetic opening bars.

2. THE SECOND SERIES OF "SLAVONIC DANCES", OP. 72

The version for piano duet was written between June 4th and July 9th, 1886, the score between the middle of November of the same year and the beginning of January 1887.—Dances 1, 2, and 7 were first performed on January 6th, 1887, at a concert of the Czech National Theatre in Prague, with *Dvořák* conducting. Score and parts published by Simrock, Berlin, in 1887.—Duration of the whole series, including intervals: about 42 minutes.

The first series of "Slavonic Dances", for which Simrock paid a fee of three hundred marks, very soon brought Simrock in thousandfold profit, and it is, therefore, not surprising that this very enterprising and, at the same time, artistically far-sighted businessman should some time later urge Dvořák to create another such volume of dances. Dvořák at first declined, one reason being that he was at work on a large symphony and an oratorio, while another was that, with his strong sense of artistic conscientiousness, he was well aware of the seriousness and difficulty of the task of presenting in a new series of Slavonic Dances a work whose musical value would not fall below that of the first, which had already won world-wide fame and popularity. In a letter to Simrock (January 1st, 1886), he expressed it in his own way: "To do the same thing twice is devilishly difficult!" and so he excused himself by saying: "I am not the least in the mood to think of such gay music," adding somewhat irritably that the publisher evidently imagined composing to be a much simpler business than it was in reality, and insisting that he would be able to start the dances only when he felt the proper enthusiasm for them. This enthusiasm was, however, forthcoming when, having finished the score of the great national oratorio "St. Ludmilla", he felt the need for the creative respite that work on a lighter and more entertaining composition would afford. The creation of the new series of "Slavonic Dances", again in an original piano version and then orchestrated, was carried out with the same happy spontaneity as marked the composition of the first series. "I am enjoying doing the Slavonic Dances immensely," he wrote to his publisher at the time of their composition (June 11th, 1886), "and I think they will be altogether different (no joking and no irony!)".

And he was right. The "Slavonic Dances" of the second series are truly quite different from the earlier ones, not only in mood but also in their main expressive aspects. Dvořák not only could not repeat himself, but eight fertile years of artistic development separated him from his first series. Finally, the inner life of the composer, now eight years older, was differently coloured and conditioned. If the first series was, in the main, a pure and unaffected manifestation of vitality and gaiety, and if, in the second series, this is also true to a still greater extent of a number of dances, these qualities are partly hidden beneath a veil a poetic meditation, or yield to a mood of heartsick longing, sometimes, as in the fourth, of real anguish. And Dvořák also diverged not a little from the first series in the type of dance which he chose. Of the Czech dances introduced earlier, he returned only to the "*skočná*" (3) and the "*sousedská*" (8), adding the "*špacírka*" (5), and choosing for the rest characteristic Slovak (1), Polish (6) and Jugoslav (7) dances, supplementing them with yet another two new idealizations of his favourite "*dumka*" (2, 4).

As regards form, Dvořák kept, on the one hand, to the ternary symmetrical form, as in the first series, but, on the other, showed no small predilection for a completely free arrangement. This was prompted, no doubt, by the multiplicity of themes in several of the dances, which is also a new feature of this series (chiefly in numbers 1, 3, 7, and 8). In the character of the themes, too, it is possible to perceive a certain divergence in the fact that only some have the regular periodicity of an even number of bars, while others have an irregular form of an odd number of bars—three, five, etc. Quite new, however, is the melodic, harmonic and, in part, the rhythmic material of these dances, even though they possess all the expressive means of Dvořák's inventive and original genius, through which the second series of "Slavonic Dances", in spite of all differences of expression and mood, are organically linked with the first.

Special mention must still be made of the orchestral aspect of this second series. Here, too, Dvořák summons up new tones and colours, often so subtly compounded as to be almost impressionistic in effect, but nonetheless as splendid and glowing as in the first series. It followed from the character of the different dances that, unlike the first series in which he works throughout with a large orchestra, the second series contains only four dances written for this combination, while the remaining four are written for a small orchestra without trombones, sometimes without trumpets, and wholly without the percussion-instruments, not excepting the kettle drums. His creative imagination as a tone-poet was thus given a particularly rich, bold and strongly persuasive compass in which to display itself.

FIRST (NINTH) DANCE IN B MAJOR

Instrumentation: two flutes, two oboes, two clarinets, two bassoons, four horns, two trumpets, three trombones, kettle-drums, big drum, cymbals, triangle and strings. — Duration: 4 minutes.

The first of the second series of "Slavonic Dances" is a stylization of the Slovak "odzemek" alternating, as in the dumka, but in reverse order, explosive gaiety with melancholy. The three-part form of the dance is thus maintained by inserting between two parts of very rapid tempo *(Molto vivace, ²/₄)*, of which the second is a shortened form of the first, a calm cantabile section with an expression of dreamy melancholy *(Allegro moderato)*. The mood of the first and third part is determined by the sharply accented and wildly careering principal theme (9a), which continually returns in full force after a digression based on auxiliary ideas (9b—9d):

At the close of the first section the excitement subsides and in a sweet, melancholy two-part harmony in the wood-winds and violins, there follows the middle part, modulating between the keys of D major and B minor, the two main themes of which (9a and 9f) were taken over by Dvořák from his piano "Eclogue". This he wrote on February 7th, 1880, as the last of a group of four which he withheld from publication, so that they did not appear in print until published by the Prague "Hudební matice" in 1921.*

It is like the gentle converse of two hearts in a 'breathing-space between the wild gyrations of the dance, a dialogue in which a third the matic idea makes a declaration of love, full of tender yearning and desire:

In the last part—a shortened repetition of the first (9d is omitted), the movement of the dance is whipped up to an ecstasy of passion and ends incisively with three rapid drum-beats.

SECOND (TENTH) DANCE IN E MINOR

Instrumentation: 2 flutes, 2 oboes, 2 clarinets, 2 bassoons, 4 horns, tympani, triangle, strings.—Duration: 5¹/₂ minutes.

The Second Dance may be taken as representing a new variety of dumka such as was the second dance in the first series. The symmetrical parts in ternary form are in the same introspective and

* Here we would point to the interesting affinity of theme 9*f* with the principal theme from the first movement of the String Quartet in F major, op. 96.

slightly melancholy strain, developing from a theme with an emotional and strongly oscillating melodic line:

10a Allegretto grazioso

In the middle section the expression is enlivened by a swinging mazurka-like theme (10b), or by the unaffected phrases of a theme which is actually the melodic development of the second pair of bars from the preceding theme (10c):

10b

10c

The delightful melodic and ardent emotional quality of this dance has made it a great favourite among audiences of every kind.

THIRD (ELEVENTH) DANCE IN F MAJOR

Instrumentation: the same as for the first (ninth) dance, but without triangle — Duration: 3¹/₄ minutes.

In this dance Dvořák revived very happily the Czech "skočná" (Allegro, ²/₄). Here it is conceived in the form of an irregular rondo, in which the essentially three-bar principal theme alternates with new auxiliary ideas of varying expression, movement and mood, ranging from bustling animation to melancholy sensibility. The main theme, consisting of two resolute chords followed by a gay little skipping motif,

11a Allegro

is then joined by a theme with the humorously mincing step of an ascending fifth in successive rhythmical diminutions:

11b

After the second entry of the principal subject, the violins sing a gravely melodious theme of five bars, embroidered with a figural semiquaver motif from theme 11*a*:

11c Un pochettino più lento

The principal theme returns once more in a new combination of instruments whereupon, after a short preparative passage on the semiquaver motif from 11*a*, another theme is delivered in the delicate tone of the flute and oboe developed from a melodic inversion of the preceding theme:

11d

Scarcely is the period concluded when a new theme appears, calmer in movement and melodically reminiscent of part of a Czech folk-song "Below the oak, behind the oak":

11e Un pochettino lento

The theme takes itself rather seriously; at first the harmony is somewhat dry and ill-tempered but, in the course of its fairly long development, it becomes livelier and gayer, finally dancing away in perfectly good spirits. The coda, which works with only the principal theme, winds up the dance with characteristic speed and abandon.

FOURTH (TWELFTH) DANCE IN D FLAT MAJOR

Instrumentation: 2 flutes, 2 oboes, 2 clarinets, 2 bassoons, 4 horns, tympani, strings.—Duration: $4^3/4$ minutes.

For the third time in the Slavonic Dances, Dvořák returns to his beloved Ukrainian "dumka", and in this form the fourth of his second series possesses musical charm of rare purity and originality. It is one of the most intimate and deeply felt of the whole sixteen dances (*Allegretto grazioso*, $^3/_8$), an expression of yearning intensified at times to a cry of anguish. The principal theme, which dominates the first and the third part, gives the clue to the character of the whole with its flatly contoured melodic line (lower part in Ex. 12*a*) modulating between E flat minor, G flat major and D flat major, while, especially in combination with its counter-subject above a characteristic first inversion of a chord of the seventh, it has an expression of almost plaintive lament:

The basic mood of the dance is not greatly influenced even by the theme of the middle part although it is perceptibly brighter and enlivened with ornamental figures:

12b

The dance ends as it began, the last bar if anything still more anguished in expression.

FIFTH (THIRTEENTH) DANCE IN B FLAT MINOR

Instrumentation as for the first dance (9th) —Duration: $2^3/_4$ minutes.

The thirteenth of the "Slavonic Dances" is among the shortest and most unusual in origin. It is the stylisation of a Czech folk dance, one half of which is executed in a slow step and the other half as a quick round dance known as the "špacírka". Dvořák once happened to see the village lads and lasses dancing it in the manor meadow at Vysoká by Příbram, where he had his summer retreat.* In his stylization of this little-known dance, Dvořák not only retained the formal two-part arrangement (with a double exposition), but also the core of the main melodic line, with important compositional modifications. In the slow introductory part (*Poco adagio*, $^4/_8$), which comprises only eleven bars, the original major mode is softened to the minor, and the first four bars are embellished with figurations at the fourth beat of each bar:

* Dvořák heard the dance in this variant:

The quick part *(Vivace)* develops the simple pattern of the original subject at first in this form:

and then in a number of variants, each of which presents new imitational and figural features, and each in a different combination of instruments, but all contributing in equal degree to the fiery and impetuous verve of village festivities. The whole two-part form, closing on an agitated diminished chord *(g-b flat-c sharp-e)* is then repeated with an abundance of new ideas in composition and orchestration and worked up to a passionate climax.

SIXTH (FOURTEENTH) DANCE
IN B FLAT MAJOR

Instrumentation: 2 flutes, 2 oboes, 2 clarinets, 2 bassoons, 4 horns, 2 trumpets, tympani, strings.—Duration: $3^1/_2$ minutes.

Here Dvořák added yet another dance to the types which make up the two cycles of "Slavonic Dances"—the Polonaise. It is again written in ternary form, the quiet symmetrical parts *(Moderato, quasi Menuetto, $^3/_4$)* contrasting with the livelier and more agile middle part *(Un poco più mosso)*, each being built up on two themes.

The symmetrical parts, in contrast to the lightly stressed rhythm
and refined elegance of the main theme, (14a), have a broad, spacious secondary theme, with an expressively flexible melodic compass and a yearning warmth of feeling (14b):

The two themes of the middle part stand to each other in a similar relation, the first not without a touch of dalliance and co-
quetry (14c), while the second sounds the intimate note of a lover's
confession (14d):

The general character of the whole dance is reflected in the frag-
ile colour nuances of the orchestration and the controlled delicacy
of the conclusion, suggesting very clearly the ballroom atmosphere
of elegant society.

SEVENTH (FIFTEENTH) DANCE IN C MAJOR

Instrumentation as for the first (ninth) dance, but with piccolo. —Duration: about 3 minutes.

The last but one of the "Slavonic Dances" is an art stylisation of the Serbian "kolo", a tremendously fiery, high-spirited, rhythmical and sharply accentuated dance (*Allegro vivace*, $^2/_4$), which an audience rarely hears without demanding an encore. Dvořák presents it in a completely free form, the thematic ideas, like a display of fireworks, following one another in quick succession, alternating, combining, growing out of each other to form a composition of remarkable organic unity carried through with unflagging verve from start to finish. It is sufficient to quote the themes in the order in which they appear:

15 f

The binding material is provided by the first theme (15a), which returns several times and finally brings the dance to a brilliant close.

EIGHTH (SIXTEENTH) DANCE IN A FLAT MAJOR

Instrumentation: 2 flutes, 2 oboes, 2 clarinets, 2 bassoons, 4 horns, 2 trumpets, little bell tuned to A flat, strings. —Duration: about 7 minutes.

Dvořák concluded his "Slavonic Dances" with a dance which is the most sweetly grave and poetical of all. In substance it is again a "sousedská" (*Grazioso e lento, ma non troppo, quasi tempo di Valse,* $^3/_4$), but as if seen through the spectrum of poetic contemplation or heard at a distance, and awakening poignant memories of a youth that is past. It is a dance no less rich in themes than the preceding one. The exposition of these themes is divided into independent paragraphs, which follow each other in the order indicated below: one in a tone of dreamy comtenplation, another impulsively agitated, and among them a particularly delicate and dream-like episode in the paragraph based on theme 16e.

In the final paragraph 16*d*, 16*a* and 16*b* are repeated, the dance closing quietly with the last of these, whereupon two smashing chords of the dominant seventh and the tonic put a full stop to the "Slavonic Dances", irrevocable for both composer and publisher.

VI

LEGENDS, OP. 59

Written in the original version for piano duet, between February 12th and March 22nd, 1881, and scored between November 13th and December 9th of the same year.—Nos 1, 3, 4, first performed on May 7th, 1882, at a concert of the Prague Conservatoire, conducted by Antonín *Bennewitz*; Nos 2, 5 and 6 for the first time on November 26th, 1882, at a concert of the Vienna Philharmonic conducted by Wilhelm *Jahn*.—Published by Simrock, Berlin, in the piano version in 1881, in score and parts in 1882. Time of performance of all ten Legends: about 40 minutes.

The volume of ten "Legends", embodying moods of an epic character, form an intimate and more serious counterpart to the "Slavonic Dances". Both cycles of compositions, chronologically not far apart, have a common origin in as far as both were originally written as piano duets for the intimate atmosphere of house music, and only later were given the orchestral setting in which they were first presented to the public. They differ, however, in that the "Legends" were not written at the instigation of a publisher, but as the result of the composer's spontaneous creative impulse. There is no evidence to show how the idea came to Dvořák of writing a cycle of small works with a poetic and mystically suggestive title, though his deeply religious disposition is a quite sufficient explanation. One thing is certain: the idea was already in his mind when he was working at the last pages of the preceding D major symphony, which he completed on October 15th, 1880, for the day before, in a letter to Simrock informing him that the symphony was finished, he intimated that he intended to begin work on piano duets which would be entitled "Legends", and that he hoped to have them finished the following month. It might appear that it was just the buoyantly happy mood of the large symphonic work which made him think about composing something which would offer a contrast, both in its intimate character and in its mood. But four whole months were to pass before he set to work on the "Legends", during which time his pen lay idle.

The "Legends", however, have close affinities of musical expression with the "Slavonic Dances". There is a clearly observable similarity of thematic ideas and of other specific compositional features, which are characteristic of the first series of "Slavonic Dances"—not excepting the natural contrapuntal bracketing of the principal subject with the countersubject. Only here everything is on a much more intimate and dainty scale, from the compass of the form, in principle again binary or ternary rondo, and, in spite of the spaciousness of the themes and their presentation, suited to the limited size of the orchestra. This consists of the wood-wind and strings, with the addition only of horns and the occasional use of trumpets, the harp, and the kettle drum or triangle. Everything is determined by the content of these compositions, which are illuminated by a truly legend-like tenderness, and, whether they sing of love or longing, suffering or sacrifice, of enthusiasm or glory, always tell their story with a warm fervency, and are always shrouded in the same shadowy mysticism which gives them their special quality: a particular sweetness and spirituality of expression. Dvořák's musical inventiveness found here, too, full opportunity to produce works of highly individual charm, nor did he find it difficult, even with the self-imposed economy of orchestral means, to give the "Legends" a tone-colouring of fascinating beauty which, in its expressiveness and harmoniousness, imparts to the whole cycle its characteristic style. Thus the "Legends" have found favour not only with the broad community of music lovers, but also with specialists of very fastidious taste. The Viennese critic, Dr. Eduard Hanslick, wrote of them on publication: "Perhaps this is the loveliest of the ten Legends; perhaps another—for on this point there will be different opinions, but only within one general opinion—that all are lovely!" And Johannes Brahms could not refrain from remarking in a letter to the publisher Simrock, "Please give my kind regards to Dvořák and tell him what pleasure his 'Legends' continue to give me. It is a charming work and one cannot but envy the man his fresh, gay and fertile invention."

FIRST LEGEND IN D MINOR

Instrumentation: 2 flutes, 2 oboes, 2 clarinets, 2 bassoons, 4 horns, tympani, strings.—Duration: 2³/₄ minutes.

The first of the "Legends" (*Allegretto*, ²/₄) is written, as are also the three following, in rondo form and comprises three themes, of which the first steps out firmly with an expression of festive solemnity not without a certain archaic colouring in the harmonic texture:

The imitation of the countersubject, which joins the theme in the upper part on its return, shifts later to the bass in which it strongly underlines the heroic dignity of the theme.

The second theme sounds softer, more lyrical and tinged with warm desire (1*b*), but in a later variant (1*c*) approximates more towards the tone of the first theme:

The third seven-bar theme (1*d*) is broadly lyrical and emotionally coloured, its delicately swelling melodic line intensifying the
fervency of the middle part of the "Legend" and giving to its conclusion a luminous refinement of expression:

SECOND LEGEND IN G MAJOR

Instrumentation: 1 flute, 2 oboes, 2 clarinets, 2 bassoons, 4 horns, strings.—
Duration: $3^3/_4$ minutes.

The second Legend (*Molto moderato*, $^3/_4$) opens with a quiet theme
possessing an air of chaste, meditative resignation:

The second theme *(Poco animato)* has a double character: the
first two bars assert themselve. in syncopated rhythm, the sforzando of the drawn-out notes like cries of anguish, while the next
pair of bars, which are later used independently, suddenly raise the
intensity of the expression to one of deep religious fervour:

The two paragraphs alternate twice, the second time with a still
more agitated presentation of theme 2*b*, whereupon the clarinet and
the bassoon, later joined by the violins, introduce a third theme,
again breathing the spirit of humble resignation to the divine will:

2c.

The mood is once more heightened by a new and ecstatic delivery of the second figure of theme 2*b*, whereupon the Legend closes on a note of quiet inner joy and mystic exultation.

THIRD LEGEND IN G MINOR

Instrumentation: 2 flutes, 2 oboes, 2 clarinets, 2 bassoons, 4 horns, triangle, strings.—Duration: 3½ minutes.

The third of the series of "Legends" is, in general, idyllic but is distinguished from its two predecessors by the opening and closing sections (*Allegro giusto*, ²/₄) which, by way of contrast, show a pleasing liveliness of movement and playfulness of expression. This is apparent in the first two themes in rondo form, and in the minor key of the first:

3a. Allegro giusto

3b.

The idyllic calm of these parts extends then to the middle part (*Andante*, B flat major, ⁴/₄) of which they form the symmetrical

framework. Here the movement is considerably slowed down and
the expression assumes the fervent tone of blissful inner exaltation.
The section is broadly melodic and is built up out of this theme:

3c. **Andante**
tranquille e molto espress.

FOURTH LEGEND IN C MAJOR

Instrumentation: 2 flutes, 2 oboes, 2 clarinets, 2 bassoons, 4 horns, 2 trumpets,
tympani, triangle, strings.—Duration: 5 minutes.

The fourth of the "Legends" is crowned as it were by the softly
glowing halo of the saint and hero. The tone of the whole composition is one of solemn pathos, both in movement and key (*Molto
maestoso*, $^4/_4$), as well as in the character of its three thematic ideas.
The first of these has the unadorned chorale-like simplicity of psal-
modic declamation, or is interwoven with a harmonically contoured countersubject:

4a. Molto maestoso

At times, however, the level of expression rises to a sharply rhythmic march or a noble hymn of praise.

The second thought, which comprises the next part in rondo
form, is considerably more animated in movement (4*b Piu animato*),
but in the simple alternation of tonic (C major), dominant (G ma-

jor) and subdominant (F major) is no less solemn, especially when
it is overlaid with the shining glow of a broadly vocal melody in the
high-pitched instruments:

An intermezzo, with an undertone of dramatic agitation, paves the
way for the third idea developing out of a restless *ostinato* of chords
in triplets:

A return is then made to theme (4*a*), in a splendidly festive variant delivered by the full orchestra, with the lively embroidered
theme 4*b* in the middle, whereupon the glowing emanations of
theme 4*d* bring the Legend to a calm and dignified close.

FIFTH LEGEND IN A FLAT MAJOR

Instrumentation: 2 flutes, 2 oboes, 2 clarinets, 2 bassoons, harp, strings. —
Duration: 3 minutes.

A complete contrast to the preceding number is provided by the
fifth of the "Legends", which calls to mind the sweet and delicately
tinted portrait of a female saint. In simple ternary form, lively in
movement throughout (*Allegro giusto*, $^4/_4$), it develops from a pair of

thematic ideas, of which one, melodically supple in its outline, is accompanied by canonic imitation (5a), while the other is introduced by the interval of an ascending fourth in characteristic rhythm (5b):

Throughout the "Legend" the dominant expression is one of pastoral tenderness and spiritual mysticism, exquisitely rendered in tone by the ensemble of wood winds and strings with no other addition than pearly runs and arpeggios in the harp.

SIXTH LEGEND IN C SHARP MINOR

Instrumentation: 2 flutes, 2 oboes, 2 clarinets, 2 bassoons, 2 horns, harp, strings.—Duration: $5^3/_4$ minutes.

In the sixth of the series of "Legends" in three-part form there is something romantically mysterious and restless. The restlessness emanates from the triplets, which provide an *ostinato* running through the whole Legend,—the quality of mystery from the principal thematic ideas, whether they keep to the tonic key of C sharp minor in the symmetrical parts (*Allegro con moto*, $^4/_4$), or brighten in the middle part *(Moderato)* into the key of D flat major. It is out of the triplet movement in the symmetrical parts, largely entrusted to the harp, that the main theme evolves and is delivered with passionate impetuosity by the violins and violoncellos, the clarinets interpo-

lating an expressive little final comment which later occurs independently (6*a*). The calmer subordinate theme is given only the
passing prominence of an episode unable effectively to tranquilize
the generally agitated character of the composition (6*b*):

In the middle part of the work the triplet *ostinato* settles on a
pedal point above which is drawn the softly melting line of theme 6*c*,
to the accompaniment of the light arpeggios of the harp. For the
closing section, descending as from mystic heights, Dvořák uses one
of the thoughts contained in the middle part of the slow movement
of the third symphony in E flat major, written in 1873 (See above
Ex. 12*b*, p. 63):

The last part of the Legend is a shortened repetition of the first
part, only, instead of the thematic figure 6*b*, a sudden modulation to
the key of F major introduces a new theme of strongly tranquilizing
tendency (6*e*), which forecasts the clear luminous mood of the conclusion.

SEVENTH LEGEND IN A MAJOR

Instrumentation: 2 flutes, 2 oboes, 2 clarinets, 2 bassoons, 2 horns, tympani, strings.—Duration: $4^1/_2$ minutes.

The next Legend, again in simple ternary form, is of a much calmer character. It opens straight away with a courtly principal theme (*Allegretto grazioso*, $^2/_4$) underlined in the middle by the sharply rhythmic steps of the lower instruments:

And though the middle part is marked by an acceleration of pace (*Poco più mosso*) and the livelier character of the theme in gay little triplets,

the greatly shortened repetition of the first part restores to the Legend its original gravity.

EIGHTH LEGEND IN F MAJOR

Instrumentation: 2 flutes, 2 oboes, 2 clarinets, 2 bassoons, 4 horns, strings.—Duration: 4 minutes.

The expression of the eighth Legend of the cycle (*Un poco allegretto e grazioso*, $^6/_8$) is again altogether idyllic. It is written in irregular rondo form, with thematic ideas of greater variety but slighter structure, now quieter, now more animated, appearing in the following order:

The modulations of key range widely and the successive figural enrichment of the themes does much to strengthen the impression of the manifold sensations which Nature evoked in the sensitive, reflective spirit of the artist.

NINTH LEGEND IN D MAJOR

Instrumentation: 2 flutes, 2 oboes, 2 clarinets, 2 bassoons, 2 horns, tympani, strings.—Duration: 2½ minutes.

The ninth of the Legends (*Andante con moto*, $^3/_4$) achieves in form as in themes the highest degree of idyllic simplicity. It grows out of a single, pleasingly pastoral theme which passes by way of canonic imitation from one instrument to another and which—except for a few bars in the middle—is repeated in different variations over a deep tonic pedal on D in the horns and tympani:

The whole Legend is, in its inspiration and craftsmanship, a miniature masterpiece and is possibly Dvořák's most intimate "*sousedská*".

TENTH LEGEND IN B FLAT MINOR

Instrumentation: 2 flutes, 2 oboes, 2 clarinets, 2 bassoons, 4horns, strings.—
Duration: 4 minutes.

The tenth Legend concludes the whole cycle on a note of bitter-
sweet reflection, which alternates twice with a lyrical theme breathing sighs of wistful desire. The first mood is interpreted by the softly
melting key of B flat minor (*Andante*, $^4/_8$) and a gently undulating
theme in sixths:

The second mood is rendered by the yearning song of the horn
in the warm key of B flat major interwoven with a delicate-textured
accompaniment in the high register of the violins:

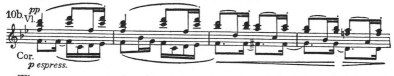

The two paragraphs alternate twice, thus giving the composition
a simple two-part form, full of tender feeling and of humble sub-
mission to a higher will.

VII

VARIATIONS AND SCHERZO

1. SYMPHONIC VARIATIONS ON AN ORIGINAL THEME, OP. 78

Instrumentation: piccolo, 2 flutes, 2 oboes, 2 clarinets, 2 bassoons, 4 horns, 2 trumpets, 3 trombones, tympani, triangle, strings.

Written in score between September 6th and 28th, 1877, as opus number 38.—First performed under opus number 40 by the orchestra of the Czech Interim Theatre in Prague on December 2nd, 1877, with Dr Ludevít *Procházka* conducting.—Score, parts and four-handed piano arrangement (by the composer) published by Simrock, Berlin, in 1888, as opus 78.—Duration: 24 minutes.

A fondness for the most varied treatment of thematic ideas and the most exhaustive exploitation of their melodic, harmonic and rhythmic substance, was a characteristic feature of Dvořák's compositional art. It is to be observed in almost every one of his works, and we had special occasion to remark on it as one of their characteristic traits in the analysis of the "Slavonic Dances". It was, therefore, only natural that Dvořák should include in his work the form of variations, and not only within the framework of cyclic works but also as an independent form of composition. His first excursion into this field was the *Variations on an Original Theme for Piano* (op. 36, written towards the end of 1876) and—possibly because of the pleasure this kind of work gave him—shortly afterwards, the *Symphonic Variations on an Original Theme for Full Orchestra.* Following the "Peasant a Rogue", op. 37, it was his thirty-eighth work, but, on publication seven years later, was given the misleading opus number 78, in accordance with the publisher's wish.

For the theme of this composition Dvořák chose the melody of the first part of his own work for male choir, "I am a Fiddler", to words by Adolf *Heyduk,* which he had composed in the middle of January 1877 (included in the collection "Choral Songs for Male Voices"

11. Facsimile of the first page of Hans Richter's letter to Dvořák.

12. *Facsimile of the second page of Hans Richter's letter to Dvořák.*

published by "Hudební Matice", Prague, 1921). The theme, of which the first nine bars are identical with that of the choral song, is as follows:

Theme:

It is possible, though the surmise is otherwise unsubstantiated, that Dvořák's choice was influenced by the text itself, which tells of the inward happiness that fills the care-free heart of a wandering musician. His choice was, however, also a very happy one in respect of the purely musical shape of the theme in as far as it possesses a number of features which allow of interesting variational treatment. The structural articulation of the theme is in itself unusual, consisting as it does of three strains stated in the order *aba*, of which the first and third extend to seven bars and the second to six; in all a theme of twenty-two bars of irregular periodicity. Melodically the first strain is the more interesting, not only because of the intervals of the first two bars, but chiefly because of the raised fourth (so-called Lydian fourth) which affords rich possibilities for a wide range of harmonic colourings and, at the same time, preserves the original flavour of the theme even in those variations most divergent from it. The first strain is also made most use of (it is the core out of which all the variations evolve) while the second strain, providing a melodic and rhythmic contrast to the first, is only prominent in a few of the variations.

There are twenty-eight variations in all—a far from small number. They begin with a very simple statement of the theme, the expression of which is transformed by a variety of counterpoints (the first three variations); thereupon the melodic and rhythmic aspect of the theme changes, diverging more and more from the theme, while keeping to the tonic key of C major and the original duple time (variations 4—16); at the seventh variation there is a break; triple and duple time alternate; from the eighteenth on there are digressions into other keys (18 is in D major, 19 in B flat major, 20—24 in B flat minor, 25 in G major and 26 in D major), till at length the second but last variation returns to the original key and to a restatement of the theme whose well-defined character dominates the spaciously worked out final variation.

The way in which Dvořák handles the theme and its constituent elements in the course of the compositional plan provides ample and convincing proof of the wide compass of his creative imagination. Beginning with the fourth variation, the theme undergoes ever new and increasingly daring transformations, both melodic and rhythmic, in which, the composer's mastery of figural work and imitation is balanced by his unique art of delicate and wonderfully colourful instrumentation. In connection with the latter, it is worthy of note that at first Dvořák gives chief prominence to the strings, adding here and there, for colour, the horns and only very occasionally the trumpets and trombones, whereas these latter groups of instruments, headed by the horns, gradually assume more importance from the fifteenth variation, till they display themselves in full splendour in the glorious *maestoso* climax of the work.

It is however, necessary to stress that all this kaleidoscopic variety of expressive means was not determined purely by Dvořák's musical fantasy but, to a considerable extent, by the emotional content of the composition. And that content is extremely variable and diversified, in keeping with Dvořák's disposition, with its strong tendency to change rapidly from serious, dreamily contemplative or passionate moods to sudden outbursts of unaffected gaiety. In the Symphonic Variations the mood changes with almost every variation; one is serious, another delightfully playful, a third full of unhappy memories, another overflowing with high spirits, while yet another contrasts the expression of dour defiance with a devoutely humble prayer. Simple marching airs alternate with supple dance rhythms, the twilight of fairy-tales with the gloom of ballads, the simple folk-song, too, makes itself heard and, finally, the mood is whipped up to a whirlwind presto of unrestrained merriment and boisterous fun. Important, moreover, is that all these nuances of mood possess a specifically Czech colouring underlined at the close, with telling effect, by the introduction of a gay polka in the middle of a fugato developed with immense verve and endless inventive resource.

The twenty-eight variations are worked out in the following order:

The first three variations give a literal repetition of the theme accompanied by varied counterpoints: in the first the counter-point is provided by a light, playful bird-like motif fluttering above the theme, in the second, entrusted to the strings alone, a more serious tone is imparted by the calm cantabile of a viola and cello duet, while in the third, where the theme is declaimed in unison by all the wood wind, its calm line broken into by a sharply ac-cented triplet motif in the strings. (In each of the following exam-ples, the seven bars of the main theme must be mentally supplied.)

A digression from the original version of the theme is contained in the fourth variation, in which the melodic arch of the first strain *(a)* is raised by the low-pitched instruments to the accompaniment of a melody in the upper part in contrary motion, while the second strain *(b)* finds expression in the languishing sighs of the cellos, over which the flute and oboe imitate figure *n* from the first variation:

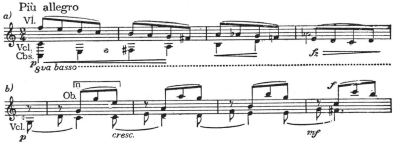

In the fifth variation, lively in character, the theme splits into rapid running figures in the violas and cellos on the one hand, and, on the other, into a persistently repeated rhythmic figure in the wood wind, which, when superimposed on the other, gives the variation a charmingly playful colouring maintained despite the literal repetition of the first part of the theme at the close of the period.

Var. 5.

Similar in tone, too, is the s i x t h variation in which the undulating movement of the triplets in the strings, derived from the cadence figure of the previous variation, answer the gay bird-trills of the wood wind and with this answer bring themselves into the picture.

The phrase concludes with a resolute three-bar motif, which may be regarded as a variant of bars 5—7 of the basic theme, with a characteristic descending second *(o)* at its close, which is made use of in further variations.

Var. 6.

Nor does the s e v e n t h variation, in which the wood-wind and strings are joined for the first time, at least in the form of interpolations by the horns and trumpets, show any deviation from the lively, playful tone of the preceding variations. In the lightly alternating skipping steps of the wood-wind above the undulating tremolo of the strings, this variation also grows out of the descending interval of a second *(o)* from the preceding variation, the period always closing with a diminution of the first two bars of the theme.

Var. 7.

A calmer mood comes in with the e i g h t h variation, in which the theme is wrapped in the soft dreamy harmonies of long-sustained

chords in the wood-winds (bracketed in the example under *n*),
drawn over the reiterated figure *p* of the seventh variation.

With the ninth variation, however, a return is made to the tone
of youthful vigour and gaiety imposed by the expressive rhythmical
transformation of the second strain of the theme *(b)*.

The same rhythm, but at a considerably accelerated pace, is also
retained by the tenth variation, in which the light springing step
of a diminution of the beginning of the theme rises successively from
the lowest instruments to the highest, while a short digression into
B major in the middle of variation is the first serious departure from
the harmonic base of the whole composition.

An abrupt change of mood is announced in the eleventh variation. Out of a tiny motif of three notes, in which the interval of
a second can be related again to figure *o* in the sixth variation, there
develops a meditative, emotionally-coloured dialogue between violoncello and oboe:

The dialogue becomes increasingly agitated, with restless modulations of key expanding into an ascending passage in the first violins
which, however, comes down to earth again and quietly opens into
the twelfth variation. This takes the form of a smooth, passionate
violin solo which unfolds with expressive intensity:

Var. 12.

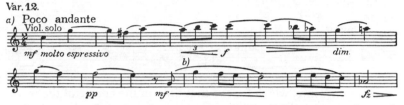

A strong and, in its abruptness, truly Dvořák contrast of mood
is presented by the thirteenth variation. Here, the no longer
easily recognizable transformation of the theme is punctuated by
gay bell-like trills and assumes a dancing rhythm:

Var. 13.

It is, however, only a short-lived outburst of joyousness which
gives way with equal suddenness to a mood of the utmost seriousness in the fourteenth variation. In the calm chords of the strings,
alternately underlined by the muted horns, this variation sounds
like a prayer, over which the imitation in the flute evokes the impression of a vesper bell:

Var. 14.

On its repetition the quavers of the flute change to three semiquavers, accompanied by the bassoon which sings the first strain (a):

A new sharp contrast is provided by the next variation, the fifteenth, with its expression of stubborn unyielding pride. In it a new modification of the theme, related to that in the fourth variation, delivers itself in an angry unison of the lowest-pitched instruments, while the rest of the orchestra accompanies it with crashing chords on the weak beats of the bar.

Var. 15.

The trombones, which for the first time in the course of the work are given a melodic function, bring this variation to an end with an immensely powerful statement of the basic theme in this new harmonic variant.

The last two bars lead by rising sequences in the strings to the short but very quick-paced and vigorous sixteenth variation, again concealing in its sequence of chords the whole beginning of the original theme (marked >):

Var. 16.

The seventeenth variation also keeps to the tonic key of C major, like all preceding variations, but marks a new departure from the general plan by alternating the duple time, in which all the variations have so far remained, with triple time which, the eighteenth excepted, dominates all the variations up to the twenty-sixth. The seventeenth variation is described as a Scherzo and grows out of the three-note motif including the element *o* while the flute and clarinets step out over the delicate staccato of the bassoons and horns in a measure having the dainty quality of an elfin dance.

At the close of the variation the dance gradually seems to recede into the distance and the bass modulates in descending sequences into the key of D major—the first shift from the tonic key of C major —in which the eighteenth variation is delivered by the horn, here used for the first time in a melodic function. The character of the variation is a soft, nocturne-like love-song reminiscent of Czech folk-music in which, high above the only slightly altered melody of the theme in the horn, there flutters the bird-like figuration of the violins.

The key of D major leads without transition to the key of B flat major, in which the nineteenth variation appears as a folk-coloured waltz based on the motif of the fifth bar of the main theme:

The next five variations form a group, being not only all in the same key of B flat minor and having the same rhythmic base ($^3/_8$,

$^6/_8$, $^{12}/_8$), but forming new variations of the theme of the preceding nineteenth variation. In mood, too, all are tinged with fantastic fairy-tale grotesqueness; each as if portraying in sound some well-known character of fairy-tale—a dancing gnome (21), the daring Honza-hero (Jack in the Beanstalk) (22), in which the horn energetically climbs up two octaves with a thematic variation reminiscent of the fourth variation or the "Sad Princess" (the gloomy 24th variation). It is worth noting, too, that the softly melting melody of variation 23 is supported by a rhythmic accompaniment derived from the closing element of theme 22 (indicated in the example by a bracket). We quote the thematic idea of all five variations in order:

The next variation, the twenty-fifth, retains the triple-time wavy figuration of the preceding one, but the expression brightens considerably with a change to the hard key of G flat major and also gains emotional warmth from the ardently lyrical transformation of the theme, the middle part of which (a variant of the original *b* figure) has a pleasing folk naïvety of colouring:

The twenty-sixth variant develops from the same transformation of the theme, beginning in the key of D major but working round, through a modulating process, to that of C minor, in which a calm augmentation of the fifth bar of the basic theme is presented with repeated uncertain questionings above it in the form of the semi-tone figure *o:*

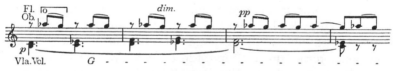

A return is now made to the original key and the original theme of the variation. The second last of these, the twenty-seventh, presents the first strain of its theme *(a)* in the form of snatches of conversation between the pizzicato of the strings and the staccato of the winds, again combined in the cadence with the semi-tone *o:*

This is actually a short introduction to the final variation which crowns the whole work. At the beginning of the first part, the violins, taking off from the semi-tone figure -*o*, break into a rapid run leading to a diminished quotation of the theme and closing into an energetic fugato handled with admirable originality and resource. This is no longer fairy-tale or day-dreaming, but real life, vigorous high-spirited country life, as is confirmed by the character of the second strain of the theme, a typical, lively Czech polka combined with the main theme in counterpoint.

Var. 28.

Meno mosso

The gay mood of the finale rises in the following part, the tempo is accelerated, the festive mood heightened by the broadly melodic entry of the harmonically simplified theme in the trumpets and trombones, the whole then culminating in a short jubilant *stretto*.

No account of the Symphonic Variations would be complete without a few words about their history. The first performance of the work, which took place in 1877 under the baton of Dr. Ludevít *Procházka*, was followed by a period of apparent neglect. Dvořák, however, returned to the unpublished work nine years later, and not only conducted the Variations himself at concert given in Prague on March 6th, 1886, but, after mature consideration, offered them to the celebrated conductor of the Vienna Philharmonic, Hans *Richter*, for performance. The latter immediately accepted them as "a splendid addition to his programme" and gave them their first performance abroad at his concert on May 15th, 1887, in the Crystal Palace in London. "It's a splendid work", he wrote after his first rehearsal to Dvořák in Prague "these variations can take an honoured place among the finest of your compositions," and after the actual concert in a letter reporting on the "magnificent success" of the Variations added, "at the hundreds of concerts which I have conducted no novelty has ever had such a success."

Not long afterwards, on December 4th of the same year, he repeated the Symphonic Variations with no less success at a concert of the Vienna Philharmonic, and Dvořák, who was present at the concert, wrote to his Berlin publisher: "The playing was splendid and the work was loudly applauded by the audience," nor did he forget to add that Brahms had given him "a present of a lovely cigarette-holder", as a souvenir of the occasion. As was only to be expected, Simrock immediately accepted the Variations for publication and brought them out at the beginning of the following year 1888, and, as if they were a composition of recent date, gave them the opus number 78, in direct opposition to the author's wishes. Since then the Symphonic Variations have held the position which Richter accorded them in the foremost rank of Dvořák's work. Among the celebrated conductors who have included them in their repertoire is also Arturo *Toscanini*.

2. SCHERZO CAPRICCIOSO, OP. 66

Instrumentation: piccolo, 2 flutes, 2 oboes, cor anglais, 2 clarinets, bass clarinet, 2 bassoons, 4 horns, 2 trumpets, 3 trombones, tuba, tympani, bass drum, cymbals, triangle, harp, strings.

Written in score between April 6th and May 2nd, 1883.—First performed by the National Theatre Orchestra, conducted by Adolf *Čech*, on May 16th, 1883, in the New Czech Theatre in Prague.—Score, parts and four-handed piano arrangement (by the composer) published by Bote & Bock, Berlin, 1884.—Duration: 12^1/$_2$ minutes.

The Scherzo Capriccioso was composed at a time when Dvořák was inwardly not predisposed for the creation of works of a gay and care-free nature. On the contrary, his inner consciousness was darkened by those gloomy and passionately defiant moods which gave birth to the Piano Trio in F minor and, somewhat later, to the D minor Symphony, op. 70 (see page 111). If, in spite of this special frame of mind he set to work on such a composition, which from its very designation indicates a tone of capricious humour, it is little wonder that, instead of the expression of the joy of living the spirit of the work is one rather of stubborn defiance, of passionate questioning or gloomy meditation. In the Scherzo the character of these moods determines the relative complexity of the subject-matter and also the structure of the work, which is in ternary form, and of which the spaciousness of design, the richness and boldness of the imitation, figuration and contrapuntal treatment of the themes is unusual in a work of this kind. The sombre range of moods also imparts to the Scherzo its special tone-colouring which, in the full orchestra, gives particular prominence to instruments of a dark timbre, such as the English horn and the bass clarinet.

The first part of the Scherzo (*Allegro con fuoco*, D flat major, $^3/_4$) is composed of two strongly contrasting themes, the main theme, of which most use is made throughout the composition, consisting of two periods. The first eight-bar strain makes a stormy, impetuous entry underlined by strong rhythmic syncopation, and then undulates flexibly in rapid semiquavers (1*a*); the second six-bar period is stampingly defiant in its octave steps in the first half, and softly ar d expressively lyrical in the second half (1*b*):

The actual entry of the main theme in the full orchestra is preceded at the beginning of the composition by a twice-repeated imitation of the opening four-bar phrase, first by a fanfare of two horns and then, like an echo, by the flute. The interval of a second in the fourth bar is extended the first time to a third, mysteriously repeated in the cellos, and the second time to a fifth, repeated by the horn.

The theme itself then bursts out in full force of expression and tone, but not for long, for the stream of sound suddenly diminishes and upon it is borne in, after a few transitional bars, the second, subordinate theme, which, in contrast to the first, sings a lovely and spontaneously expressive melody with an undercurrent of passionately coloured alternated harmonies, first in G major and then in A major.

2.

The closing paragraph comprises a short development of the first four-bar phrase of the main theme (1a), tossed from one instrument to another, whereupon the whole introductory section is repeated with occasional extension and enrichment of certain passages and frequent rescoring.

Towards the end the mood becomes calmer, with a delicate repetition of the first and fourth bars of the principal theme in preparation for the entry of the middle part (*Poco tranquillo*, D major) which, in contrast to the predominantly stormy and agitated mood of the first part, has a contemplative air of reverie emanating from its lovely, leisurely theme of fully thirty bars, delivered first by the cor anglais and repeated higher in the flute and clarinet with the violins weaving a delicate figuration an octave above it:

3.   **Poco tranquillo**
     Cor. ingl.

The expression here, too, becomes livelier but not gayer, for the new theme 4, rhythmically and harmonically related to theme 2, is darkened by its presentation in the minor mode and, combined in a further variant 4a with proud fanfares in the trumpets and trombones and accompanied by a stormy sequence of quaver chords in the other instruments, even assumes a hard and defiant expression.

4.

The whole of this middle part of the Scherzo is placed within repeat marks, after which there follows a lively development of figures from 1a and 4, interrupted only by an episode in which the first four bars of theme 1a, crooned softly by the bass clarinet, bassoon and cello, develops into this slightly undulating variation of theme 4:

4b.

The development, worked up with rising dynamic intensity, leads to a fairly regular recapitulation. The only important deviation is that the opening run-up of the principal theme in this variant starts not from the dominant but from the tonic:

1a.

The Scherzo closes with a coda which begins peacefully in the form of a softly reminiscent dialogue embracing the first four-bar phrase of 1a (in the horns) and theme 2 (flutes, oboes and clarinets), when unexpectedly a harp cadenza develops out the chord of the seventh (*a-c sharp-e-g*) and finally seizes on theme 1a, with which it sweeps forward to a passionate, accelerated and excitingly brilliant culmination.

VIII

PROGRAMME MUSIC

An independent and fairly large group within the body of Antonín Dvořák's orchestral works is represented by the compositions comprising that branch of music known as programme music, by which we understand compositions whose content is related to some extra-musical background, whether poetic, dramatic or descriptive.

It is well-known that Dvořák, though essentially a neo-classicist with a predilection for the form of pure, so-called "absolute" music in which he also proved himself a master, was capable in his creative versatility of a keen appreciation of, and fondness for, the characteristic features of musical neo-Romanticism. This was due especially to his unaffected admiration for the music of the greatest representatives of this important period tendency—*Wagner* and *Liszt*—an admiration which was strongly reflected in those works produced towards the end of the first decade of his creative activity i. e. at the beginning of the seventies of the last century and revived at intervals, eventually playing its most significant role in the last decade of the composer's life.

Thus Dvořák proved to be a child of his time in not remaining indifferent even to programme music, and it was equally characteristic that his interest in this branch of musical composition shows distinct stages of development: from the semi-dramatic and semi-concert overture he passed on to the purely concert overture, with a programme-content of deepening significance, and thence to Symphonic Poems of unmistakably programme character. His liking for this form does not arise out of any need of his creative imagination for extra-musical inspiration, but is quite simply due to the fact that his reflective and sensitively reacting mind was attracted and stimulated by the problem, as it appeared to him, of combining "absolute" music with extra-musical subject matter, whether epic or dramatic or even illustrative of a certain mood. We have already indicated his interest in this problem in a number of compositions of a more intimate character, principally for piano, and he devoted all the more thought to it in his orchestral works, which are not only the most natural and most effective medium for programme music, but the medium in which his musical imagination was fondest of expressing itself.

Dvořák's concert overtures follow closely on the operatic overtures and even merge with them so intimately that certain dramatic overtures lost their original function in the course of time and became mainly or altogether concert overtures.*

Here, however, we have undoubted examples of a type of overture with an independent subject and poetical content which form a clear transition to the symphonic poem as conceived by Liszt or Smetana.

In the process of his creative development, Dvořák also arrived at this neo-romantic form of musical composition, but not until the very close of his orchestral production. That this step was an inward creative necessity is proved by the fact that he composed no less than five great Symphonic Poems in quick succession, four of which drew their themes from Czech folk-coloured fairy-tale and ballad poetry, as contained in the popular collection entitled "The Gar-

---

* Such is the overture to the first opera "Alfred", published posthumously under the title "Dramatic Overture"; another is the original overture to the opera "Dimitri", which Dvořák removed from the sphere of the theatre, having replaced it by a considerably shortened version, which was also published after the author's death; a third example is the well-known overture "My Home", originally the overture to the popular play "Josef Kajetán Tyl", which became a regular feature of concert and radio programmes when interest in the play itself declined. We shall, therefore, include these three overtures in our analysis, which, of course, does not rule out the appearance of the overtures to some of Dvořák's other operas as independent works in the orchestral concert repertoire; they retain, however, their connection with the stage.

land" by Karel Jaromír *Erben,* while for the last he chose his own, in a large measure autobiographical, subject matter, for that reason also very close to the folk tradition.

What has been said earlier of the purely musical core of Dvořák's non-illustrative orchestral works, of the artist's relation to the orchestra, and of the mastery with which he handled it, can be applied without reservation to his overtures and symphonic poems. His art of instrumentation, his sensitive feeling for the natural possibilities of each instrument and for their effective combination, in short, his rare sense of the magic of pure, spontaneous, intoxicating, unexpected tone colour, are typical features of all his orchestral works, no matter what the inner impulse out of which they arose. And if those qualities were an integral part of Dvořák's art from its very beginnings, then the impressionistically colourful character of extramusical themes was itself sufficient to vouchsafe in the five symphonic poems a unique level of achievement richly corroborating the reputation of one of the greatest masters of instrumentation in the whole history of music.

The group of Dvořák's orchestral works of programme character may thus be considered to differ from the others for the most part only in being associated with a certain thought-content and in the solution of the formal problems which such a connection implies. The differences in the latter point do not go so far, however, as to invalidate the dependence of these compositions upon the formal laws of "absolute" music, especially when, as in a number of cases, Dvořák could employ traditional musical forms without much modification. And yet we find differences here such as strengthen the impression of a special form in connection with this group of compositions, which works itself out with increasing clarity as the series progresses. In what nuances this special form manifests itself will be indicated in the analyses of the compositions themselves.

DRAMATIC OVERTURE

Instrumentation: piccolo, 2 flutes, 2 oboes, cor anglais, 2 clarinets in B flat, 2 bassoons, 4 horns, 2 trumpets, 3 trombones, tuba, tympani, bass drum, cymbals, triangle, harp, strings.
Completed on October 19th, 1870.—First performance by the Czech Philharmonic, with Oskar *Nedbal* conducting, on January 1th, 1905, in Prague.— Score, parts and four-handed arrangement (Roman *Veselý*) published posthumously by Simrock, Berlin, first under the designation "Tragic", then "Dramatic" Overture.—Duration: 15 minutes.

The "Dramatic Overture" originally designated by the composer "Tragic Overture", is one of Dvořák's very early works. It is actually the orchestral overture to his first opera, written in 1870 and based on the dramatic poem, "Alfred the Great", by the German Romantic, Karl Theodor *Körner* (1791—1815). Dvořák himself withheld this opera during his life-time as unsuitable for performance, and it was not till 1938 that it was produced by the Municipal Theatre in Olomouc.

The plot of the opera is an episode in the Anglo-Danish Wars of the end of the ninth century, in which the English King Alfred defeated the Danish Princes Harald and Gothron, thus winning the hand of his beloved Alvina. This work was written at a time when Dvořák was still quite unknown, when his still unformed and undirected creative energy was strongly under the spell of Wagner's music and favoured non-periodic and otherwise erratically developed thematic ideas. This, too, is the compositional style of the "Dramatic Overture", first performed after the composer's death. It is one of the best parts of the opera, the composition being very lively, in spite of its loose and rambling structure, and impressing the listener with its strong, effectively built up dynamism, as also with its individual conception of the content. Working almost exclusively with the thematic material of the opera, the overture is conceived not only as a symphonic pre-view of the drama itself, on the model of

Beethoven's "Leonora" or Wagner's first overtures, but its significance is raised by a shift of accent from the struggle to win a woman
to the historic background, which is the struggle for national freedom and independence. Herein lies also its higher national purpose, anticipating that of not a few of Dvořák's later works.

The overture consists of a short, slow introduction and a quick
movement on a broad plan. The grave introduction (*Poco adagio*,
G flat major, $^{12}/_8$), which suggests the heroic character of the composition and the seriousness of the struggle described, develops out
of two themes not used in the opera itself: after a crashing chord
of the sixth in G major and a short imitation of the curiously undulating second of this pair of themes (2), the cor anglais comes forward first with the dignified, calm and Wagneresque theme 1, in
the tonic key of G flat major, the violoncellos then following up
with the irregularly contoured, rhythmically restless and gloomily
tinged second theme.

The main part of the overture (*Allegro molto appassionato*, $^2/_2$) is in
a kind of free, indeterminate rondo form. It is worked up out of a
whole series of thematic ideas, taken over, without exception, from
the opera itself. Most prominent among them are the fighting themes
of the two nations, the terse, passionately rising theme of the Britons
(3), and the broad, rhythmically lively theme of the Danes (4).

These two themes keep returning in the course of the overture, contending and in constant rivalry with each other to the very close. Alternating with them are the other thematic materials consisting, on the one hand, of the two themes (1 and 2) quoted above from the slow introduction, and then all the others derived from the chief characters and dramatic episodes of the opera. They include the group of motifs connected with Alfred's bride, Alvina (5a), the presages of her victory (5b), her love (5c) and her heroic self-sacrifice (5a and 5e):

And then the themes of the two rivals, Harald (6) and Alfred (7), of which the common rhythmic core is to be heard every now and again in the thematic intricacies of the overture, and out of which Alfred's theme rises to an impressive culmination before the close of the composition in rhythmic augmentation, finally bursting forth festively in the clashing sounds of trumpets and trombones.

The above-quoted themes mingle in gay kaleidoscopic fashion without greater structural unity or order, the main tendency being to express the swift course and fanatical passion of the struggle. And this is the basic impression created by the composition, which work up to a fully effective and powerful close.

"DIMITRI" OVERTURE

Instrumentation: 2 flutes, 2 oboes, 2 clarinets, 2 clarinets in B flat and A, 2 bassoons, 4 horns, 2 trumpets, 3 trombones, tuba, tympani, triangle, harp, bass drum, cymbals, strings.

Written between September 5th and 25th, 1882, partly at Sychrov and partly in Prague.—First performance along with the opera at the New Czech Theatre in Prague, on October 8th, 1882, with Mořic *Anger* conducting.—Score published by "Hudební matice" in Prague, 1946.—Duration: 15 minutes.

The historic opera "Dimitri" is Dvořák's seventh musical drama. The libretto by Marie *Červinka-Rieger* (1854—95), based partly on Friedrich *Schiller's* dramatic fragment "Demetrius" and partly on the historical drama "Dimitr Ivanovič" by the Czech writer, Ferdinand *Mikovec*, is a direct continuation of the plot of *Mussorgski's* opera "Boris Godunov": the false Dimitri enters Moscow after the Tsar's death, seizes the throne and, by his liberal attitude to the Russian people, wins their support. He then, however, falls ardently in love with Boris's daughter Xenia, which provokes the furious anger and jealousy of his Polish mistress, Marina, who betrays his real origin to the assembled people, and at whose suggestion the Boyar Shouisky, loyal to the late Tsar, shoots the Pretender.

Dvořák's opera had originally an independent orchestral overture, with which it was also performed a number of times. A year after the first performance, Dvořák realized the unsuitability of a long formal overture before a tragic opera, and cut out the whole allegro part leaving only the original grave introduction, to which he gave a new conciliatory ending, and which now always forms the prelude to the opera.

The original full overture is thus limited to concert performance, for which it is well suited as a composition of solemn pathos and symphonic dignity of style. Its slow introduction is built up of themes connected with Russian events previous to Dimitri's entry into Moscow, while the following quick part is worked out in fully developed sonata form in which the themes are related to the principal character and to what brings about his downfall.

The whole slow introduction to the overture (*Largo*, E flat minor, $^4/_4$) evokes the impression of great solemnity in which the moods, however, alternate rapidly and the restless, strongly agitated melodic line predicts the stir and tumult of coming dramatic events. The first two bars mark the entry of the strings in unison with the solemn theme (1), of which the opening motif *m* is clearly derived from the principal Dimitri theme (1*a*—see later). The heavy marcato rhythm gives the opening theme 1 an ominously tragic air, underlined in the closing figure by the harmonically divergent interval of a diminished fourth (*g-c* flat):

As if in reply to the questioning tone of this diminished fourth, the oboes and bassoons introduce, in the next three bars, a soft, almost timidly vacillating theme which, in the opera, is associated with Boris's youthful daughter Xenia, not a little frightened and confused by all that is going on around her:

The whole of this five-bar phrase is repeated a fourth higher, whereupon a short, energetic gradation leads to the incisive entry of the chord of F sharp minor, in which the above-quoted figure *m* in the trombones twice replies very expressively with the motif related to the passage in the first act where Xenia, deeply shocked, describes the murder of her brother, Tsarevich Fedor:

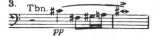

After a further short dynamic rise, motif 1*m* is heard once more, delivered this time with special emphasis and majesty in the trumpets and trombones, broadly spanned in the high pitched instruments by an agitated phrase delivered from the opening figure *n* in theme 2.

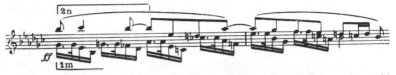

The quicker part of the overture (*Allegro vivace*, E flat major, $^4/_4$) is in fully developed sonata form, with exposition, development, recapitulation and coda.

The exposition describes the central character of the drama and the two between whom his passion vacillates: the timid passive Xenia and the passionate, proudly imperious Marina. The principal theme is derived from the powerful swinging melody of the large ensemble at the close of the first act and its two opening bars are regularly quoted throughout the opera as Dimitri's heroic theme:

The subordinate theme is here represented by the above-mentioned theme associated with Xenia, its variant 2*a*, above wavy sextolets in the harp, taking the form of a duet in the flutes, first in the key of B flat major and then, combined with the oboes and clarinets, in the more melancholy key of B flat minor.

The group of final phrases comprises Dimitri's love-song to Marina at the beginning of Act II,

and then an allusion to the vigorously rhythmic theme of Marina's Mazurka from the same scene in the full orchestra:

The development, in which agitation and uncertainty alternate with the expression of proud resolution, has the character of open conflict between all the themes cited. The recapitulation is an almost regular repetition of the exposition, with the usual shift to the tonic. The overture is brought to a close by a coda in accelerated tempo *(più mosso)* in the full orchestra, based on the buoyant principal theme (1*a*), which appears in its original form, then in its augmented form in the trumpets and trombones, and, finally, in jubilant diminution.

"MY HOME"

(Domov můj)

Overture to Šamberk's play "Josef Kajetán Tyl", op. 62.

Instrumentation: 2 flutes, 2 oboes, 2 clarinets, in B flat, 2 bassoons, 4 horns, 2 trumpets, 3 trombones, tympani, triangle, strings.
Written between January 21st and 23rd, 1882, at Vysoká by Příbram.— First performed along with Šamberk's play at the Interim Theatre in Prague, on February 3rd, 1882, conducted by Adolf Čech.—Score, parts and four-handed arrangement (Dr. Josef Zubatý) published by Simrock, Berlin, 1882.—Duration: 8 minutes.

Dvořák was at work on the score of the opera "Dimitri", when the management of the Czech Theatre in Prague asked him to write the entr'actes and other incidental music for the folk play *Josef Kajetán Tyl* by the popular Czech actor František Ferdinand *Šamberk*. The play itself is a dramatically simple and moving picture of the hardship and persecution which fell to the lot of the greatly beloved folk-play writer Josef Kajetán *Tyl* (1808—1853), with the comico-tragic background of an actor's life at the time of the birth of a National Czech Theatre, in which each of the three acts presents a variant of the theme depicting how the author of the nationally popular song "Kde domov můj?" ("Where is my home?") (the first part of the present-day Czechoslovak national anthem) is driven from place to place unable to find a home.

Dvořák wrote some smaller pieces for this play, charming in their melodic thought and completely appropriate in mood, the two short and rhythmical entr'actes and finally a large orchestral overture. In accordance with Šamberk's wish he took as the thematic material for this play the melody of the song "Where is my Home?" and, as a contrasting element, he himself chose the Czech folk song "In the farmyard everything is crowing and cackling", suggested to him by the passage in the play in which Tyl, dismissed from the ensemble of the Prague Theatre, is seeking for himself and his own theatrical company a refuge in the Czech countryside.*

* We quote here at least a few bars of the original versions of these songs.
"Where is my Home?"

"In the farmyard":

These two songs, bound by the common element in their musical line of an ascending and descending second (see the bracketed element *m* in the example) provide the thematic material for the orchestral overture which Dvořák wrote as the introduction to the play. It is a lightly sketched composition, without any particular thematic intricacies, but with all that delightful freshness and spontaneity demanded by the subject of the play and the character of the two songs used as leading motifs, as well as possessing a specifically Dvořák dynamism of sound and movement. It was, therefore, not at all surprising that the overture was very soon frequently and successfully performed on concert platforms, usually under the title "My Home", the designation given it by the composer in the manuscript score.

This overture, too, keeps to the classical scheme, with a slow introduction and a quick part in strictly regular sonata form based on the simple conception of two thematic ideas. These are introduced straight away in the introductory part (*Andante maestoso, quasi adagio*, C major, $^3/_4$), which opens with two statements of the first strain of the song "In the farmyard" in metrical augmentation (1*a*), and alternately in the major and minor mode, modulating then into E flat major, in which key some development is made of the elements of the song "Where is my Home?"

Element *m* is the germ of a short dynamic rise which leads to the first imposing presentation of the theme 2*a* by the full brass to which the minor key gives additional pathos.

Thereupon a new dynamic rise, worked up with the material from the same songs, paves the way for the quick part of the overture (*Allegro vivace*, C major, $^6/_8$), of which the sonata form makes do with the above-quoted two themes.

The very animated character of this part derives from the skipping rhythm of the six-quaver bar in which first of all a variant of the melody "In the farmyard" disports itself vivaciously as the main theme:

The opening phrase of this theme and its skipping rhythm, used in the function of imitation, disturbs the more serious expression of the melodically flowing subordinate theme, here represented by the whole melody of "Where is my Home?", transposed now to the key of A major, and with the additional attraction of unusual harmonic modulations (2*b*).

The development alternately presents the two themes, or occasionally combines them, with immense variety and resource, the composer displaying, in the variational and imitational work, his inexhaustible fertility of technical invention.

The recapitulation repeats the exposition with the usual change of key in the subordinate theme (now in C major). Onto it is grafted a broad coda, which finally presents in full a hymn-like and splendidly built-up declamation of the song "Where is my Home?" (*Allegro con fuoco*, $^4/_4$). A victoriously jubilant final passage based on elements from theme 1*b* brings the overture to an effective close.

"HUSSITE OVERTURE"

Dramatic ouverture for large orchestra, op. 67

Instrumentation: piccolo, 2 flutes, 2 oboes, 2 clarinets in B flat, 2 bassoons, 4 horns, 2 trumpets, 3 trombones, tuba, tympani, bass drum, cymbals, triangle, harp (ad. lib.), strings.

Written between August 8th and September 9th, 1883, at Vysoká.—First performed at the inauguration of the Academy in the new National Theatre in Prague, on November 18th, 1883, with Mořic *Anger* conducting.—Score, parts and four-handed arrangement (by the composer) published by Simrock, Berlin, 1884.—Duration: 14 minutes.

The dramatic overture entitled the "Hussite" was intended, in the same way as "My Home", for the theatre, but ceased to fulfil that function even before its first performance, so that it immediately assumed its place as a concert piece. Its original purpose, however, dictated the content and, at the same time, predetermined its fate as one of the musically and nationally most noble works in Czech concert music. It was one of those works which was created shortly before the opening of the new National Theatre (after the fire), and was permeated with the spirit of hopeful confidence in the future of the artistic and national life of the Czech nation linked with this event.

The impulse to the "Hussite" was given by the director of the

National Theatre, František Adolf Šubert, who was preparing to write a dramatic trilogy for the new theatre dealing with the Hussite Age, and who asked Dvořák, even before he himself had started work on it, to write the orchestral overture. Šubert summarised for the composer the content of the trilogy, of which no more than the first act was completed, as "The origin of the Hussite movement, the Hussite wars and, after the wars, the restoration of peace". The theme of the composition was thus tersely expressive in character, the action showed a natural inner development, while the matter was essentially suited to the musical medium. In addition, Dvořák grasped its inner purpose and tendency so that, in transposing it into the musical medium, he did not confine himself to the description of the storms of war, but deliberately laid the stress on its national ethical aspect, conceiving it as the expression of the struggle for the noble idea of national freedom, evoked by the death of the hero-martyr who had given this thought life and meaning, and finally achieved a solemn victory.

Outwardly the form of the classical overture again sufficed for the composer's treatment of this subject, with its slow introduction and broadly-planned quick part in sonata form. He gave musical expression to the associated thought-content of the subject in two of the five basic themes of the overture, the first of which comprises the opening two-bar phrase of "Ye who are God's valiant warriors":

and the middle motif of the melody of the "Saint Wenceslas" chorale:

Both these songs were favourites of the Hussite soldiery at the beginning of the fifteenth century, since when they have never diminished in popularity or significance, but are frequently quoted in modern Czech music.* Thus in the "Hussite", Dvořák rightly quoted and combined fragments of both chorales. If the choice of these two themes was evidently a matter of personal bias, Dvořák's completely individual conception is also apparent in that, while not making either of them the principal theme of the sonata form, for which he chose new, independent ideas, he yet attributed to them a decisively important place, especially as regards the motif of the Hussite song, in the structure of the movement.

As has already been indicated, the overture begins with a slow introduction (*Lento ma non troppo*, C major, $^3/_4$) illustrating, we may presume, the rise of the Hussite Movement. The wood-wind open the overture with a grave, broadly-phrased theme in a tone of elevated pathos embodying as it were the greatness and nobility of the ideas which kindled the movement:

The inner significance of the theme is very soon convincingly underlined by thematic fragments from the two chorales which follow the first theme in this combination:

The movement becomes somewhat quicker (*Piu animato*, C major, $^3/_4$), and, over the movement of the harp passages and the pizzicato

* The chorale "Ye who are God's valiant warriors" was splendidly employed by Bedřich *Smetana*, in the last two parts of his monumental symphonic cycle "My Country", while Josef *Suk*, for instance, created his "Meditations on the Saint Wenceslas Chorale" an intimate chamber-music work for string quartet, and Vítězslav *Novák*, again, his impressive "St. Wenceslas Triptych", originally for organ, later transcribred for orchestra.

in the strings, the violins, flute and oboe draw this intimation of the later subordinate theme from the quick part of the overture (5), combined again with a fragment of the St. Wenceslas motif:

Thereupon it rises to a climax marking the re-entry of the introductory theme 1, which, in the glorious, hymn-like harmonies of the full orchestra, sounds like a great chorale wherein thousands of voices join in ecstatic prayer.

The quick part (*Allegro con brio*, C minor, $^2/_2$) retains the main features of sonata form, the exposition and development being charged with dramatic tension foreshadowing the hard impact of conflict and struggle. The principal theme, with which the exposition opens, begins with two wide intervals of ascending fifths and then breaks into a diminished version of the Hussite motif, concluding quietly with an allusion to the St. Wenceslas chorale:

The development of this, in which the germ of fighting action is implicit and which, besides working up the materials of motifs 2a and 2b, also exploits the sharply accented rhythms of the thematic idea 4, is of considerable length and strongly agitated, rising to a powerful, defiant climax with the Hussite motif 2a:

The dynamic tension is first relaxed before the entry of the sub-ordinate theme, which sings a melody of warm pathos, lively in movement and with a progressively rising melodic line:

This theme, too, is in places interwoven with a motif from the St. Wenceslas chorale (2*b*), and closes with a new, impressive statement of the Hussite motif (2*a*), the whole orchestra underlining the strong rhythmic accents, followed by a decrescendo passage based on the principal theme (3).

The development, which is perhaps the longest and most complex to be found in any of Dvořák's sonata movements, begins with a calm quotation of the two chorale motifs, motif 2*b* maintaining its grave and elevated character, while motif 2*a* appears in a restless diminished version. Both these motifs are then intertwined with several repetitions of the opening bars of the principal theme (3), while an alternating exposition of all the themes works up an atmosphere of bustle and stir and active preparation for battle. Ever and anon fragments of the Hussite motif are delivered in the sharp penetrating tones of fanfares rallying to the attack, while the excitement rapidly spreads to the whole orchestra which beats out, with thunderous hammer-strokes, the rhythmic pattern of the same motif. It is a passage of immense dramatic tension in which the last flames of struggle seem to shoot up, casting shadows before of the closing act of the tragedy of the defeat of the Hussite movement at Lipany. This is confirmed in the rapidly following dynamic collapse and feebleness of expression with which—in the transition to the recapitulation—above a deep pedal point, successive allusions are made to the spacious subordinate theme into which a muted horn, faintly, as from a great distance, interpolates a quotation of the Hussite motif.

Dvořák, however, did not see the Hussite drama end tragically: in the afterglow of the flames of war, crimson-tinged with blood spilt in the fierce conflict, he senses the rosy dawn of a new national life and the victory of the idea for which the fight was waged. And so the recapitulation of the allegro part of the "Hussite" is borne forward on a rising tide of joyful aspiration. It is all in the festively bright key of C major. The principal theme, originally proud and defiant (3), is transformed into a delicate pastoral in the oboe, accompanied by the sinuous movement of the flutes and bell-like strokes on the triangle:

In the same glorious key the two chorale motifs sound forth triumphantly, as does also the subordinate theme (5) above the restless rhythm of the kettle drums, with an undercurrent of anticipatory excitement building up to an imposing coda in which, once more, like the symbol of the victorious future of the nation, there is declaimed with full and festive solemnity the noble introductory theme (1), a short *stretto* bringing the Overture to a brilliant close.

If the "Hussite" is a powerful and deeply moving work in respect of its music and content, its high purely musical values are amply testified to by the success it has had and continues to meet with on its performance abroad. Nor can we omit to recall that it was especially the celebrated German conductor, Hans von *Bülow*, who cherished a particular admiration for this work and performed it on innumerable occasions, countering any objections offered by his impressario with his decided: *"What I perform I stand by. Dvořák is for me, along with Brahms, the most outstanding musician of the present day.."* (in a letter dated November 27th, 1887).

"NATURE, LIFE AND LOVE"

(Příroda, život a láska)

Three Overtures, op. 91—93

Although he was still to manifest his bent for absolute music in a number of compositions after the "Hussite" Overture (the D minor Symphony op. 70, the G major Symphony op. 88 and the second series of the "Slavonic Dances"), Dvořák first found an outlet for his growing bias towards programme music in three concert overtures. These are important, among other reasons, not only because they have their own emotional content independent of, and uninspired by any extra-musical source, but because in their musical and thought content they were conceived as a connected cycle with a common title, *"Nature, Life and Love"*. Only later did each part get its special designation, the first being entitled *"In Nature's Realm"*, the second *"Carnival"* and the third *"Othello"*.

Nor was it mere coincidence that Dvořák created this special cycle of works in his fiftieth year. In a number of previous works of larger and smaller compass he had already shown an inclination towards poetic and philosophical contemplation, and now, having reached maturity of years and experience, there grew on him the fondness and disposition for solitary reflection, which made him feel more than ever the need to ponder as an artist over the eternal problems of Life and Nature to which he had all his life stood in the closest relation. Deeply religious in feeling, he saw in Nature, above all, the unfathomable work of a Divine Will, but, in a certain pantheistic sense, he also saw in it the chief source of life and all that it comprises of Good and Evil. And it is this view which he expressed in his cycle "Nature, Life and Love", which is equally the manifestation of the strength of true spiritual experience and of the creative imagination of a musician-poet.

As may be judged from several titles in the sketches and scores, and partly also from a number of statements inspired by him, Dvořák wished, in the form of a cycle of overtures, to paint musical pictures evoked by the most powerful impressions which the human soul can know: the solemn silence of a summer night, the gay whirl of life and living, and the passion of great love poisoned by jealousy. Briefly, to portray Nature herself from both the bright and the seamy side. Dvořák was for long uncertain what designation to give the parts of this cycle. The first sketch of the overture bears no less than four suggestions for titles. At the top of the first page of music the composer has written: "*Ouvertura lyrica*" or "*In Nature's Realm*" or "*A Summer Night*", while on the title-page "*Solitude*" is added as sub-title. The score of the second overture has, besides the title "*Life*", also the sub-title "*Carnival*". The third is headed "*Love*" and "*Othello*". It is of interest, too, that the manuscript score "In Nature's Realm" bears a dedication to the University of Cambridge and "Carnival" to the Prague Czech University. (Both universities had shortly before conferred honorary degrees upon the composer.) These dedications are not reproduced in the printed score.

The idea forming the common base for all three overtures (Nature and her powers for good and evil) is given musical expression in a theme of nature (see Ex. 1), which is the principal theme of the overture "In Nature's Realm", appears in short reminiscences in "Carnival" and is again given greater prominence in "Othello". A detailed analysis shows the changes that theme undergoes in harmonic and tone colouring in its different thought-contexts. Otherwise the overtures are, both in content and musically, independent compositions keeping in general, as regards form, to the classical type of overture, and only diverging from it within the limits demanded by the context. Each has its own character and mood, built up with all the expressive means of musical art, from the quality of the melodic, harmonic and rhythmic material to the thematic design and structure and the range of orchestral colour-values.

This expressive differentiation of the overtures, however, in no way disturbs the inner unity of the cycle. Being the reflection of the elasticity and wide compass of Dvořák's musicality and of his highly developed sense of contrast, which finds scope for display even within the framework of a well-integrated whole, it only strengthens the spontaneous effectiveness of the whole cycle, especially since the composer has succeeded in unifying the content and its purely musical expression, thereby attaining the highest degree of conscious artistic organisation. The bucolic freshness and clarity of the overture "In Nature's Realm", which is the simplest in form and content, contrasts sharply with the fiery passion of the "Carnival", in whose theme, rhythm and tone-colouring there surges an intoxicating youthfulness and joy of living, while the climax of the cycle, the tensely dramatic and tragically accented "Othello", is the most complex and daring in structure. All three are distinguished by those qualities which determine the beauty as well as the individual and national originality of Dvořák's musical art.

"IN NATURE'S REALM"

(V přírodě)

Overture for large orchestra, op. 91.

Instrumentation: 2 flutes, 2 oboes, cor anglais, 2 clarinets in B flat, bass clarinet, 2 bassoons, 4 horns, 2 trumpets, 3 trombones, tuba, tympani, cymbals, triangle, strings.

Written in sketch between March 31st and April 18th, in score by July 8th, 1891.—First performed, along with the other two overtures at Dvořák's farewell concert before his departure to America, on April 28th, 1892, by the augmented orchestra of the National Theatre conducted by the composer.—Score, parts and four-handed piano arrangement (Josef *Suk*) published by Simrock, Berlin, 1894.—Duration: 13 minutes.

The subject-matter of the overture "In Nature's Realm" can be outlined as follows: We go out into the quiet of a summer evening when the sounds of day have died down and silence has fallen on the world around us. Soon, however, our ear picks up an indeterminate long-drawn-out tone—the voice of Nature as she sinks to rest—and here and there a bird-call falls upon the ear. *(Short introduction.)* All at once, however, when the mind has thrown off the weight of daily cares and surrenders itself to the embrace of the universe, the inner voice of Nature makes itself heard in the soul. At first faintly, as from a distance, but rapidly growing in strength, multiplying and expanding till it sounds forth in a tone of pure and exalted happiness: here Nature sings the symphony of her sublime mystery, the Symphony of Life and Love, purifying and strengthening the human spirit and raising it to a hymn-like ecstasy of joy. *(Exposition, development and recapitulation.)* Inwardly purified, the spirit returns to reality, while Nature is again manifest in a deep, all-pervading long-drawn-out silence broken only by the occasional voices of birds. *(The closing section is a repetition of the introduction.)* Thus in general it is the simple, but musically rich and colourful emotional expression of inner perceptions, to which only the prevailing mood and the narrow frame of the introduction and close give the general features of programme music. In form the overture keeps to regular sonata structure while stressing the group system in its thematic material.

The overture, with the same time indication (*Allegro ma non troppo*, F major, $^6/_4$) throughout, begins with a delicate pedal point of the tonic above which, in the bassoons and violas, there moves the basic theme of Nature in this still embryonic form.

The flutes and oboes reply to variant 1*a* alternately with short bird-calls derived from the closing figure of the principal theme *(m)*, which then breaks into a calm rippling passage in preparation for the first soft entry of the theme of Nature in the clarinet (1):

The theme is repeated, with a trill on the first note, by the oboe in the key of B flat major and is then passed on to the cor anglais, along with the bass clarinet and again to the horn, while the violins repeat the third bar of the theme with increasing urgency, until, after a short gradation on the chord of the dominant seventh (in the basic key), the theme blossoms out in the full orchestra, this time with a more decorative version of figure 1*b* and with a continuation in which the trills ring out as clear and bell-like as children's laughter (1*c*):

Broadly, as if in one breath, the song of the theme grows in expressive power, culminating in the unannounced entry of a new vigorous theme with strong rhythmic contours:

Two further themes follow, the first of which is divided into a broad and elevated dialogue, between the low-pitched instruments and violins (3), disturbed by the syncopated rhythm of the horns, while the second tranquilizes the musical stream with its softly idyllic tone (4):

A quotation of the theme of Nature (1) in the delicate tone-colouring of the wood-wind swings the movement into the key of A major, in which the violins at last present the playful and delight-fully rhythmic subordinate theme:

The gay tone of this theme is stressed on repetition by light syn-copations in the bass and, in its further course, still more so by the persistent repetition of the rhythmic figure *p*. A short theme tinged with passion:

provides the transition to the final theme which, at first, soars lightly as a bird in the flute and clarinet, while the cor anglais and bassoon reply with a yearning, softly sighing melody in the inner part:

7.

The emotional stream then mounts and increases in volume till it overflows in bursts of jubilation in the full orchestra, finally rising to a mighty climax with a majestic presentation of the basic theme of Nature (1).

The development works up the materials of the principal theme (1, 1*b*, 1*c*), which combine a great variety of variously coloured counterpoints, makes passing allusions to themes 7 and 5, and then, having modulated through a number of remote keys, returns to the tonic, in which the theme of Nature (1) is again heard in its simple and calm original form.

The recapitulation is a literal repetition of the exposition with the traditional shift of the main themes to the basic key. The sole deviation is the idyllic motif 4, which now appears in the key of D flat major modulating into B major. The dynamic culmination of the recapitulation, built up with great resource, is, itself, splendidly effective. A powerfully graded exposition of the final theme (7) is followed by the theme of Nature (1), in jubilant fanfares of trumpets and horns, while its continuation (1*c*) jigs along firmly three octaves deep in the winds and strings, the four horns emphatically reiterating the interval of a third from the same theme, while the majesty of the passage is still further underlined by the sudden transition from F major, by way of F sharp minor, to the radiant key of F sharp major, with an equally sudden change back to F major.

We have, however, by now reached the beginning of the coda. The short chorale-like motif in the strings:

8.

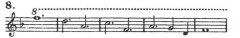

rapidly falling off in tone, closes the joyful and lively symphony of the inner voices of Nature, a clarinet cadenza calmly descends to the pedal point of deep *f*, over which, as in the introduction to the overture, the germ of the theme of Nature (1) gently rocks, while high above are the faint twitterings of bird-voices. With the theme of Nature opening into theme 8, the overture ends in a mood of shimmering delicacy.

"CARNIVAL"

(Karneval)

Overture for large orchestra, op. 92.

Instrumentation: piccolo, 2 flutes, 2 oboes, cor anglais, 2 clarinets in A, 2 bassoons, 4 horns, 2 trumpets, 3 trombones, tuba, tympani, cymbals, tambourine, triangle, harp and strings.

Written in sketch between July 28th and August 14th, and score completed by September 12th, 1891, at Vysoká.—First performance as for the overture "In Nature's Realm" (p. 295).—Score, parts and four-handed piano arrangement (Oskar *Nedbal*) published by Simrock, Berlin, 1894.—Duration: 9 minutes.

The second overture of the cycle "Nature, Life and Love", entitled "Carnival" (originally "Life") has no more definite or detailed programme than the overture "In Nature's Realm", and, with one small deviation, is also very similar in form. Still filled with the elevated feeling of solitude, man finds himself, all at once, caught up in the gay whirligig of life — and is happy! Willingly he yields to the carnival mood of merriment and, throwing reserve to the winds, he enters into the spirit of youthful revelry with care-free abandon, grateful for all its joys and beauties. Thus, in a few words, we may describe the general atmosphere of the first part of the overture, which comprises the exposition of the sonata form

(*Allegro*, A major, $^2/_2$). The orchestra enters in full force with the vigorous principal theme spread broadly over a two-part paragraph.

After a short modulating digression, the second principal theme, equally radiant, is presented in undiminished strength, but still grander and prouder in its conformation.:

The theme concludes with a swiftly-moving unison passage in the strings whereupon, with admirable invention, the violas create out of its metrically augmented figures the rising sequences of a mock-pious melody:

Its obviously caricatured gravity turns into a grimace in the violins above the diminished chord of the principal theme (9), and a short tranquillizing passage in the syncopated rhythm of the first bar of the same theme provides the transition to the paragraph containing the secondary theme. The passionately swelling melodic line of this lovely motif is worked out in dialogue through a full thirty bars:

It is first given to the violins, with counterpoints in the wood-wind, but on its repetition the groups of instruments exchange roles. Scarcely has the song with its expression of longing and desire died away than the violins break in with the second subsidiary theme which, to the accompaniment of the light rhythms of the wood-winds, strings, tambourine and delicate fanfares of trumpets, combines with the rhythmic figure *s* from theme 10, acquiring in the process an air of carnival gaiety and abandon:

This theme is presented by the violins in the key of G major, then with a richer accompaniment by the clarinet in E major, finally rising by a steep gradation to the final theme in which the whirling gaiety of the dance seems to reach its climax.

After a continuation of theme 13 has been presented in rising sequences, the wild revelry is suddenly cut short: above the eddying movement of the diminished chord *e-g-b flat-c sharp* in the harp, the first two bars of theme 9 appear in the violins. The swinging quavers of the second bar rise sharply, then gradually lose force, subside and ebb away till they settle at last on the sharply struck *g* of the horns. It is as if a man, having torn himself away from the giddy vanity of life's fair and withdrawn into inner contemplation, should put the question: Where then is the true source of all this happiness; who is the giver of all this life and intoxicating joy? And the reply rings out—Nature! A stroke of genius is the short, lyrical intermezzo (*Andantino con moto*, G major, $^3/_4$) interpolated at this point in the composition, the pure poetry of its mood dying away in a silvery beam of sound. Above the *ostinato* of the cor anglais, which repeats the rhythmic figure *r* from the principal theme, there sound in the inner harmonies the meltingly soft chords of the divided and muted violins and violas, and over them, again, the flute draws a dreamily beautiful line of melody (15), to which the clarinet significantly adds the gentle motif of Nature from the first overture (1):

The poetic charm of this passage is further heightened when the solo violin repeats the melody (15) and the cor anglais concludes it, whereupon a few bars in the same mood bring the intermezzo to a close.

And then, as if the vision had faded and the spirit were back again in the reality from which it had withdrawn itself, the harp, along with the clarinets and the bassoons, start the eddyings of a diminished chord, above which the violins deliver the first two bars of the principal theme (9). The development begins. The key (G minor) and the mood have their special significance. On returning to the whirl of gaiety, the impression evoked by that moment of inner contemplation still persists as, on passing from darkness into a brilliantly lit ballroom, we see its outlines blurred and bizarrely distorted. The chief role is given to theme 10 which, in its original form and in rhythmic diminutions, passes from one group of instruments to another, finally appearing in combination with the principal theme (9) and even with allusions to the theme of Nature in the deep brass instruments (1).

The blurred and distorted outlines suddenly come into focus. Once more theme 10 is delivered in full strength and, in combination with theme 11, presented with great pomp by the trombones. A rapid gradation based on the first principal theme (9) leads to the recapitulation, which is a regular repetition of the first part of the exposition but, in its further course, is considerably shortened and concentrated. All the more unified and powerful in effect is its rise to a short coda, which works up in an accelerated tempo *(Poccopiumosso)* the opening figure of theme 9, the composition ending in a final whirl of intoxicating gaiety.

"OTHELLO"

Overture for large orchestra, op. 93

Instrumentation: 2 flutes, 2 oboes, cor anglais, 2 clarinets, 2 bassoons, 4 horns, 2 trumpets, 3 trombones, tuba, tympani, bass drum, cymbals, harp and strings.
Written in sketch between November 1891 and January 14th, 1892, and in score between December 10th, 1891 and January 18th, 1892, in Prague.—First performance and publication as for the overture "In Nature's Realm".—Duration: 14 minutes.

The third overture of the cycle "Nature, Life and Love", the "Othello" ("Love") overture, has the most clearly defined programme, and therefore is the more free in its formal divergences, although it, too, keeps in general to the sonata form. The programme does not follow the Shakespearean drama closely. It is conceived on more general lines, and Othello is not so much an individual as a type: but just because the stage drama is also the artistic solution of a human tragedy such as Dvořák presents in his music, the overture was quite rightly given the same designation. The Othello overture, as in Shakespeare's great tragedy, does not speak of love as of something ennobling and benign, but of its dark side, of that

13. Antonin Bennewitz, the first conductor of the symphonic poems "The Water-Goblin", "The Noonday Witch" and "The Golden Spinning Wheel".

*14. The House of Artists (formerly Rudolfinum) where Dvořák's
symphonic poems were performed for the first time.*

evil passion which mars the happiness of human hearts—of the malignant weed of jealousy. And because it speaks of love as an evil begotten by Nature, it, too, grows organically out of the basic programme of the cycle. For it is Nature that awakens the brute instincts in the human soul, that corrodes and corrupts the purest and highest of feelings—that begets the jealousy which destroys love. The theme of Nature (1), therefore, again plays an important role. It is frequently quoted, although never in its clear poetic form as in the two preceding overtures, but harmonically and instrumentally somehow demonically distorted. The force that Nature here calls into being is terrifying and contains in itself the seed of death and destruction. It begins to germinate and grow, breaking harshly into the hymn love sings of its happiness, undermining it and finally triumphing over it. This parallelism in the basic idea and its development between the Shakespearean drama and Dvořák's work makes it possible to bring the two works into a certain relationship based on these similarities. Who wishes may find in the overture a portrait of Iago, of Othello's mighty love for Desdemona, the passionate flaming-up of his jealousy, the terrible deed of destruction and his own death. In its purely musical aspect, a striking feature of the overture is the great fertility of thematic ideas presented in sonata form, in which both the principal theme and especially the subordinate theme are introduced along with a whole group of related themes.

The work opens with a grave introduction (*Lento*, F sharp minor, $^4/_4$) of considerable length. In the soft chords of the peaceful chorale delivered by the muted strings, we sense the boundless happiness of love flooding the human soul (Othello's happiness).

16. Lento

This expression of sweet bliss is suddenly rent by a sharp sound
of evil portent, like a flash of lightning coming from a cloudless sky.
In his mind the seed of black passion planted by Iago springs into
life. The strings repeat the jagged rhythms of figure 17a three times,
each time an octave lower, out of which develops the principal theme
of the overture symbolizing the disintegrating force of jealousy
(17b). The figure, having served its purpose, creeps away in an augmentation in the bass and the spirit tries to recover its former tranquillity (second entry of theme 16), and succeeds—but not for long.
An incisive diminished chord persistently disturbs the mood, and,
as if intimating in what soil that ill-fated seed is germinating, the
wood-wind repeats three times the theme of Nature (1) in a characteristically harsh harmonic colouring. The clear sky becomes overcast, the clouds gather thicker and blacker: darkly and yet majestically the theme of jealousy (17b) sounds forth in the strings and,
after a short and agitated rise to a sharply accented diminution of
the second pair of bars of the same theme, the 'cellos and basses in
unison storm in with the theme of Nature (1), which concludes
with a thunderous clap in the full orchestra, dying away to a tremolo
in the tympani.

The quick part of the overture now follows in sonata form (*Allegro
con brio*, F sharp minor, ³/₄). In the exposition, passion straightway
begins its destructive play: the two themes of jealousy and Nature

enter into a dialogue, the former (17*b*) in the sharp unison of flutes, oboes and clarinets, the latter (1) very expressively in the dark depth of the bassoon and cellos. The monstrous instinct grows apace, the movement rises in emotional intensity and expressiveness, to which a sharp diminution of figure -*t* in rising sequences contributes very notably, the whole orchestra then opening into a powerfully passionate variant of the principal theme of the overture (17*c*), reminiscent in its shape of theme 10 from the preceding "Carnival" overture:

17c.

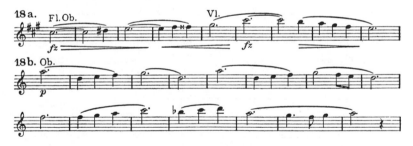

But then a new and numerous complex of related thematic ideas is announced. These, in sonata form, build up paragraphs with the secondary and concluding themes, all of which possess a predominantly ardent melodic character as well as sharing the characteristic element of three rising seconds.

18a. Fl.Ob.

18b. Ob.

The clouds begin to disperse, rays of warm sunshine break through, and light enters and illuminates the spirit. Theme 18*b* delivered in the melodic tones of the violins, closes with a sequel of intensified ardour (18*c*), of which another variant presented by the woodwind below the airy figurations of the violins breathes only love's sweet desire (18*d*):

The same expression of a lover's happiness is then embodied in a short paragraph which reviews the three last-quoted themes (18*b* to 18*d*), while a tone of sensuous desire colours the paragraph containing the closing theme (18*e*) which, melodically and rhythmically, again grows out of the preceding themes as a new variant:

The strength of love seems so far to have prevailed over evil suspicion. The metrically augmented closing theme 18*e* in the transitional passage to the development swells in the wood-winds into a hymn of love (18*f*) whose purity of feeling repulses even the sharp thrusts of jealousy (opening figure of 17*b*) which keep intruding in the violins:

At the beginning of the development, the hymn, on its passage through a wide range of keys, increases in intensity of expression.

The heart has quite forgotten the temptings of an evil voice and exults in the glorious happiness of love.

But just at that moment the demon of jealousy appears in all its majesty. The victoriously soaring theme of love (18*f*) is suddenly arrested by the blow of a diminished chord, beneath which all the deep instruments raise the same theme harmonically caricatured, and a dynamic passage derived from the triplet figure of the theme of jealousy (17*b*), delivered by the strings in unison, ruthlessly turns the whole of the soul's happiness to ashes. (Undoubtedly by a coincidence, but none the less interesting for that, is a passing reminiscence of the principal theme of Dvořák's "Requiem" in the long tones, *a-b flat-g sharp.*) Almost like a grimace, the theme of Nature (1) is given out by the muted horns below the delicate undulations of the flutes three times in succession, each time a minor third higher and with increasing force. The theme of jealousy (17*c*), combined with 17*b* joins it, advances with resolute step, and to the accompaniment of sharp figurations and malicious trills in the violins, steadily growing in force until, on opening the recapitulation, it storms along in its original form of 17*b*.

Its wild careerings, however, are brought to an abrupt stop by a triplet figure in the deep octaves of the violoncellos, double basses and finally—in augmentation—in the trombones. The theme, stifled in the wood-winds, is heard for the last time, the original rising second leading into the fourth bar significantly replaced by a descending fourth (Desdemona's death). The spirit staggers beneath the terrible blow from which it cannot recover—its happiness gone beyond recall. There remains only the memory of it penetrating the mist in which the themes of love and happiness take shape, but as in a trance and tinged with an ineffable melancholy (18*a*, 18*c*, 16, 18*e* mostly in F sharp major). Even the theme of jealousy (17*b*) intermingles with them, but without any of its original terror and passion. Memories, however, cannot bring back lost happiness. The thought sears his soul—and in a short agitated coda Nature com-

pletes her work of destruction (Othello's suicide): Nature's theme
(1), still more distorted than before, appears in the low registers of
the 'cellos over a tremolo in the tympani and the alarming blare of
the tuba, till, after a steep gradation and terrifying shrieks in the
whole orchestra, the theme of destruction (17b) rears its head in the
horns, trombones and lower-pitched strings. The last three bars
swerve suddenly into F sharp major and bring the work to an incisive close.

SYMPHONIC POEMS

The last group in the programme music of Antonín Dvořák consists of five compositions of the class that is most typically and exclusively associated with programme music—the Symphonic Poem.
Dvořák's very considerable creative interest in programme music
took him into this sphere at the very close of his orchestral production, and quite naturally as the final phase and culmination of his
development. He thereby gave yet another proof of his creative
versatility, of the lively way in which his imagination reacted to
everything which might give him the chance of full and sincere
musical expression, and also of his ceaseless search for new creative
impulses.

Dvořák created, in all, five symphonic poems in close succession.
The first four form a related group as drawing their themes from
the collection of poems (created in the spirit of folk-verse), "The
Garland" ("Kytice"), by Karel Jaromír *Erben* (1811—1870). Dvořák had shown a special liking for this highly original poetical work
since his early youth when he wrote his longest collection of songs
"The Orphan's Couch" ("Sirotkovo lůže"), (1871) and then, again,
much later when he created his ballad cantata "The Spectre's
Bride" ("Svatební košile") (1884). "The Garland", as a work of art
created in the same spirit and having the same specific qualities as

the folk poetry of which he was so fond, attracted him by the un-affected seriousness and truthfulness of its moral base, by the magic charm of its mythological subject and figures as created by the lively imagination of the people, and by the originality of content and form which was very close to him, not only in feeling but also in musical expression. It was thus perfectly natural that he should return to it when he finally resolved—and certainly not without careful consideration—to link his musical inspiration to this literary, extra-musical source of inspiration, especially at a time when he showed in other directions, too, a strong predilection for the folk-tale.

The four symphonic ballads of this group (although each is con-ceived and worked out in a different way and has its basic mood proper to the subject), are akin not only because they are a typical expression of Dvořák's musical individuality, distinguished by the beauty of thought which is its hallmark, but principally because they completely correspond to Erben's conception and expression. Like the ballads of this poet, Dvořák's four symphonic poems on the themes of these ballads are remarkable for their specifically Czech character and as having at the same time a broad human appeal, for, in spite of their dignity and stylisation as works of art, they are imbued with a rare simplicity and depth of feeling. It was the throroughly Czech spirit of Erben's themes which set up sym-pathetic vibrations in the soul of the composer, and it was Dvořák's musical genius which comprehended these themes in their whole highly differentiated range of feeling and mood.

The symphonic poems based on Erben's themes set Dvořák a new and very delicate task as regards their formal arrangement. Previous compositions in the sphere of "programme" music had all had a poetic framework of a very general character or limited to certain basic features for whose transcription into the musical medium the most highly developed musical form of the sonata could be suitably employed. Now, however, the subjects were very definite, and their episodic detail equally precise and extremely varied; thus it was inevitable that they should determine the musical form. And though the epic breadth of Erben's poems did not make Dvořák's task any easier, he mastered it so successfully that these compositions, too, form a worthy part of his life's work. With the exception of "The Golden Spinning Wheel", the longest and least dramatic of the four ballads, he succeeds in a remarkable way in identifying the form of the poetic pattern with a certain musical form, whether that of the rondo, as in "The Water Goblin", or a form deriving organically from a cyclic composition of four movements, as in "The Noonday Witch" or "The Wild Dove". While the composer in his striving after a faithful musical transcription may have seized now and again on too subordinate details in the action, it cannot be looked upon as a fault in as much as it does not impair the organic structure of the movement, for it is in reality immaterial whether the listener takes in such a detail or not. The main thing is that the composition should give the impression of a musically organic and artistic unity, that it should evoke the mood and create the main outlines of the action of the poem, as well as communicating its ethical substance. Dvořák's symphonic poems based on Erben's themes satisfy these requirements and in a way that is in complete conformity with his creative genius. Musically they are among the loveliest works that his rich invention and original mind created, while in content they bear eloquent witness to the noble power of complete singleness and purity of emotion, as well as to a highly developed feeling for the dramatically expressive and flexible musical transcription of the poetic pattern.

A special place in the group of Dvořák's symphonic poems is held by the fifth and last of them, entitled "The Hero's Song". This work, unlike the others, is not related to any particular poetic background, but is based on an independent conception of the composer's personal experience. What that personal experience was, we shall learn in the musical analysis of the composition. Here it suffices to mention that also in the transcription of his own theme he employs the same individual style as in the preceding symphonic poems, and that, in form, too, he keeps to a one-movement synthesis of the symphonic four-movement cycle, on a well- thought-out thematic plan, thus creating in "The Hero's Song" a work bearing the unmistakable stamp of his creative genius and forming a worthy epilogue to his purely orchestral production.

"THE WATER-GOBLIN"

(Vodník)

Symphonic poem for large orchestra after the ballad by Karel Jaromír Erben, op. 107

Instrumentation: piccolo, 2 flutes, 2 oboes, cor anglais, bass clarinet, 2 clarinets, 2 bassoons, 4 horns, 2 trumpets, 3 trombones, tuba (2 tuba ad lib.), tympani, bass drum, cymbals, triangle, tam-tam, bell, strings.

Written in sketch between January 6th and 10th, in score between January 24th and February 11th, 1896.—First performed along with "The Noonday Witch" and "The Golden Spinning Wheel" at a public performance of the Prague Conservatoire conducted by Antonín *Bennewitz*, on June 6th, 1896.—Its first concert performance by the Vienna Philharmonic in Vienna, on November 22nd, 1896, with Hans *Richter* conducting, and then at a concert of the Brno Philharmonic Society, in Brno, on April 11th, 1897, conducted by Leoš *Janáček*.—Score, parts and four-handed piano arrangement (Dr. Vilém *Zemánek*), published by Simrock, Berlin, 1896. Simrock's English translation of the title was "The Water-Fay".—Duration: 19 minutes.

Erben's ballad of the Water-Goblin is composed in a uniformly gloomy and tragic tone. The fairy-tale ruler of the watery kingdom is portrayed as a terrifyingly powerful and destructive character. Hungrily he waits at the lake side for the girl who, having disregarded her mother's warning, goes to the lake to do the washing on an ill-fated Friday. He drags her down to the bottom of the lake and there makes her his wife. Not even love for the child that is born to them can make the poor woman happy in his kingdom. She longs to see her mother again and begs the Water-Goblin to let her go home at least for one day. The Water-Goblin at first angrily refuses to grant her request, but finally gives way on condition that the child stays with him. But he awaits his wife's return in vain. Her mother will not let her out of the house and the Water-Goblin, in a frenzy of rage, takes his revenge on his own child and, amidst the shriekings of the storm as it lashes the lake to fury, throws the child's body, riven in two, onto the threshold of the cottage.

The Water-Goblin with his treacherously murderous intent and his vindictive rage is the central figure of the ballad in which the scenes representing the daughter with her mother and her child are mere episodes, deepening by their contrast of mood the gloomy atmosphere pervading the whole poem. Dvořák solved the problem of conveying the atmosphere and content in two ways: first, by tinging the whole composition with the expression of deep inconsolable sadness, he creates the uniformly gloomy mood of the poem; and, secondly he brings out the significance of the Water-Goblin as the central figure by making the scenes with him the main paragraphs in the rondo form in which the episodic scenes with the mother and daughter and with the daughter and child form the subsidiary paragraphs, the whole being welded into an artistically harmonious unity. The composition shows the following arrangement: 1. Water-Goblin above the lake (principal paragraph A); 2. Mother and daughter (subsidiary paragraph B); 3. The Water-Goblin gets the girl into his power (A); 4. The young mother sings to her child and longs for home (subsidiary paragraph C with partial development); 5. The Water-Goblin permits his wife to visit her mother (A); 6. Mother and daughter (B); 7. The Water-Goblin takes his revenge (A as development); 8. Epilogue (coda). Dramatic tension and climaxes are achieved by representing each new paragraph of the ronde form, in conformity with the content of the ballad, as a new and characteristic variant, both in its dynamic and expressive features.

The first paragraph of "The Water-Goblin" (*Allegro vivo*, B minor, $^2/_4$) introduces the ruler of the watery realm and at the same time creates the whole setting in which the action will unfold. Dynamically, it is one great crescendo and decrescendo, in its orchestral colouring as bewitching as a picture by Böcklin. The atmosphere of the night scenery at the edge of the lake, into whose gently splashing waves the moonbeams dip, and beside it the terrifyingly grotesque figure of the Water-Goblin sewing himself a pair of shoes, is recreated in tone with extraordinary realism. The introductory Water-Goblin theme comprising two periods (1*a* and 1*b*) seems to portray the bizarre appearance of the little man with green hair, its grace-notes and trills in the same rhythm as that of the song he sings to the moon: "*Shine, little moon, shine, so that my thread may twine*". (The stereotyped undulating motif in the strings gives this scene its characteristic undertone.)

But as the passage grows in tone, reinforced by the penetrating whistle of the piccolos and the clashing of the cymbals, the basic theme of the Water-Goblin assumes a terrifying character, so that when its second part changes into the rhythmically hard and threatening rising sequences of variant 1*c* we sense the whole terrible potentialities of the Water-Goblin which are further underlined by the lapidary motif of his power (1*d*) and the dynamic culmination of the paragraph.

The first subsidiary paragraph which follows (*Andante sostenuto*, B major) describes the scene in the cottage in which the mother begs her daughter not to go to the lake. Dvořák treats this episode as a three-part song. The simple, folk-coloured line of the melody, full of sweet girlish charm (Leoš *Janáček* alluded to it as "a theme of such delightful child-like simplicity that it floods the whole soul with warmth"), describes the daughter and the trustfulness of her resolve to go to the lake:

The theme of the mother and her warning in the minor middle part (2*b*), though thematically related to the preceding theme (note the similarity in figure *m* and *n*) is tinged with an expression of sad presentiment underlined by the accompanying chromatic line:*

---

* Dvořák himself wrote in the words "daughter" and "mother" in the sketch of the composition to indicate to which figures they corresponded.

Theme 2*b* is repeated thrice in something like diminished variations; the first time the violins sing both lines of melody; the second
time the theme, in the rhythm of semiquaver sextolets, descends into
the violas and violoncellos, while the contrapuntal line is taken over
by the flutes along with the clarinets; the third time the theme is
delivered by the piccolo with the trumpet and trombone, the second
line taking the form of demi-semiquaver figurations in violins and
violas. The expression of the theme grows in intensity as if empha-
sizing the increasing urgency of the mother's entreaties.

Last night I had an evil dream,
Don't go, daughter, down to the stream,
A white dress betokens sorrows
Tears are concealed in pearls
And Friday is unlucky, I deem.

But warnings and entreaties fall on deaf ears: the girl's theme (2*a*),
sung once again in the warm key of B major is heard now in fuller
and deeper orchestral colours and even more trusting and resolved
than before. Only the rhythm of the Water-Goblin motif monotonously kept up in the tympani indicates that the mother's fears
are not unfounded.

The Water-Goblin is sure of his victim. The new principal paragraph breaks in with his grotesque theme, the hard motif of his un-
earthly power (1*d*) ominously threatens the girl, and a rapid gradation leads up to a presentation of the Water-Goblin theme bla-
zoned forth in all its terrifying majesty and accompanied by victorious fanfares of trumpets and trombones in which it is possible to
detect a derivative of the girl's theme:

Scarce had she dipped the first garment in,
Than the plank she stood upon caved in.

As in the opening paragraph of the composition now the steep decrescendo floods the expression with a deeply affecting sadness, and the passage rising from the depths *("the waves surged up from below")* concludes the paragraph with a long-drawn-out shriek in the violins, dyimg away in the hollow echoes of the clarinets and horns.

Another paragraph in rondo form *(Andante mesto come prima)* introduces us to the cold, cheerless kingdom of the Water-Goblin. The clarinet and viola sing a sad, slow, chromatically descending melody, as if scanning the words of the poem:

Melancholy and mournful is the watery realm
Where fishes play beneath the foam: *

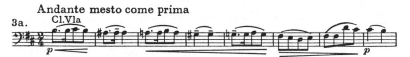

And the wind instruments then take over, in prolonged gloomy chords, the chromatic progression of the preceding melody into which the 'cello significantly fits a pizzicato accompaniment of the opening figures of the Water-Goblin theme:

---

* It is of interest to note that the rhythm of the majority of Dvořák's motifs corresponds exactly to the metrical rhythm of Erben's lines in the original.

3b.

This whole part is then repeated twice, each time in a different combination of instruments (theme 3a is given the second time to the piccolo and clarinet and the third time to the violins), and finally expires in an agony of spiritual anguish. All the despairing hopelessness of the fate of the Water-Goblin's wife is here given expression. Alone the sight of the infant with green hair sheds a gleam of comfort. Touchingly, above the undulating accompaniment of chords of the seventh, there rises the soft line of a lullaby:

"Sleep-a-by, lullaby, dear little son of mine,
Dear little Water-Goblin."

over the fifth and sixth bars of which Dvořák wrote in the sketch the words of the poem:

"Smiling you look at me."

And again this is repeated three times, each time a semitone lower (in E, E flat and D major), while in the modulating transitions there is significantly announced, in the bass, the motif (5a) out of which is developed the theme of the wife's supplication in the following paragraph (see 5b below):

The Water-Goblin, with his motif in the full strength of the orchestra, expresses his anger at his wife's song and addresses her roughly:

> *"What are you singing, wife of mine?*
> *I do not like this song of thine!"*

(These words, too, are written in above the following motif of the Water-Goblin's anger.)

The wife appeases the Water-Goblin's wrath with the words:

> *"Be not angry, be not vexed,*
> *Water-Goblin, husband mine!"*

which is expressed in a softly soothing quasi-recitative melody:

but immediately it is followed by the urgent entreaty to be allowed to go up and see her mother for a little while at least, the violins pleading beseechingly in the expressively contoured outline of theme 5*b*, while the Water-Goblin's motif is persistently reiterated:

The Water-Goblin, his rising irritation finding outlet in explosions of rage (1*e* and 1*a* in a great variety of forms working up the

tension), at last agrees to allow his wife to visit her mother, but with the strict injunction that she must not embrace anybody at home and must return to the lake before the bell rings for vespers (a solemn emphatic exposition of his theme in B major, dying away in delicate allusions to the motif of anger 1*e*).

Another subordinate paragraph *(Lento assai)* represents the short dialogue that takes place between mother and daughter in the cottage. The theme of the daughter (2*a*) sounds sad in the violoncellos above the grave chords of the trombone and the two tubas, and sad but increasingly emphatic is a variant of the mother's theme (2*b*) interpolated between its figures by different members of the wind in succession:

The mother is determined not to give up her daughter to the Water-Goblin. In this sketch, at the end of the phrase delivered by the solo flute, Dvořák quotes the lines from the poem:

> *"I shall not suffer you to stay*
> *in thrall to a water-fay."*

The drama hastens towards the catastrophe; the deep tremolo of the violoncellos and double basses warningly recall the request made by the girl to the Water-Goblin (allusion to theme 5*b*). And the last big paragraph of the composition *(Allegro vivace)* begins. Dvořák's note in the sketch: "The Water-Goblin comes, a great scene, development, principal theme," sums up the character of the whole of this part, both as regards its thought and its musical content. The final principal paragraph is again in rondo form, but broadly worked out and richly embroidered. The dynamic line, is, however, no longer a crescendo and decrescendo as at the beginning, but rises in one single steep gradation till the catastrophe is reached. While the waves of the lake swell angrily in passages of rising dramatic sequences, the Water-Goblin, represented by his theme (1*a*), impatiently prowls around the cottage, whence the fear-stricken tones of his wife's voice reach his ear (5*b*). A number of times the "*bang, bang, bang*" of his fist on the door sounds frighteningly in the 'cellos and double basses, and this motif, taken from the same theme and combined with the motif of the Water-Goblin's power (1*d*) and of his anger (1*e*), betray the wrath of the infuriated man-goblin trying to break into the cottage:

The whole atmosphere seethes with terror. The waves of the musical stream rise powerfully and the wild "*bang, bang, bang*" now thunders forth in the chords of the whole brass, while interpolations of motifs 1*d* and 1*e* break in with ever more terrifying accents. For the last time the Water-Goblin reminds his wife of her entreaty and her promise (5*b*), but in vain. And now he rears himself in all his destructive and horrible monstrosity (trumpets and trombones in full force and in the dark key of D minor give out his theme 1*a* in a powerful metrical augmentation) and four shattering blows of a diminished chord struck by the full orchestra mark the climax of the tragedy. On the threshold of the cottage:

> *Two things lie here in a pool of blood—*
> *The flesh creeps with horror and dread:*
> *A child's head without a body,*
> *A child's body without a head.*

Thus ends Erben's ballad but Dvořák adds a few bars of coda, which tell what Erben left untold and submerges the terrible conclusion of the drama in a flood of immeasurable sadness. After the Water-Goblin's act of revenge it is stiflingly close, both in the cottage and at the lake's side. The cor anglais, along with the bass clarinet, moan reminiscences of the mother's theme (2b), while the piccolos and flutes dully and monotonously tap out the rhythm of the Water-Goblin's motif (1a). In the oboe the daughter sobs inconsolably over the dead body of her child and—in the distance— the Water-Goblin, his wrath somewhat abated by the terrible revenge he has taken, is yet filled with unrelenting gloom as he disappears into the depths of his desolate watery realm (3b and 3a). With his motif picked out in scarcely audible pizzicato in the violoncellos and double basses and a gloomy B minor chord in the bassoons, trombones, and tuba above the subdued tremolo of the tympani, the composition comes to an inexpressibly sad close.

"THE NOONDAY WITCH"

(Polednice)

Symphonic poem for large orchestra after the ballad by Karel Jaromír Erben, op. 180.

Written in sketch between January 11th and 13th, in between January 14th and February 27th, 1896.—First performance in Prague as for the preceding "Water-Goblin". First concert performance by the Vienna Philharmonic in Vienna, on December 20th, 1896, with Hans *Richter* conducting, and then at a Dvořák concert in Brno, on May 8th, 1897, by the orchestra of the Prague National Theatre conducted by the composer.—Score, parts and four-handed piano arrangement (Julius *Spenge*) published by Simrock, Berlin, 1896. Simrock's English translation of the title was "The Noon Witch".—Duration: 15 minutes.

"The Noonday Witch" is the shortest and most concise of the ballads by Erben of which Dvořák produced a musical transcription. Its action is confined to a few short episodes. The mother preparing the midday meal is angered by the child's fretting and, unable to quieten the child, threatens it with the Noonday Witch. Scarcely have the words passed her lips than the frightful hag appears in the doorway and with her *"Give me the child!"* strikes terror into both mother and child. When the father returns home in a little while he finds the mother in a faint with the smothered infant at her breast. Erben encompasses the whole drama in a few verses, in incisive and dramatically effective diction, without episodes or digressions to hold up the action. Dvořák had therefore to supplement the original to some extent to prevent the musical transcription from appearing fragmentary or musically formless. He did not begin with the child's naughtiness as does Erben but, by way of introduction, gives an idyllic picture of domestic happiness, the bright tranquillity of its mood making the theme itself all the more tragic by contrast. The scene picturing the apparition of the Noonday Witch is conceived in the form of a bizarre dance, which introduces an important dynamic and rhythmical element into the structure of the tone-poem. This is then developed into an organically unified whole, the first part of which comprises the scene with mother and child; the apparition of the Noonday Witch is represented by an *Andante sostenuto*, her wild whirlings round the child take the form of a small scherzo, while the scene marking the arrival of the father provides the tragic conclusion. It follows, too, from the character of the poem, that the musical themes of "The Noonday Witch" do not conform to the literary text but are freely invented ideas. They are all short and can be divided into four main groups: the themes related to the scenes with the child (examples under number 1), with the mother (2), with the Noonday Witch (3) and with the father (4).

The beginning of "The Noonday Witch" conjures up a picture of peaceful domesticity, the mother busy with household cares and a child playing beside her. The idyllic theme 1*a* in the harmonies of the wood-wind, with delicate tinklings of the triangle, give to this part of the composition a charming pastel softness of colouring which betrays no hint of the approaching drama:

Nor is there as yet any indication of it in the child's first outbreak of restlessness (1*b* in the oboe), especially when it passes away in a childishly sweet and smiling cadence of the same instrument. But when it comes again, a peevish fit of ill-humour seems to seize the child and the motif of restlessness is abruptly taken over by the strings in unison (1*c*):

The mother who, in Dvořák's conception, is the central figure of the composition, and whose theme undergoes a great variety of psychologically subtly differentiated transformations, at first chides the child good-humouredly (2*a*):

But in vain. The child screams all the louder in the motif of ill-humour (1*d*), at which point Dvořák notes in the sketch "The child begins to scream", and in chromatically rising lamentations, so that the mother has no choice but to scold the little rebel sharply (2*b*), (the sketch contains the note 'the mother is angry and scolds'). When even that has no effect she threatens in an unguarded moment to call the Noonday Witch (3*a*).

This threat has its effect. For a while peace reigns once more in the room and the idyllic mood of the opening returns. Here Dvořák repeats a considerable part of the introductory music, not only out of a feeling for musical form, but with a deliberate, gradational purpose. For the child, once again becoming naughty and noisy, no longer heeds his mother's chiding, but peevishly throws down the toys his mother gives him. At this the mother loses her temper and harshly calls for the Noonday Witch. But alas!

Somebody lightly lifts the latch of the parlour door. With the creeping chords of the muted violins and violas and above the quavering tone of the bass clarinet (3*b*), there stands in the doorway the apparition that has come in answer to her call. A wizened little figure with a sheet drawn over her head, her presence strikes terror in the gravely expressive theme 3*c*. According to Leos Janáček the musical description is "so truthful that one can almost clutch at the terrifying shadow in these weird, halting, unwonted and unimagined harmonic steps."

Andante sostenuto e molto tranquillo

* In connection with the theme of the Noonday Witch it is of interest to note the similarity between it and part of the introductory theme 1*a* in the following variant:

3c. Cl. Fag.

And when, at the beginning of this theme, the trumpets rap out, as if in the words of the poem, the imperious demand: *"Give me the child!"*, the mother all at once realizes the terribleness of the moment and beseeches the Noonday Witch to have pity (2c).

2c. Più animato Vl.   2d.

(Dvořák repeats the scene so that the mother's supplication may burst out still more passionately).

The Noonday Witch, however, knows no pity. On the contrary, malevolently gloating over the terror she inspires, she begins to dance round her victim with grotesque steps increasing the torture of both mother and child. In alternate triple and duple time, this weird dance develops from the theme of the Noonday Witch (3d and 3c) and the supplication of the mother (2d), till it culminates in the aldritch shriek of triumph of the little witch-woman, its rising chromatic sequences being very aptly likened by Janáček to the outstretching of a long skeleton hand (3e).

3d. Allegro   3e.

The beseeching cries of the mother die down to the sobs (2c) which, in the second interval of the last bar of the motif (bracketed in the example), still moan in anguish when the sound of the noonday bell drives the apparition away.

2e.

Calm and unconcerned the father returns home:

A terrible sight meets his gaze:

In a dead faint the mother lies,
And to her bosom presses the child.

(*2d* in sequences in the oboe, clarinet and flute). The father restores his wife to consciousness (theme *2f* in which the semitone sighs of the flute lead up in a fervently ascending line of relief to the descending theme of the mother)

only for them to realize together the tragic reality that the child is dead. With an expression of boundless grief, the whole orchestra delivers a variant of the mother's theme (*2g*),

followed significantly by the two themes of the Noonday Witch: *3c* in the imposing presentation of the trumpets and trombones and the grotesque dance motif *3d* in the wood-wind which then, with a swiftly moving passage, brings the composition to a close.

"THE GOLDEN SPINNING-WHEEL"

(Zlatý kolovrat)

Symphonic poem for large orchestra after the ballad by Karel Jaromir Erben,
op. 109.

Instrumentation: piccolo, 2 flutes, 2 oboes, cor anglais, 2 clarinets, 2 bassoons, 4 horns, 2 trumpets, 3 trombones, tuba, tympani, bass drum, cymbals, triangle, harp, strings.

Written in sketch between January 15th and 22nd, in score between March 4th and 25th, 1896.—First performance in Prague as for "The Water Goblin" (see p. 313).—First concert performance by the Czech Philharmonic (Prague National Theatre orchestra) on May 8th, 1897, in Brno, with the composer conducting.—Published as for "The Noonday Witch" (see p. 313).—Duration: 18 minutes (with cuts listed in the footnote on p. 331).

The third of Dvořák's symphonic poems based on Erben's ballads is "The Golden Spinning-Wheel". The content of the ballad derives from a well-known fairy-tale motif: The king, who has been out hunting, reins up on his horse on a cottage at the edge of the forest to ask for a drink of water. In the cottage there dwells a mother with her daughter and her step-daughter, and it is the step-daughter who, sitting at home at the spinning-wheel, so fascinates the king with her beauty that he falls in love with her on the instant and asks for her hand. On his second visit, he instructs the mother, an old hag, to bring her step-daughter Dornička to the castle. The mother and her daughter, however, kill Dornička on the way through the forest, take with them her eyes, feet and hands and make for the Castle where the mother passes off her own daughter as her step-daughter. The king, not seeing through the deception, welcomes his bride with delight and celebrates the wedding. Soon after, however, he must go to the wars. Dornička's body has meantime been found in the forest by a mysterious old man who thrice sends a youth to the Castle to ask for the feet in return for a golden spinning-wheel, for the hands in exchange for a golden distaff and for the eyes as the price of a golden spindle. The young queen, coveting the possession of these remarkable objects, successively gives in exchange for them the parts of Dornička's body with which the old man in the forest is then able by means of living water to bring the dead girl back to life. The king returns victorious from the wars, and his wife in welcome sits down to the golden spinning-wheel. But it fares ill with her. The spinning-wheel creaks out a song which betrays the crime committed in the forest by the women. The king then finds Dornička in the forest alive and well, takes her to the castle as his true wife and throws the murderesses to the wolves.

Erben's versification of the fairy-tale is a broadly conceived poem in six parts, with a large number of verses in almost each of which is described some detail of the action of importance for the story. Dvořák, in deciding to make a musical transcription of this ballad, had also to decide to give it a predominantly descriptive character, which, on the other hand, led to a certain amount of formal looseness of structure and diffuseness but, on the other hand, offered Dvořák the welcome opportunity to give full rein to his musical imagination in minor fairy-tale detail, and to create passages of fascinating charm of thought and harmonic colouring which are among the loveliest things to come from his pen. Formally Dvořák made things somewhat easier for himself by confining the thematic material of the composition to three basic groups of which the first (examples under number 1), germinating thematically from a single nucleus, is connected with the powers of good and evil as represented by the figures of the king and the mysterious old man on the one hand, and by the figure of the mother-hag on the other. The second links up the motifs of the lovely Dornička and her spinning-wheel, while the third expresses the King's passion for Dornička's unsullied beauty (3). He then heightened the significance of the content of "The Golden Spinning-Wheel" by enveloping its whole musical expression in a mantle of truly fairy-tale poesy and by imbuing this expression in places with the irresistible charm of folk-music at its loveliest.*

The beginning of the composition describes the King's arrival at the cottage. Above the lively patter of staccato triplets (2) representing the gay ring of horses hoofs, the horns intone the basic folk-coloured theme of the King (1a).

Theme 1a is repeated a number of times with dynamic rises and falls, while in the middle of the paragraph a new central thought is introduced, clothed in a melody which already intimates the King's enravishment (3a).

In the violins and violas three knocks at the door of the cottage and a violoncello passage based on the spinning-wheel theme (2b) announce the appearance of the lovely young spinner, whose key theme (2c), sung by the solo violin above the undulating spinning-

---

* It may be noted that, in Czechoslovakia, "The Golden Spinning-Wheel" is generally performed with cuts made in the score by the composer Josef *Suk*, Dvořák's pupil and son-in-law, in order to make the symphonic poem shorter and formally more concentrated in those parts where, out of fidelity to the literary pattern, Dvořák repeats certain parts to conform with Erben's poem. These cuts are: a) from number *(Meno mosso, larghetto)* to bar 13 following number 8 *(Larghetto)*; b) from the 28th bar following number 12 (bar 16 in *Molto vivace)* to bar 10 preceding number 6 14; c) from bar 9 following number 15 *(Poco piu mosso)* to bar 8 following number 16 *(Un poco piu mosso)*; d) from bar 6 preceding number 17 (bar 2 following *Poco allegro)* to bar 6 preceding number 18 (bar 2

wheel figure, is a wonderfully apt transcription of the words of the
poem

A girl like a blossom then came out
Of beauty such as the world had no thought!

The next scene is also worked out in symmetrical form. At the
King's wish the girl sits down at the spinning-wheel and the orchestra sings a song of tender charm based on the spinning-wheel
theme (*2b*) above the delicately sinuous accompaniment of the strings
and harp.

The huntsman stood as if spellbound
His great thirst quite forgotten.

In the ardently yearning melody (*3b* and *3c*), orchestrated in
glowing colours, the King declares his love to the girl. (In the instrumentation of this passage of intoxicating beauty, in which the
violins sing the melody in octaves, only the strings take part, sup-

following *Poco allegro*); e) from bar 13 following number 24 to bar 9 following
number 25.—While it may be possible to agree with the cuts listed under c)
and d), i. e. in the places describing in the same musical terms the sending of
the messenger to the Castle with the parts of the Golden Spinning-Wheel three
times in succession, it may be said that the other cuts encroach dangerously
upon the musical organism of the poem by omitting the theme in which the
mother-hag welcomes the king on his second visit to the cottage and, along
with it, an important musical thought, not otherwise made use of in the composition, and then by deleting the characteristic wedding music with a special
variant of the King's basic theme.

ported by the soft chords of the trombones and tuba, and interwoven
with the undulating staccato of the wood-wind.)

3b. Poco animato, ma non troppo

3c.

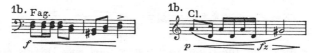

The song of the spinning-wheel and the girl's theme (*2b* and *2c*)
close the charmingly tender love-scene as they had opened it.

Again the King comes riding on his prancing coal-black steed,
and again he knocks at the cottage door and longs for a sight of
his sweet bride. But instead of lovely Dornička, "*a hag came out, all
skin and bone*":

The themes alternate in the ensuing dialogue, the King's passion
flames up and he instructs the mother to bring Dornička to the
Castle. Dornička's tender theme (*2c*) closes this scene, too, the music
finally melting away in the soft arpeggios of the harp.

The stealthy, creeping tones of the deep 'cellos and basses gloomily introduce the next paragraph describing the ill-fated walk
through the forest. The scene has the character of a diabolical
scherzo, in which the leading role is taken by the motif of the evil
deed (*1c*) which, like the motif of the hag, is a distortion of the
King's theme (*1a*).

1c. Molto vivace
      Legni

Along with it there then appears, as a subordinate motif, a theme of softer character, beside which Dvořák noted in the sketch the stepmother's cajoling words "*At the King's Castle there will be fighting!*"

At the culmination of this part, when the motif of murder is whirling at its wildest, there sounds forth as its counterpoint in the trumpets and trombones the theme of the King-warrior—(1*a*); as if the last thought of the murdered Dornička were of her noble bridegroom. The stream then subsides and only the dance-rhythm motif of the vengeful spinning-wheel (2*d*) ominously disturbs the mood of the close of the paragraph.

In the meantine the King, in a festive variant of his theme, welcomes his presumed bride to the Castle:

and to the accompaniment of dance music, based on yet another variant of the same theme, they celebrate their nuptials:

But here, too, the spinning-wheel motif intrudes significantly into the music and is interwoven in the following passionate love scene between the King and his false bride which is built up of new thoughts to form a flowing paragraph of great ardour and impassioned urgency.

This scene, which is among the musically most fascinating parts of the score, ends with the King's theme in the trumpets and horns dying away in the distance as the King departs for the wars (1*a*). With a jump from A flat major into E major, the next section opens with the theme of the unknown old man in the grave chords of the brass-instruments, representing a variant of the King's theme.

The old man sends a young serving-lad to the Castle to sell the golden spinning-wheel for a pair of feet: against the sinuous theme of the spinning-wheel in the violins, his command sounds serious and resolved in the horns and violas (*a*), and its descending seventh is then echoed in the lad's offer: *"Buy, my lady, dear it's not, only two feet is all its cost" (a)* :

Between these two figures the step-mother's squawking motif (1*b*) is harshly interpolated by the bassoons, while the lad's haste and the Queen's interest in the spinning-wheel find expression in a softly undulating motif in the flutes *(b)*:

In Erben's ballad the old man sends the lad on two more occasions with the golden distaff and the golden spindle, and Dvořák, in the intention of the poet, also twice repeats the whole paragraph embodying the scene with the old man and the serving lad, the first time a major third and the second time a minor third higher, concluding the whole section with the old man's theme in the trombones and tuba (1*f*) and the motif of the resurrected Dornička (2*c*).*

With gay fanfares of his theme (1*a*) and a festive augmentation of its variant (1*e*), the King returns from the wars. At his request, his wife sits down to show off the golden spinning-wheel, but, to the accompaniment of terrifying trills in the violins, it unexpectedly creaks out the horrid secret of the forest murder of poor Dornička (2*e*):

The crime of the two women is brought to light (motif 1*c* in the penetrating tones of the trumpets and horns alternates in a wild confused whirl with motif 2*e*) and the King rides into the forest from whence comes his anxiously repeated call: *"Where, my Dornička, where art thou?"*:

* For the cuts carried out in this part of the score by Josef *Suk* see page 331.

15. Facsimile of a page from the manuscript score of the symphonic poem "The Wild Dove".

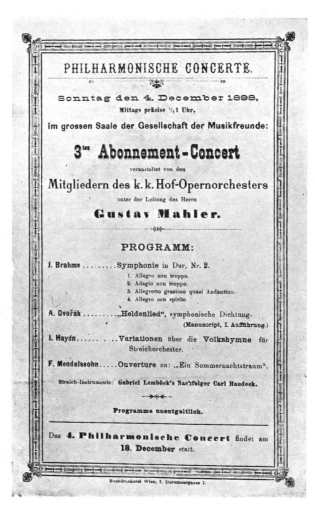

PHILHARMONISCHE CONCERTE.

Sonntag den 4. December 1898,
Mittags präcise ½1 Uhr,

im grossen Saale der Gesellschaft der Musikfreunde:

3ᵗᵉˢ Abonnement-Concert

veranstaltet von den

Mitgliedern des k. k. Hof-Opernorchesters

unter der Leitung des Herrn

Gustav Mahler.

PROGRAMM:

J. Brahms . . . . Symphonie in Dur, Nr. 2.
   1. Allegro non troppo.
   2. Adagio non troppo.
   3. Allegretto grazioso quasi Andantino.
   4. Allegro con spirito

A. Dvořák . . . . „Heldenlied", symphonische Dichtung.
   (Manuscript, I. Aufführung.)

J. Haydn . . . . Variationen über die Volkshymne für
   Streichorchester.

F. Mendelssohn . . . . . Ouverture zu: „Ein Sommernachtstraum".

Streich-Instrumente: Gabriel Lemböck's Nachfolger Carl Haudeck.

Programme unentgeltlich.

Das 4. Philharmonische Concert findet am
18. December statt.

Buchdruckerei Wien, I. Dorotheergasse 7.

16. Programme of the Philharmonic Concert in Vienna, where the
symphonic poem "The Hero's Song" was performed for the first time.

The King finds his Dornička and in tones of impassioned ardour once again sings his love for her—first in that rapturous key of A flat major, as when he first kissed the false bride (themes 2*f* and 2*g*) and then in the key theme of love from the beginning of the composition (3*b* and 3*c*) now declaimed in tones of intensified ardour. The whole orchestral ensemble then joyfully sing Dornička's theme (2*c*), combined with the spinning-wheel motif (2*b*), and the happy King, to the accompaniment of the jubilant tones of his own theme (1*a*), leads his true wife to the Castle.

"THE WILD DOVE"

(Holoubek)

Symphonic poem for large orchestra after the ballad by Karel Jaromír Erben, op. 110

Instrumentation: piccolo, 2 flutes, cor anglais, 2 clarinets in B flat, bass clarinet, 2 bassoons, 4 horns, 2 trumpets, 3 trombones, tuba, tympani, bass drum, cymbals, triangle, harp, strings.

Written in sketch between October 22nd and 25th, in score between October 26th and November 18th, 1896.—First performance at the concert of the Brno Philharmonic Society in Brno, on March 20th, 1898, conducted by Leoš Janáček.—Score, parts and four-handed arrangement by the composer published by Simrock, 1899.—Duration: 18 minutes.

As the fourth of his symphonic poems based on ballads by Erben, separated from the third by an interval of six months, Dvořák made a very happy choice in the ballad entitled *"The Wild Dove"*. The ballad as related by Erben has the following content: A funeral procession is making its way to the village churchyard, and following the coffin is the young widow sobbing inconsolably. Her lamentations, however, are not sincere, for if truth be told it was she who had dispatched him to another world. Nor is it long before her pretty face assumes a more cheerful expression and she yields to the amorous addresses of a handsome young man and marries him. The wedding takes place and all is gaiety. But the sense of her guilt suddenly seizes upon the woman and sharp pangs of conscience drive her to the grave of her poisoned husband where the lamentations of a wild dove in the tree that has grown above his grave shake her soul with remorse. In despair, she takes her own life, knowing herself and her name to be under an eternal curse.

Dvořák could safely base his tone poem on this highly condensed and dramatically effective ballad without being tempted into any kind of descriptive digression, and could also freely develop the poetic content as his feeling and ethical ideas directed. On the one hand he aggravates the seriousness of the wife-murderess's crime by stressing her guilt from the very beginning (Erben does so only later); on the other hand, when she has paid the penalty for her crime in suffering and remorse, he lifts from the guilty soul the curse with which the close of the poem burdens her and ends the composition in a mood of reconciliation. If he was fortunate in the choice of a subject, he was no less so in its musical expression. And that not only in the inventive resource of his musical imagination, which was inspired in all its aspects to manifestations of unusual beauty, power and originality, but also in the way he succeeded in identifying the formal outline of the musical structure with the dynamic outline of the action and in giving it an organically unified form. According to the short *mottoes* which he had printed in the score, the thought-content of his tone-poem builds up into five main paragraphs, arranged in conformity with the principle of c y c l i c s y m-p h o n i c f o r m, and is further unified by all the themes being derived from a single thematic cell. In his "Wild Dove" he thus achieved an ideal balance between the purely musical content, the thought content and the musical form, on the one hand, and the values of tone-poetry, on the other, thereby achieving with this work not only the culmination of his creative efforts in this category of music but creating one of the most perfect and powerful works of its kind in musical literature.

The thematic core out of which the whole music of the "Wild Dove" grows is the curse motif, as Dvořák straightway designated it in his first sketch of the composition, but which might equally well be called the motif of guilt:

a.

The composition itself begins with this theme in its original form. Dvořák describes the opening scene of the funeral in the form of a funeral march (*Andante funebre*, C minor, $^4/_4$), of which the leading theme is an independent variant of the motif which the flutes and violins weave in tones of lamentation over the *ostinato* rhythms of the bass:

b. Andante funebre

Four gloomy chords struck pianissimo by the trombones not only interrupt this mournful dirge, but shift its repetition a semitone higher into the key of C sharp minor in which the funeral song assumes a new colouring. Only when it has died away does there rise in the oboe and trumpet—like a march trio—the key-theme of guilt *(a)*, this time softer and more pathetic in quality, into which the simulated lamentations of the widow-murderess break with the dissonances of chromatically descending sequences in the flutes and violins *(c)*. Here the characteristic features of village funeral music are as truthfully and convincingly rendered as the widow's feigned grief.

Motif *c* is then taken over by the violins together with the clarinets, once more theme *b* is heard, now in the key of E minor, and a
two-bar gradation based on its diminution leads to a massive six-
four chord in the tonic key of C minor, forming a curtain of sound
against which the trombones—with terrible emphasis—declaim the
motif of guilt *(a)*. This marks the culmination of the first part
which, in four bars of a descending fragment of the same, in successive diminutions, provides the transition to the second part, the music
of which describes the meeting of the widow with a handsome youth
(*Allegro*, A major, $^2/_4$).

The clear A major struck by the strings and the harp indicate a
sharp contrast of mood, which is confirmed by the swaggering, youthful theme of the young man *(d)*, gaily interpolated by a distant solo
trumpet in the rhythm of Erben's lines:

> *From the white manor,*
> *Over grass and meadow,*
> *Rides a handsome youth,*
> *In his hat a feather.*

(This theme, too, is again a melodic variant of the basic motif and
closely related to variant *(b)*):

A passing allusion to the theme of guilt in the clarinet does not
deter the young man from letting his eyes rest with favour on the
lovely widow. The sad funeral theme *(b)* takes on a new feeling
in the sixth bar, the expression may be a kindling look of amorous

desire (the first two bars of theme *e*), which the young man does not hesitate to answer with a confession of love in the melody of his theme (third bar of *e*) :

The music does not in any way hold up the action of the impetuous courtship, even though the composer, for purely musical reasons, repeats it a minor second higher. And the widow's expression also grows brighter with a coy variant of the theme of mourning in the flute:

This is in keeping with Erben's ballad:
That self-same week all thoughts of the dead had flown,
Scarce a month passed before she was sewing her wedding gown,

By way of a simple crescendo in the strings on the trill *g-a flat*, Dvořák leads straight into the wedding music, which comprises the third part of the composition (*Molto vivace*, C major, $^3/_4$). It begins with gay fanfares in the trumpets and trombones, with energetic interpolations of variant *f* by the strings, to which the piccolo together with the flute and oboe reply exultingly with theme *-d*. The animated mood of a happy honeymoon is characteristically underlined by the combination of $^3/_4$ and $^2/_4$ time. And then a bagpipe player breaks into a folk-coloured melody with its equally characteristic raised subdominant, which is again a variant of the basic theme *(g)*, as is also the fiery three-bar figure which alternates playfully with the bagpipe melody *(h)* :

h.

This whole dance is rhythmically effervescent with life and movement. But there is then a sudden quietening down as it passes over to the calmer and more flowing line of a walz tune. *"A wedding there was, a wedding, sweet music the band was playing, To his breast he pressed her, and she kept smiling, always smiling,"* are the key lines written in by Dvořák for this middle part *(un poco meno mosso)*, in which a delightful lyrical augmentation of the basic theme soars above its bagpipe variant, to the softly undulating accompaniment of the harps, violas and violoncellos:

Un poco meno mosso

i.

And it is truly "sweet music". In its rapturous, soaring and ardent melodic and harmonic lyricism, and in the glowing tone-colours of its orchestration, the whole passionate love scene which now unfolds, modulating through the keys of A flat, B and back again to A flat major, is a passage of bewitching beauty. All too soon, it seems, this scene ends, disappearing after a third repetition like an enchanted vision to be followed by the lively recapitulation of the dance music of the bagpipe. The wedding scene then concludes with a quiet variant of the basic theme, developed in variation form with something intimate and unaffected in its tone, which at the same time is also strangely disquieting:

j. Allegretto grazioso

The next paragraph of the composition speeds to the catastrophe *(Andante,* ⁴/₄*)*. Melody *j* dies away unfinished above the terrifying

tremolo of the chord of a diminished seventh *(d flat-f-g-b)* and the
Wild Dove, on the little oak tree over the grave, begins its haunting
song: the two flutes, separated by an intermittent semi-tone trill in
contrary motion, the oboe weaving in and out its mournful interval
of a second, while, high above, the harp delicately thrums a high
a flat:

The weirdly mysterious impression of this tone-painting is intensified by the crushing entry of the basic theme of guilt in the
bass clarinet and then in the horns.

Time passes, passes away, a year like a day,
But one thing passes not away: for guilt comes to stay.

is the quotation Dvořák writes into the score at this part, underlining the words which give it its significance. Again, and ever more
urgently, the dove repeats the theme of guilt *(a)*, while a new variant in the violins comes through, its anguished note of supplication
expressing the tortures of the woman's soul:

The pangs of conscience become more and more terrifying in
their insistence, the motif of guilt is given out in unison by the four
horns and in a threateningly grotesque diminution by the double
basses, and vainly the theme of beseeching entreaty rises a last time
in a despairingly agitated gradation. Like the voice of implacable

judgement, the theme of guilt (which is also the theme of the curse) thunders out in the trumpets and trombones with the massed strength of the brass instruments in the dark key of C minor, while the wildly descending passage of the strings tells how *"the unhappy woman seeks herself a grave"* (the line is quoted by Dvořák in the score), passing judgement on herself for the crime she has committed.

Thus the crime is expiated and redeemed. Over softly radiant harmonies, the solo violin carries into the heights a new variant of the basic motif bearing the redeemed soul away into the unknown:

The theme of guilt is heard threateningly once more in the horns and bassoons, but then it assumes an expression of sad resignation in the tranquil melody of the violins above the dark pizzicato of the other string instruments. A sequence of clear, warm major chords, into which the gentle, reconciled cooing of the wild dove are delicately interpolated, steer the last bar of the music into the home tonic of C major, and the composition, dying away in the deep octaves of the woods-horn, ends as it began.

"THE HERO'S SONG"

(Píseň bohatýrská)

Symphonic poem for large orchestra, op. 111.

Instrumentation: 2 flutes, 2 clarinets, 2 bassoons, 4 horns, 2 trumpets, 3 trombones, tuba, tympani, bass drum, cymbals, triangle, strings.
Written in sketch between August 4th and 23rd, in score, between August 24th and October 25th, 1897.—First performance at a concert of the Vienna Philharmonic held in Vienna, on December 4th, 1898, with Gustav *Mahler*

conducting.—In Bohemia, the composition was first performed at a concert of the Czech Philharmonic (the Prague National Theatre orchestra) on January 28th, 1899, conducted by Oskar *Nedbal*.—Score, parts and four-handed piano arrangement by the composer, published by Simrock, Berlin, 1899. Simrock's English translation of the title was "Heroic Song".—Duration: 24 minutes.

After an interval of almost a year had elapsed since the composition of "The Wild Dove", Dvořák once more turned his creative thoughts to the sphere of symphonic poems and, with the completion of another and now the fifth such work, he also concluded a life-time of symphonic creation. This time he no longer bound himself by a subject from Erben, nor from any other literary source, but gave the new symphonic poem a programme of his own expressed in the designation *"The Hero's Song"*.

According to certain information provided by the composer himself, the content of "The Hero's Song" may be summed up as a picture of the composer's own artistic destiny, having roughly the following plan: At the beginning of the composition, there are the indications of a keen courage and readiness to go out and conquer. But the élan is only of short duration and is, as it were, struck down in its first flight. Disappointment and trial sing a sorrowful and despondent song. But even so, a voice of comfort and hope breaks through and grows in strength and volume till it bursts forth in the tones of a great festive hymn. Nature, too, adds her word of consolation and encouragement. Courage returns and with it the will to work and fight: at first in the strong, untamed tones of the introduction and then, as if aware of its own strength, the spirit sets out with a buoyant, warm, folk-coloured tune, going from one success to another, and breaking out at last into the strains of a glorious song of victory, its exultation and triumphant splendour rising to powerful heights. Such in its main outlines was the life of Dvořák, the composer. And at a time when his artistic works were successfully conquering the concert platforms of the Old World and of the New, while at home he was already beginning to make a name for himself in the sphere of opera, he had certainly every justification for looking back upon his own past achievement with proud satisfaction and, on looking back, to sing his own "Hero's Song".

He set about the work with all the happy enthusiasm of his creative genius and, in order to bring out very clearly that the composition celebrates the life of an artist sprung from the people and always true to his simple origins, he coloured a number of the thematic ideas and some parts of the composition with the typical tone of Czech folk-music, also making abundant use of the clarinet, an instrument very popular among Czech folk-musicians. In form, "The Hero's Song" is again based on the cyclic unity of the four movements of the classical symphony, of which the individual parts are clearly differentiated in mood: after a quick introductory part, there follows a broadly designed *Poco adagio lacrimoso* as a slow part, a transitional passage with echoes of the introduction leads to the scherzo, whereupon a typical finale concludes the composition. These parts are not, however, conceived as independent units but, in their thematic structure and treatment, are linked to and derived from each other in the manner of sonata-form developments. The musical content of "The Hero's Song" is embodied in three basic themes, of which the first two appear in a wide range of variants which undergo innumerable changes and transformations according to the content of the composition. The first of these themes, itself the basic theme (quoted under number 1 in the examples), may be termed the theme of courage, combat, happiness and victory. The second (group 2), the theme of disappointment, trial and grief but also of victory over them, and the third, subject to least change in the course of the composition (3), the theme of consolation and hope.

The first relatively short paragraph of the composition (*Allegro con fuoco*, B flat minor, $^3/_4$) works mainly with the basic theme, which enters straight away in the energetic unison of the violas, violoncellos and double-basses (1*a*), but then moves nimbly enough, skipping from one member of the wood-wind to another, alternating, on the one hand, with the care-free variant 1*b*, and, on the other, combining contrapuntally with the passionate, full-blooded variant 1*c*.

The thematic core of the succeeding slow part *(Poco adagio lacrimoso*, B flat minor, $^3/_4$) is the second theme, expressive of suffering and sorrow even in its original form *(2a)* and not without a hint of despair in its continuation *(2b)*.

The whole of this section, with its song of grief, is repeated in a still richer range of emotional gradations and orchestral colouring. The expression then becomes calmer and, as an auxiliary thought in the key of D flat major, there rises the warmly comforting melody of the third theme (3):

3.

This theme dies away in the clarinets and oboes and, by way of an emotionally tender augmentation, leads to motif 1*b*, out of which, after a number of modulations, the variant 1*d* is evolved. Its playful pastoral tone in the scale of F major seems to indicate that Nature herself is anxious to soothe the wounded spirit with her healing balm.

1d.

It seems, therefore, perfectly logical that the musical stream should then swell, with forces revived and restored, into a festive *grandioso* of the whole orchestra, in which the theme of hope (3) is combined with a counterpoint of the theme of disappointment (2*a*), transposed into the bright key of D flat major. A short, delicate sequel combining motifs 3 and 1*b* concludes the whole paragraph at a reduced pace. The re-entry of the basic theme 1*a* also marks a return to the introductory *Allegro con fuoco* which, with a steep gradation and equally steep descent, paves the way for the next important paragraph.

The remaining part of the composition, combining the character of a symphonic scherzo and finale, now flows in a unified stream which steadily rises in pace, volume and expression. It opens quietly with an *Allegretto grazioso* (E major, $^2/_4$), in march rhythm, derived from a melodious, folk-coloured variant of the basic theme (1*e*):

The theme unfolds in three-part song form, with a middle part in the key of G sharp minor and a folk-coloured final phrase:

This whole song is repeated in richer orchestral colours, combining on its third entry with the theme of hope (3) in the following two-part counterpoint:

A dynamic gradation forms the transition to the next part, with somewhat accelerated tempo, which at first grows out of a new variant of the second theme (2c), but then returns to theme 3 which, with its brisk pace and new key setting in C and A major, is now in good heart and full of youthful self-confidence.

The spectre of stubborn struggles and bitter disappointments finds expression for the last time in the agitated line of motif 1c, and a new short development of the basic theme (1a) opens out into the finale, which signals the entry of the song of victory proper *(Molto vivace,* B flat major, duple time). In this part the basic theme appears in ever new variants and transformations. After several bars of introduction based on the energetic variant 1*f*, a short passage leads to a fairly extensive *Piu mosso* passage, in which the happy variant 1*g* and its more grave and festive augmented variant 1*h* alternate and combine in a lovely modulating process, not omitting to present at last, over a rhythmic *ostinato,* a victorious variant of the second theme (the theme of difficulties vanquished 2*d*).

    A bold gradation leads to a new *Poco più mosso* with the exultant fanfares of variant 1*k* and ends with a spirited *Vivacissimo.* If the first half of "The Hero's Song" impresses the listener with the beauty and grave pathos of its deeply emotional plasticity, the second part fills him with admiration for its boldly designed structure which, in one breath as it were, speeds swiftly and irresistibly to its splendid and victorious conclusion. In "The Hero's Song", Dvořák has created a work which is not only a worthy memorial to his great artistic achievements, but which, in the complexity and ingenuity of its thematic construction, is one of the most remarkable creations of his genius.